FREE RIDE

Robert Levine has been the executive editor of *Billboard*, as well as a features editor at *Wired* and *New York*. His writing has appeared in the *New York Times*, *Businessweek*, *Rolling Stone* and *Vanity Fair*. He covers technology and the culture business from New York and Berlin.

ROBERT LEVINE

Free Ride

How the Internet is Destroying the Culture Business and How it Can Fight Back

VINTAGE BOOKS
London

Published by Vintage 2012

2 4 6 8 10 9 7 5 3 1

Copyright © Robert Levine 2011

Robert Levine has asserted his right under the Copyright, Designs
and Patents Act 1988 to be identified as the author of this work

First published in Great Britain in 2011 by
The Bodley Head

Vintage
Random House, 20 Vauxhall Bridge Road,
London SW1V 2SA

www.vintage-books.co.uk

Addresses for companies within The Random House Group Limited
can be found at: www.randomhouse.co.uk/offices.htm

The Random House Group Limited Reg. No. 954009

A CIP catalogue record for this book
is available from the British Library

ISBN 9780099549284

The Random House Group Limited supports The Forest
Stewardship Council (FSC®), the leading international forest
certification organisation. Our books carrying the FSC label are
printed on FSC® certified paper. FSC is the only forest certification
scheme endorsed by the leading environmental organisations,
including Greenpeace. Our paper procurement policy can be found
at www.randomhouse.co.uk/environment

TO KERSTIN

Everyone has the right to the protection of the moral
and material interests resulting from
any scientific, literary or artistic production
of which he is the author.

ARTICLE 27, UNIVERSAL DECLARATION OF
HUMAN RIGHTS, 1948

CONTENTS

[FREE RIDE]

There was a time when NBC lived up to its old slogan, "Must See TV." For most of the 1980s and 1990s, the network dominated television with iconic hits that shaped the culture of the time: *Miami Vice*, *The Cosby Show*, *Cheers*, *Seinfeld*, *Friends*, and more. It had *The Today Show* in the morning, *The Tonight Show* in the evening, an unbeatable lineup of sitcoms for Thursday night, and *Saturday Night Live* every weekend. For some of that time, it also showed Major League Baseball, NFL football, NBA basketball, and the Olympics.

The network earned its ratings by pushing the boundaries of television: *Miami Vice* brought MTV visuals to the police drama, *Hill Street Blues* incorporated gritty realism, and *Seinfeld* brought self-awareness to sitcoms at a time when most half-hour shows still ended with a hug. These shows made NBC one of the most profitable divisions of General Electric,[1] to which the network returned $800 million in profit in 2003.[2]

In 2010—just seven years later—the network expected to lose more than $100 million.[3] When Comcast agreed to acquire 51 percent of NBC Universal, it was mostly interested in the company's cable channels—Bravo, Syfy, and others.[4] The proposed deal assigned the broadcast network an on-paper value of *zero*.[5]

As NBC has faltered, other companies that rely on its programming have thrived. In early 2006, more than five million people watched the famous "Lazy Sunday" *Saturday Night Live* sketch on YouTube, which was bought for $1.65 billion by Google later that year.[6] *Heroes*, one of the network's recent hits, became one of the most popular shows on file-sharing services.[7] And telecom companies built empires selling bandwidth that lets consumers download or stream pirated television shows without commercials.

NBC isn't the only media institution that has seen its value plummet in the last few years. MGM, with its iconic roaring-lion logo and library of James Bond films, sold for $5 billion in 2004 but drew bids of less than $2 billion in 2010.[8] The EMI Group, which owns Capitol Records and the classic Beatles and Frank Sinatra recordings, ended up in the hands of Citigroup after a private equity buyer couldn't make its debt payments.[9] The *Washington Post*, which set a high-water mark for U.S. journalism when it published the Pentagon Papers and uncovered the Watergate scandal, has reduced its newsroom staff, closed its national bureaus, and—perhaps most painfully—declared, "We are not a national news organization of record."[10]

While each of those companies had its own issues, they all faced the same underlying problem: they weren't collecting enough of the revenue being generated by their work. The material they put out was certainly popular. But like "Lazy Sunday" and *Heroes*, that material built other businesses, including the Pirate Bay, Apple's iTunes Store, and the *Huffington Post*.

The damage isn't limited to major media conglomerates. Independent film companies are struggling, and studios have cut divisions devoted to smaller films. Music sales in the United States are worth less than half of what they were in 1999.[11] Newspapers have seen ads decline by 43 percent since 2007,[12] the Tribune Company entered bankruptcy in 2008, and the *Seattle Post-Intelligencer* laid off most of its reporters and started publishing only on the Web. It's time to ask seriously whether the culture business as we know it can survive the digital age.

As recently as 2008, the Electronic Frontier Foundation could say that "the music industry is the only industry that appears to be unable to adjust their business models to take file-sharing into account."[13] Even at the time, this wasn't entirely true: the DVD sales that drove movie studio profits were already falling.[14] At this point, with newspapers losing readers to Web sites that summarize their stories, and the television and book businesses threatened by online technology, it's time to ask whether any significant professional media business can thrive in an environment where information can be taken so easily. When nearly a quarter of global Internet traffic consists of pirated content, according to a study by the Envisional consultancy commissioned by NBC Universal but based on data from other companies, it's time to ask whether there's actually much of a new market to adjust to.[15]

Piracy isn't new, of course, and it's hardly the whole problem. But the easy, illegal availability of all kinds of content has undermined the legal market for it, in a way that affects the entire media business. Sites that use pirated material to draw an audience drag down the price of online advertising to the point where companies that produce new material have trouble competing. Media companies that sell products online have to lower prices in order to compete with pirated versions of those same products sold by companies that bear none of the production costs. By making it essentially optional to pay for content, piracy has set the price of digital goods at zero. The result is a race to the bottom, and the inevitable response of media companies has been cuts—first in staff, then in ambition, and finally in quality.

This devaluation could also hurt the Internet, since professional media provides much of the value in a broadband subscription. A 2010 study by the Pew Research Center's Project for Excellence in Journalism found that more than 99 percent of blog links to news stories went to mainstream media outlets like newspapers and networks.[16] File-sharing services are filled with copyrighted music.[17] Seven of the ten most popular clips in YouTube history are major-label music videos.[18] Amid the Internet's astonishing array of choices, statistics show that most consumers continue to engage with the same kind of culture they did before—only in a way that's not sustainable for those who make it.

So far, the conflict over the future of online media has been framed as one that pits media conglomerates against a demanding new generation of consumers who want music and movies their way—available online, at any time, in every format, and at no additional cost. This may not be much of a business. But like most ideological arguments about the Internet, the idea that consumers want free media has an economic agenda behind it.

The real conflict online is between the media companies that fund much of the entertainment we read, see, and hear and the technology firms that want to distribute their content—legally or otherwise. For the past few years, helping consumers access content has been one of the best businesses on earth: Apple's iTunes Store made it the most valuable technology company in the country,[19] Netflix's stock rose nearly 219 percent over the course of 2010, and YouTube dominates online video. But these companies depend on a ready supply of content that consumers want, and the lack of a functioning market online has already endangered this. Like TV, the Internet is only as good as what's on.

The one thing everyone can tell you about the Internet is that "information wants to be free." This memorable phrase, coined at a 1984 hacker convention by the influential technology thinker Stewart Brand, evolved into a media business mantra that shaped the online world as we know it. This is why newspapers gave away web content, why Hulu doesn't charge users, and why music fans expect albums to be free for the taking.

Unfortunately, we've forgotten the rest of Brand's quotation:

> On the one hand information wants to be expensive, because it's so valuable. The right information in the right place just changes your life. On the other hand, information wants to be free, because the cost of getting it out is getting lower and lower all the time. So you have these two fighting against each other.

Brand's own information wanted to be expensive, and he made a small fortune in the publishing business. A bohemian intellectual who befriended both Buckminster Fuller and Ken Kesey, Brand appeared as a character in Tom Wolfe's *Electric Kool-Aid Acid Test* and campaigned for NASA to release a picture of Earth from space. As living off the land became part of the post-hippie zeitgeist, he created the *Whole Earth Catalog*, an influential compendium of advice that Steve Jobs once referred to as "sort of like Google in paperback form." [20] He started out peddling an early version from the back of his truck and went on to sell more than a million copies of a later edition. In 1983, a year before Brand said that information wanted to be free, he got a $1.3 million advance to create the *Whole Earth Software Catalog*.[21]

From the perspective of the technology world, information wants to be free "because the cost of getting it out is getting lower and lower all the time." The idea that online media will inevitably be free comes from the theory that the price of any good should fall to its marginal cost. Since digital distribution gets cheaper every year, the marginal cost of media keeps approaching zero. That's why *Wired*'s editor Chris Anderson, in his book *Free: The Future of a Radical Price*, argued that "free is not just an option, it's the inevitable endpoint."[22]

There are two main problems with this argument. First, it's only a theory—and one economists normally apply to commodity goods. Second, and more important, if the price of culture fell to its marginal cost, movie studios would have no way to cover their production expenses. They'd have three choices: close up shop, turn films into advertising for other products, or sell the first copy of every movie for $150 million and make online downloads free after that. If none of these ideas sound like promising strategies, it's because pricing media at its marginal cost just doesn't work in the real world.

Much of the enthusiasm for free media comes from mistaking the packaging for the product. If you believe people once paid $15 for silver plastic discs, it's only natural to think online distribution will revolutionize the recording business. But if you realize people were paying for

the music *on* those discs, it's obvious that someone still has to make it—
and that someone probably wants to get paid.

Many very intelligent people seem to have a hard time understanding that making music is harder than distributing discs. In Ken Auletta's
Googled: The End of the World as We Know It, Google's co-founder
Sergey Brin tells Auletta that more people would read his book if he put
it online for free. Auletta points out that this would make it difficult to
pay for reporting, editing, and a marketing campaign to ensure his work
reached readers. "The usually voluble Brin grew quiet," Auletta writes,
"ready to change the subject."[23]

To Google, Auletta's book is just a series of ones and zeros—and
not very many of them, compared with a movie. To Auletta, those ones
and zeros were exceptionally expensive to create—at least in terms of
time—since the technology that has revolutionized the cost of distributing text hasn't dramatically changed the nature of writing it. Reporters
can access online databases and interview sources by Skype, but they
still have to read documents and ask the right questions. In cases like
this, "information wants to be expensive."

Therein lies the conflict. Most online companies that have built
businesses based on giving away information or entertainment aren't
funding the content they're distributing. In some cases, like blogs that
summarize newspaper stories, this is legal; in others, it's not. But the
idea is the same: in Silicon Valley, the information that wants to be free
is almost always the information that belongs to someone else.

In economic terms, these businesses are getting a "free ride,"[24]
profiting from the work of others. The fact that video can be distributed practically free on YouTube hasn't really changed the amount of
money it takes to make a television show. If shows are distributed for
free, in a medium where advertising isn't worth much, the companies
that produce them won't be able to make money. Eventually, they'll
stop paying people to create them. Aggregators like the *Huffington
Post* and search engines that specialize in finding illegal downloads of
copyrighted content often say that they're providing "exposure." But
they're also providing competition, by selling advertising that used to

go to creators. As the old Catskills joke goes, "You could *die* of exposure!"

Right now, that's what's happening to the culture business.

It wasn't supposed to be this way.

The Internet was supposed to empower creators, corporate and independent alike. As it became easier to distribute entertainment and information—important U.S. exports, as well as valuable parts of our lives—technology would generate jobs. Art and commerce would benefit together.

It's time to acknowledge that this isn't happening—and that it won't until we turn the online free-for-all into a free market. Instead, the Internet as it exists now has empowered a new group of middlemen, like YouTube, that benefit from distribution without investing in artists. And while online technology has built some impressive empires, many of them don't generate that many middle-class jobs, since they either get the benefit of professional content without paying for it or depend on user-generated content—the digital-age equivalent of Tom Sawyer convincing his friends that painting the fence will be fun. The Reuters product manager Anthony DeRosa described the dominant online business model as "Digital Feudalism": we think we're using YouTube when YouTube is really using us.[25]

I'm not a Luddite who doesn't "get" the Internet. My first job out of graduate school was at the *Wired* Web project HotWired, where I started a few months after it sold the world's first clickable banner ad. I've spent most of my career covering technology, media, and the intersection between them, and I spend as much time reading original blogs as I do with a daily paper. I love the way the Internet makes so much of the world's culture accessible—from European newsweekly Web sites to Afrobeat albums on iTunes—and I think it has helped some important new voices find an audience. This isn't a book about why online technology isn't important; it's one about how we can make it more valuable.

Most Internet companies aren't getting a free ride, of course. For every file-sharing service, there are dozens of emerging artists, independent labels, and established companies using online technology to create interesting work. Inexpensive video cameras allow people to document news as it happens, garage bands upload cool songs to Myspace, and sites like the *Daily Kos* use mass collaboration to compete with newspapers on important stories. Much of the best reporting on technology and the media business can be found on sites like GigaOM and TorrentFreak. This explosion of creativity has enriched our culture immensely. But many bloggers face some of the same problems as newspapers: it's hard to make money if half the people who read your stories do so on another site.

When Napster went online in 1999, I thought the kind of mass piracy it enabled was a transitional step before digital technology helped musicians connect directly with fans who would be happy to pay for their work. I thought more online publications would follow the path of *Slate* and *Ars Technica* and invest in original reporting and writing. I thought the Internet would become a place where creators and companies with any level of popularity could figure out ways to sell information without worrying that someone else had made it available for free a mouse click away.

Gradually, I became a skeptic. A decade after Napster, technology start-ups like Grooveshark and Hotfile are still building businesses on the same model: users share content illegally while the company that allows them to do so profits. This doesn't only hurt creators whose work is taken without payment; it harms the entire online economy. Who wants to build a legitimate music business when it's easier to start an illegal one? Why would anyone invest in a staff of reporters and editors when it's so much cheaper to aggregate the work of others? How can any company compete with a rival that offers its products but bears none of the expenses? The free ride has become a road to riches.

I'm not exactly neutral on this issue: I write for a living, and that puts me firmly in the creators' camp. But this book is based less on experience than on extensive reporting that shows how giving away content online rarely adds up to a business for creators. (Although I've written for some of the publications mentioned in this book, I point out when that's the case.) And the technology companies that suggest there's money in giving away content aren't exactly unbiased, either. Google has as much interest in free online media as General Motors does in cheap gasoline. That's why the company spends millions of dollars lobbying to weaken copyright.[26]

Executives on both sides of this debate tend to see paying for content as a moral issue. Media companies bemoan a new generation of consumers who don't know they need to pay for content, while technology pundits talk about a "right" to access information that doesn't have much legal support. While it's silly to argue that lending a DVD to a friend is some kind of a moral failing, it's even more ridiculous to suggest there's an inalienable right to see *Iron Man 2*. Especially when many of those who push the idea of that right get their funding from companies that want to distribute movies for free.

The real issue is how to establish a functioning market for content online, whether that involves selling it or supporting it with advertising. The core copyright businesses—music, film, television, and computer software—account for about 6.5 percent of U.S. GDP, according to a report by the economist Stephen E. Siwek.[27] More important, given the current economic climate, they generate jobs and a trade surplus.

Technology executives like to suggest that media companies are selling buggy whips in the age of the automobile, but that doesn't hold up. As a means of distribution, the Internet is replacing plastic and paper, which represents a leap in efficiency. But that's the medium, not the message. So far, content generated by online businesses can't compete with that from traditional media companies. If *Heroes* had lost its audience to a show about individuals with superpowers that was funded by a file-sharing service, that would have been competition. So far at least, that's not what we're seeing. Traditional media companies aren't in trouble because they're not giving consumers what they want; they're in trouble because they can't collect money for it. It's the natural outcome of an online economy that transfers wealth from "each according to his ability" to "each according to what he can get away with."

It's tempting to believe that the devaluation of creativity we've seen over the last decade was somehow inevitable, that technology makes information so easy to distribute that any attempt to regulate it is futile. But it's important to remember that the Internet didn't spring full-blown from the brow of Zeus—or even the mind of Al Gore. The U.S. government developed much of the basic technology, offered favorable tax policies to encourage the development of online commerce, and passed laws that turned out to give Web sites significant advantages over their off-line counterparts.

Some of these decisions put the media business at a substantial disadvantage. While television channels would be subject to massive liability if they broadcast shows they don't have rights to, YouTube can do so with impunity as long as a user posted it. In the physical world, it would be difficult for a pirate operation based in Russia to ship hundreds of DVDs to the United States, not so much because of logistics as because of legalities. Online, digital media zooms across borders without anyone looking to see if it should be taxed, let alone whether it's legal. It's reasonable to argue whether or not this is a good thing, but it was a choice of design, not a requirement of technology.

Laws created the Internet as much as technology did, and the ones we have aren't working. I'll start my story with the Digital Millennium Copyright Act, a 1998 law that media companies first championed and technology companies managed to manipulate into a compromise that undermined the market for media online from the very beginning. It was intended to free Internet service providers from liability if copyrighted works were transmitted over their networks. But it enabled a culture in which online companies like YouTube can benefit from uploaded music or video, as long as they remove it when asked.

The first part of the culture business to get hurt was the music industry, which was destabilized by Napster and devastated by the file-sharing services that followed. In many ways, this set the pattern for what happened to the other culture businesses. An online entrepreneur would find a new way to distribute media, use professional content to build up an audience, and hope someone else would worry about whether it could grow into a sustainable business. Napster never even had a strategy. More than a decade later, no company has made a significant profit distributing music online except maybe Apple—and it makes far more money selling iStuff. This isn't creative destruction; it's the destruction of creativity.

When the music business won its court case against Napster, the technology business started fighting back—in Congress as well as in court. Attempts to defend copyright were cast as assaults on free speech, efforts to organize markets were criticized as outmoded, and piracy was confused with creativity. Much of this thinking came from organizations funded by technology companies, and some of them have as much influence in Washington as Hollywood does.

Newspapers were next. Tempted by the possibility of a larger audience and swayed by futurists who have never run businesses, they gave away online what they charged for in the physical world. The idea was that they'd make money on advertising. But the price of ad space, like that of everything else, is based on supply and demand, and the Internet has an infinite amount of it. Online ad rates started out low, fell further when the dot-com bubble burst, and now run about a tenth the price of their print counterparts.[28] Newspapers gave a valuable boost to aggregation sites like Google News but didn't capture any value for themselves. For media companies, getting advice from technology pundits was like letting the fox lead a strategic management retreat in the henhouse.

The other core media businesses—movies, television, and books—have fared better, partly because they've had time to adjust. But they're now facing the same challenges. Television could be devastated by devices like Boxee, which could erase millions of dollars in value without building a business, or even having much of a business plan. Book publishing has already faced off against Amazon's attempt to set prices for its products, much as iTunes did, with some success. And Hollywood may have the influence in Washington to fight piracy, as well as the flexibility to come up with a business model that makes piracy less attractive.

As it turns out, many of the old-media players having the most success in the new-media world ignored the conventional wisdom. The *Wall Street Journal* and the *Financial Times* are outperforming other sophisticated newspapers by charging for content. AC/DC became one of the best-selling acts of the last few years without selling music on iTunes. And AMC has won some negotiating leverage as a must-have cable channel by holding back shows like *Mad Men* from Hulu.

As the price of advertising falls, charging consumers is becoming more important than ever. Newspapers that once offered free content, including the *New York Times*, have started charging. Record companies have pulled back from advertising-supported music sites. And Comcast's interest in NBC Universal was based on cable channels like Syfy, Bravo, and the USA Network, all of which charge for programming. The future of business, it turns out, may depend on the old-fashioned strategy of selling something for more than you paid for it.

There are some reasons to be hopeful. Europe, which has a tradition of supporting its culture businesses—and an accompanying suspicion of *Le Google*—has started to take a more aggressive stance against piracy. Laws aimed at curtailing online copyright infringement in the U.K. and France have not yet had an effect, but their passage has made an important statement that some kind of order ought to apply in the digital world. And by making technology companies take some responsibility for their actions, these laws could bring them to the negotiating table.

In Europe, thinkers on both sides of this issue have found a more receptive audience for more radical solutions, such as a "blanket license" that would make a certain amount of media free with a single payment, much like a cable subscription. Such a system could grow out of private negotiations, a public mandate, or, more likely, some combination of the two. But nothing will happen as long as technology companies have free rein to distribute first and ask questions later.

The tough decisions about the future of online media don't involve the development of technology; it's inevitable that computers, bandwidth, and storage will all get faster, cheaper, and more accessible.

What's not inevitable is how that technology is used. In 2010, technology executives started saying that anyone who wanted to limit piracy was trying to "break the Internet." But the truth is that it's breaking already. Now—and perhaps not for too much longer—we have a chance to fix it.

CHAPTER 1

HOW CONGRESS CREATED YOUTUBE—
AND MEDIA'S BIG PROBLEM

I n March 2007, the former Clinton administration official who helped shape the Internet as we know it finally admitted his policy hadn't worked.

Hunched over a tabletop microphone at a copyright conference hosted by McGill University in Montreal, Canada, Bruce Lehman talked about the effects of a law hated by most of the academics in his audience. As Clinton's commissioner of the United States Patent and Trademark Office, Lehman ran the National Information Infrastructure Task Force Working Group on Intellectual Property Rights. Assigned by the White House to set rules of the road for the emerging Internet, he championed policies that became the 1998 Digital Millennium Copyright Act, a law that was supposed to extend copyright to the online world without slowing its growth. Instead, it became a prime example of the law of unintended consequences.

"Unfortunately, at least in some areas, our policies haven't worked out too well," Lehman admitted, looking vaguely uncomfortable in a tan jacket and red tie.[1] He put some of the blame on music and movie companies that didn't act quickly enough to develop new business models for the digital age. But considerable blame also goes to the law he helped design.

The Digital Millennium Copyright Act, a compromise between media conglomerates on the one hand and telecom companies on the other, devastated the first group and helped the second soar. As Lehman recommended, the law makes it illegal to circumvent copy-protection technology, such as the encryption on DVDs and some digital downloads, or distribute a tool to do so.[2] It also gives "safe harbor" to Internet service providers and some online companies so they're not liable for copyright infringement based on the actions of users.[3] That safe harbor made it easier for sites like YouTube to become valuable forums for amateur creativity. But it also let them build big businesses out of professional content they didn't pay for.

Until he started working on the Clinton administration's online policy, Lehman was best known as the first openly gay man to get a high-level government position through the Senate confirmation process. But his role as head of the patent office gave him significant authority. The top U.S. copyright official is the register of copyrights, who works in the Library of Congress, in the legislative branch of government. So Lehman emerged as the closest thing the executive branch had to a "copyright czar."[4]

Many of the professors in Lehman's audience believed the law's "anti-circumvention" provision interferes with free speech, since it makes it difficult to digitally copy music or movie scenes in order to remix or excerpt them for purposes of commentary. But Lehman was more upset that the music business was dying and other parts of the entertainment industry were facing similar problems, because the anti-circumvention policy he pushed for didn't make up for the devastation caused by the safe harbor provision to which he reluctantly agreed.

Like most of the government officials he worked with in the Clinton administration, he thought digital technology would help the U.S. media business, not threaten to destroy it.

Although it might seem hard to believe now, there was a time when copyright law was of interest mostly to copyright lawyers. It's a complicated topic, intellectually abstract even to most attorneys. But as digital technology makes it faster and easier to copy music and movies, consumers are more inclined to wonder when exactly they're breaking the law.

The answers aren't always obvious. Duplicating a CD may or may not be legal, depending on the purpose of the copy. (DVDs, which have copy protection, are covered by the Digital Millennium Copyright Act.) Many other issues raised by new technology fall into a gray area, and the prohibitive cost of litigation tends to keep some of them there for a while.

In the United States, the Constitution gives Congress the authority "to promote the Progress of Science and useful Arts, by securing for limited Times to Authors and Inventors the exclusive Right to their respective Writings and Discoveries." Over the years, that definition grew to include film and music—first compositions, then recordings. And Congress repeatedly extended those "limited Times," from twenty-eight years to, in 1976, fifty years after the death of the author.[5]

In the United States, copyright is primarily an economic instrument, a government-granted monopoly on the right to sell a work—for a limited time and with some exceptions. Until recently, the media business controlled its products by maintaining the exclusive right to copy them— hence, copy*right*. Depending on the nature of the work in question, this includes the right to reproduce, distribute, perform, and display. When media was distributed physically—on paper or on disc—the first two mattered most and almost always overlapped.

To understand copyright as a monopoly, think of a performer like Bruce Springsteen, whose recordings are owned by Columbia Records under the terms of his recording contract, which assigns those rights to the label. In practical terms, Columbia has the exclusive right to sell his recordings. Since the market has only one legitimate supplier of Springsteen albums, the label can basically set its price. This monopoly is meant to compensate Columbia for investing in Springsteen, who in turn receives royalties as well as marketing and promotional support.[6] Like any monopoly, copyright keeps the price of Springsteen albums higher than they otherwise would be, especially if they could be freely transferred online. But the monopoly is very narrow; it doesn't extend to rock anthems about New Jersey, or even to other artists' recordings of Springsteen's songs. And by allowing artists to make money on their work—either by selling it or by making an arrangement with a company that can—copyright gives them an incentive to produce more of it.

Although the logic behind copyright hasn't changed much, the laws themselves have always adjusted to new technologies, from piano rolls to cable television. Until relatively recently, most conflicts about copyright laws involved companies within, or at least close to, the businesses that depended on them. When songwriters wanted to make sure they received royalties when other performers recorded their compositions—a right they were granted in the Copyright Act of 1909—they faced off against another part of the music business. The opposing companies didn't challenge the thinking behind copyright, because their own businesses relied on it as well.

The copyright dispute that changed that—and set the stage for the battles over the online world—was *Sony Corp. of America v. Universal City Studios Inc.*, sometimes called the Betamax case. In 1976, several movie studios sued Sony to establish that the company, which did not own a studio itself at the time, would have secondary liability for copyright infringement committed with its videocassette recorder. (Sony's Betamax was a proprietary technology that quickly lost market share to the VHS.) After eight years of legal battles, the Supreme Court essentially legalized the VCR in a 5–4 ruling that held Sony wasn't subject to liability on the grounds that the device was "capable of substantial noninfringing uses."[7]

The Betamax case was the first major legal issue to set copyright holders against an industry with interests radically different from their own. Beneath all the overheated rhetoric—the Motion Picture Association of America's chief executive, Jack Valenti, famously said, "The VCR is to the American film producer and the American public as the Boston strangler is to the woman home alone"—the dispute had its roots in an economic conflict very much like the one that exists online today.[8] Movie studios wanted to sell films in a format that couldn't also be used to copy them, such as the LaserDisc technology introduced in 1978. (Whether this could have succeeded in a market without the VCR is hard to know.) Electronics makers realized that consumers preferred—

and might pay more for—a machine that could also record movies and television shows.

The Betamax case also shows why secondary liability is both important and controversial. No one disputed that it was illegal to duplicate a store-bought videocassette in order to sell copies, just as no one disputes the illegality of uploading an entire television show to YouTube today. But it's impractical, if not impossible, to police this kind of private behavior. So although neither Sony nor YouTube would commit *direct* copyright infringement, rights holders had an interest in holding them liable for *secondary* copyright infringement. In some cases, when a particular tool can be used for practically anything, this seems absurd: no one seriously suggests that carmakers should be liable if their vehicles are used in robberies. But it seems equally unrealistic to argue that a Web site called the Pirate Bay should have no responsibility whatsoever for the infringement it encourages. No auto manufacturer has ever marketed a product called the Getaway Car, complete with a device that switches license plates while the vehicle is in motion in order to evade police.

The Supreme Court's Betamax decision also complicated copyright by holding that "time-shifting"—recording broadcast television for later viewing—qualified as "fair use." The judicial doctrine of fair use provides an exception to copyright law to prevent it from placing undue limits on free speech. It allows journalists, scholars, and artists to quote or excerpt works in order to comment on them. (How much can be taken legally depends on the purpose and length of the excerpt, the nature of the work itself, and its effect on the work's value.[9]) By deciding that it also applied to consumers' use of media, the Supreme Court opened up a range of issues that are still being debated today.

Although many anti-copyright activists refer to fair use as a right, it's really an affirmative defense to copyright infringement—that is, one that acknowledges the act was committed but maintains that it's legal. "People who call it a right are just doing that to emphasize their politics," says David Nimmer, a UCLA Law School professor who with his father wrote *Nimmer on Copyright*, a treatise that has become the standard reference work on the subject for lawyers.[10]

As soon as Lehman introduced the idea of an anti-circumvention law in 1994, fair use became a rallying cry for activists who claimed that music and movie companies were trying to restrict it—along with free speech. If it became illegal to crack copy-protection systems, consumers wouldn't be able to make otherwise legal backup copies for personal use—a reasonable concern for $200 software packages but not really such a big deal for $15 DVDs. More important, some argued, it would be impossible to express ideas by remixing music or quoting text.

Courts have not agreed, since those who want to comment on a work using the work itself can retype a passage of text or record music on tape. When defendants who had distributed the code that unlocks DVDs argued that the Digital Millennium Copyright Act represented an unconstitutional restriction of fair use, the court rejected this as an "extravagant claim." "We know of no authority for the proposition that fair use, as protected by the Copyright Act, much less the Constitution, guarantees copying by the optimum method or in the identical format of the original."[11] Desirable as it might be, convenience is not a right.

As with the Supreme Court's Betamax case, the debate over the Digital Millennium Copyright Act was an economic conflict dressed up in rhetoric about rights. On one side were the major labels and studios, at the height of their power and with good connections in the White House. On the other were electronics manufacturers, telecom companies, and Internet idealists—groups that hadn't yet worked together and didn't even seem to have much in common. But they would end up influencing the law just as much.

The information superhighway became important to the Clinton administration's economic plan even before anyone actually knew what it was. Al Gore was prescient enough to see the potential of technology that could transmit information many times faster than phone lines. But no one knew what data to transmit or who would pay to get it. When Lehman first turned his attention to technology in 1993, only academics and early adopters were online, mostly with university access or dial-up connections. An e-mail address was a sign of sophistication.

In Clinton's vision, the manufacturing jobs that would be lost to trade deals like the North American Free Trade Agreement would be replaced by better opportunities in the United States. Lehman and the administration assumed that many of those jobs would come from the rapidly expanding global market for American-made entertainment. Other countries would manufacture machines; the United States could make the music, movies, and video games they played.

"They had a vision of where the country should be going as we entered the twenty-first century," Lehman says today. "It was about trying to create an economic policy that would be good for my country, and hopefully others too—to have an economy that wasn't just based on backbreaking physical labor but on the fruits of the mind."

People tend to think of the Internet as a group of private Web sites governed by consensus and computer code. But the U.S. government provided some of the science, funding, and vision.[12] Even after the Internet was essentially privatized in the mid-1990s, a 1998 law prohibited federal, state, and local governments from taxing it.[13] These decisions were made to encourage commerce, and Lehman moved in the same direction. He thought online networks wouldn't attract a mass audience without mainstream music and movies, so he pushed the anti-circumvention provision to make major labels and studios comfortable doing business online. "It wasn't the lobbyists who came to us," he says. "It was an initiative of the Clinton administration and of mine."

Technology entrepreneurs like to cast entertainment executives as out of touch with the new digital reality—old white guys who have secretaries read them their e-mail. Some are. But their Washington lobbyists started preparing for the digital world in 1994, when even the hippest prognosticators didn't know what the future would look like. That year Peter Gabriel made the cover of *Wired* for his role in defining the future of music—by releasing a CD-ROM.[14]

With Lehman's support, music and film companies started lobbying

Congress to protect their interests. The movie studios wanted the DVD format they were developing to be illegal to hack. Record labels were even more involved, and they pushed for legislation that would require "Webcasters" to pay for recordings they played online, even though traditional radio stations only paid songwriters.[15]

Lehman laid out his agenda for online copyright regulation in July 1994 with *A Preliminary Draft of the Report of the Working Group on Intellectual Property Rights*, unofficially known as the Green Paper. The proposed anti-circumvention policy caused a stir in the Silicon Valley start-up scene, which reacted as though the new guy from the corporate office confused his computer's CD-ROM tray with a cup holder: *Don't these guys know that information wants to be free?* But the Green Paper got much more attention in Washington for the way it began to define what would legally count as a copy. In the normal course of data traffic management, Internet service providers often "cache" temporary copies of files to make their networks run faster. Although individuals don't use these copies, the paper made telecom company lawyers realize that they could still be covered by copyright.

"The Green Paper was a surprise because, as I recall, it described the Internet as one giant photocopy machine," says Sarah Deutsch, an associate general counsel at Verizon. "It came to my attention because we were doing all the things it said they would hold us responsible for, like caching. It proposed that every temporary copy would be an infringement." The paper implied that Internet service providers would need permission to make these copies—in effect, to manage the flow of data on their own systems. Apart from any ideological debate, telecom companies argued—quite reasonably—that this would stall the growth of the Internet. If they couldn't run their networks efficiently, why would they invest millions of dollars to wire the country with broadband access?

The telecom companies soon had another cause for concern. In February 1995, the Church of Scientology sued the Internet service provider Netcom after a former minister posted copyrighted documents on an online bulletin board Netcom hosted.[16] Since the documents had some legitimate news value, their publication could be considered fair use, and the case rallied online activists, who warned that copyright laws could be used to suppress free speech. Telecom companies were more concerned about how the court's decision might affect their business. (Netcom and the Church of Scientology eventually settled out of court.) And they grew even more worried after a 1996 circuit court decision held that a flea market had secondary liability for sales of counterfeit recordings that took place there.[17]

With both media and telecom companies pressing Congress to define rules for copyright online, legislators were ready to listen in September 1995, when Bruce Lehman's group released a second draft of its recommendations: *The Report of the Working Group on Intellectual Property Rights*, also known as the White Paper. At least initially, Congress was more responsive to the entertainment industry. Senators Orrin Hatch (R-Utah) and Patrick Leahy (D-Vt.) championed the National Information Infrastructure Copyright Protection Act of 1995, which would have made it illegal to circumvent copy protection, and a similar bill was soon introduced in the House of Representatives. At first, their prospects for passage looked promising.

"That was the high point of our ability to enact legislation to deal with challenges to copyright," says Fritz Attaway, then the senior vice president for government relations at the Motion Picture Association of America (MPAA). "We were well organized. We had tremendous support from the administration, Bruce Lehman in particular. We had Orrin Hatch as chairman of the Senate Judiciary Committee, who took a personal interest. And we had Jack Valenti." A former special assistant to Lyndon Johnson who had run the MPAA since 1966, Valenti was one of the most influential lobbyists in Washington until his 2004 retirement.

Telecom and electronics companies weren't exactly powerless, though. Worried that an anti-circumvention law would limit the ability of its member companies to sell devices like DVD duplicators, the Consumer Electronics Association (CEA) lobbied against the law. Galvanized by the risk to their business, telecom companies asked their supporters in Congress to insert language in the National Information Infrastructure Copyright Protection Act to protect them from copyright liability and, when that effort failed, to keep the bill from moving out of committee. In an attempt to negotiate a compromise, Congressman Bob Goodlatte (R-Va.) organized a series of meetings between the two sides in the spring of 1996. But the telecom companies managed to block the bill and fundamentally change its successor.

The ongoing legal struggle between technology companies and media conglomerates has always been characterized as one of small start-ups challenging established giants. "If you look at copyright as a whole, you had a phenomenal lobby without pushback from anybody, except a little bit from us and a handful of law professors," says the CEA's chief executive, Gary Shapiro. "We're David and the content industries are Goliath."

Not exactly. The Recording Industry Association of America (RIAA) and especially the MPAA do have enormous influence in Washington, both from the money they donate and from the perception of glamour associated with their respective industries. But the computer business had an aura of innovation, and the CEA funded and ran an ersatz consumer group, the Home Recording Rights Coalition, which could generate letters to Congress. And the telecom industry, which deals with a dizzying array of federal regulations, outspends the music and movie businesses by a significant margin. They all found common cause with activists and library organizations, which framed the debate over the bill as a struggle for free speech. When Congress began debating the proposed bill, Verizon's Deutsch says, "they woke up a sleeping giant."

In a January 1996 *Wired* article about Lehman's proposals, the legal scholar Pamela Samuelson wrote, "Lehman aims to be the sheriff who will kick those anarchic digital cowboys off the Net and make the electronic frontier safe for businesses that want to set up shop there."[18] But Samuelson didn't note that the bill's opponents *also* wanted to make the Internet safe for businesses—they just happened to be different businesses. Plenty of activists wanted information to be free so they'd have an easier time selling computers, Internet access, or online advertising.

Some of the rhetoric was far more radical. In February 1996, the Grateful Dead lyricist turned digital activist John Perry Barlow published "A Declaration of the Independence of Cyberspace."[19] Barlow was reacting to the Telecommunications Act of 1996, which had plenty of faults. But he came up with one of the more overblown manifestos in the history of the Internet, which is no small distinction:

> Governments of the Industrial World, you weary giants of flesh and steel, I come from Cyberspace, the new home of Mind. On behalf of the future, I ask you of the past to leave us alone. You are not welcome among us. You have no sovereignty where we gather.
>
> We have no elected government, nor are we likely to have one, so I address you with no greater authority than that with which liberty itself always speaks. I declare the global social space we are building to be naturally independent of the tyrannies you seek to impose on us.[20]

The "Declaration" went on in that vein, mixing the wide-eyed utopianism of the New Left's 1962 Port Huron Statement with the didactic tone of John Galt's climactic speech from *Atlas Shrugged*. Since Barlow didn't have any particular authority to represent the online world, his declaration had the same legal impact as a few college kids declaring their university a nuclear-free zone. But he tapped into a powerful strain of Silicon Valley libertarianism that rejects any form of Internet regulation—except, in most cases, when it happens to help the technology business itself.

Whatever its logical flaws, Barlow's thinking became influential in shaping the idea of "online rights" as somehow distinct from those in the physical world, a concept that lacks much real legal support. In 1990, Barlow had started the Electronic Frontier Foundation with the activist John Gilmore and Mitch Kapor, who had designed the early PC program Lotus 1-2-3 and founded the Lotus Development Corporation. The organization was founded to defend civil liberties online, it works to protect privacy and free speech, and it maintains more independence from big technology companies than most other online advocacy groups. But it also came to see copyright as a barrier to free expression and to litigate against measures to protect it online.

Copyright does impose some limits on free speech, since it prevents individuals from using published works, except for purposes covered by fair use. But in the United States, which places a greater emphasis on freedom of speech than most Western countries, courts have consistently held that the two need to be balanced—partly because copyright also *encourages* free speech. "The Framers intended copyright itself to be the engine of free expression," according to the majority opinion written by Justice Sandra Day O'Connor in a 1985 Supreme Court case. "By establishing a marketable right to the use of one's expression, copyright supplies the economic incentive to create and disseminate."[21]

One reason the Digital Millennium Copyright Act inspired so much opposition was that Hollywood was also pushing Congress to again extend copyright protection. After the term of copyright was lengthened to fifty years after the death of an author in 1976, Disney and other studios lobbied for the 1998 Copyright Term Extension Act, which added another twenty years. (It would also lengthen the protection for works of corporate authorship, such as movies, from seventy-five to ninety-five years.) Since the law would keep Disney's early cartoons from passing into the public domain, opponents derisively called it "the Mickey Mouse Protection Act"—with considerable justification, since it was a giveaway to Hollywood. The law, signed in October 1998, didn't do much for media companies other than Disney, since there isn't much of a market for movies or music that old. And it's hard to say how much it even did for Disney, since Mickey Mouse's likeness would still have trademark protection after the cartoons were no longer covered by copyright.

One thing the law did do was give the moral high ground to activists like Samuelson, who wanted to weaken copyright in other ways. Technology and telecom companies were happy to take the side of public interest groups fighting against large corporations, a strategy that had its roots in the Consumer Electronics Association's creation of the Home

Recording Rights Coalition in 1981. It framed an industry dispute in terms of public interest, and this tactic has been remarkably effective ever since. Even if you believe that the Consumer Electronics Association happens to sometimes serve the public's interest, it's hardly a public interest organization.

"I represent both the technology side and the library side, and there's a symbiotic relationship," says Jonathan Band, the counsel for the Library Copyright Alliance, who has also worked for technology companies. "You always want to say what you're doing is in the public interest and not your own mercenary interest. So [the fair use ideologues] were obviously very helpful for the technology companies." Later, technology companies would return the favor with significant funding for organizations that work to loosen copyright laws.

"The principal opposition [to the bill] really came from the Consumer Electronics Association, which has always opposed copyright, and the telecom companies, which didn't want to be bothered with paying attention to content," Lehman says. Their strategy worked. The bill stalled.

When the technology business stymied Lehman's efforts in Washington, he changed the battleground. The Clinton administration had also charged him with leading the U.S. delegation to the World Intellectual Property Organization (WIPO) in Geneva, which was itself starting to look at how to update copyright law for the digital age on an international level. So he brought his ideas there, figuring he'd have an easier time, since WIPO had historically only attracted representatives from copyright industries like film and music.

"I perceived that there was an opportunity to take these treaties and turn them into something that would be to our advantage," Lehman says. "We went to Geneva and started to make a deal."

By the end of 1996, when negotiations happened in earnest, the telecom companies had followed. "For the first time, you saw all of these communications companies show up in Geneva," Verizon's Deutsch says. It was new territory for them. Deutsch remembers marveling that WIPO changed the carpets in the elevators daily. Chimes announced the beginnings of meetings, which took longer than expected. Since the negotiations took place in December, "we called it the miracle of Hanukah," Deutsch jokes, "because at WIPO they could take a day of process and make it last eight days."

Among other things, the WIPO Copyright Treaty signed at the end of 1996 required countries to pass the kind of anti-circumvention laws Lehman wanted. That put pressure on Congress to sign a bill that enacted the treaty. As anti-copyright activists point out, this is a common way of extending intellectual property protections, and they now have their own lobbyists at international bodies like WIPO.

In the summer of 1997, the Senate and the House of Representatives each introduced a pair of bills: one to implement the WIPO treaty and another to give Internet service providers safe harbor.[22] Neither had the votes to pass alone, so the two sides jousted for advantage. In September 1997, when the House Judiciary Committee's Intellectual Property Subcommittee held hearings about online liability for copyright infringement, Johnny Cash spoke about online music piracy, and Jack Valenti argued that a U.S. delay in implementing the WIPO Copyright Treaty would set a bad example for other countries with economies that didn't rely as much on intellectual property.[23] As influential as Valenti was, however, he met his match in Roy Neel, a former aide to Vice President Al Gore who had become chief executive of the United States Telecom Association. Although Neel lacked Valenti's larger-than-life personality, he made a convincing case that telecom companies couldn't possibly filter all the information on their networks. This is obviously true, but the real issue was more complicated: What, if anything, did they have to do to prevent or discourage copyright infringement?

After 1997 passed without progress, Senator Hatch hosted negotiations between entertainment industry and telecom lobbyists. As a lawyer and songwriter whose state has several big technology companies, including Novell, Hatch understood what both sides wanted. In the first few months of 1998, lobbyists came to terms with the fact that the bills would be joined. To balance the safe harbor, they hammered out the concept of the "takedown notice" (often called a DMCA takedown notice, after the bill that created it). If copyright holders found an unauthorized copy of their work online, they could send a notice to ask an Internet service provider or another neutral party to take it down.

Although telecom companies pushed the bill, safe harbor applies to a wide range of companies that transmit and store content for users. The provision does not apply to companies that control content or get a direct financial benefit from infringing activity, by selling individual movies or albums, for example. (Also, the safe harbor only protects companies from secondary liability for the actions of their users, not direct liability from their own.) Since both sides realized the Internet would develop quickly, some of the specifics were left vague: the law requires services to cut off "repeat" infringers and act on takedown notices "expeditiously." The devil, media companies would later discover, was in details like those.

Both sides felt some urgency during these negotiations. The telecom companies wanted to clarify their potential liability before a court did. Hollywood was in even more of a rush: along with some technology companies, the studios had just introduced the DVD, and they wanted to give its copy-protection system some legal teeth. The major labels were eager to introduce a copy-protected digital product themselves. Since no one wanted to miss the end of the congressional term and have to start again, both sides compromised a bit.

"This became the political price we had to pay to get the anti-circumvention stuff through," says Allan Robert Adler, the lobbyist for the Association of American Publishers. On the inauspicious day of April 1, the House Judiciary Committee merged WIPO Copyright Treaty implementation and safe harbor for copyright liability into one bill and sent it to the House.[24] About a month after that, the Senate did the same and passed the bill a few weeks later.[25]

Then, before the bill could become law, the telecom lobbyists did what Lehman did in Geneva: they maneuvered for a home-field advantage. They had the bill sent back to the House Commerce Committee, which was far more sympathetic to their interests than the Judiciary Committee. "What happened was something that has become very common since then—a competition between the Commerce and Judiciary committees," Lehman says. "Judiciary had been lobbied for years by copyright businesses—it's generally a very pro-IP [intellectual property] committee. But Commerce is very involved with telecom, so they're the big powers there."

As public advocacy groups point out, no one involved in crafting the Digital Millennium Copyright Act seems to have spent much time thinking about what was best for the public. But while those groups imply that the MPAA and the RIAA simply got the law they wanted, the truth—perhaps just as disturbing—is that it was a backroom deal between two powerful interest groups. Even the exceptions to the anticircumvention provision beloved by online groups came from lobbying the Commerce Committee. In Washington, an "activist" is often a lobbyist who happens to be on your side.

"What you try to say is 'This language is terrible,' you want to have this whole 'parade of horribles,' even though you might only really be concerned about one," says Band of the Library Copyright Alliance. "I remember one day I was in my shower just trying to think, 'How could this possibly be a bad thing?'" Ultimately, Band and his allies secured exceptions in the law for encryption research and reverse engineering. "By then," he says, "it was just to get as many carve outs as possible."

Finally, more than four years after Lehman presented his plans, Bill Clinton signed the Digital Millennium Copyright Act into law on October 28, 1998. The bill certainly helped Hollywood. The encryption on DVDs was broken the next year—in part by a fifteen-year-old Norwegian hacker.[26] The code he released online spread too quickly for studios to stop, which led activists to say copy protection was useless. But the Digital Millennium Copyright Act ensured that technology companies couldn't legally market a DVD duplication device, and that made copying DVDs inconvenient enough that most people paid for them. Within years, DVD sales dwarfed theatrical revenue.

Ironically, the industry that was most maligned for lobbying in favor of the Digital Millennium Copyright Act gained the least from it. The major record labels hoped an anti-circumvention law would offer legal protection to a new locked digital format they planned to introduce as the Secure Digital Music Initiative, but it never got off the ground. And although they eventually started selling copy-protected music on iTunes, every album they released was already available on unprotected CDs. It didn't do much good to protect iTunes files when the same music could be easily ripped from a CD.

Within a year after the Digital Millennium Copyright Act was signed, the major labels faced a piracy problem larger than they—or anyone involved in the lobbying process that led to the law—could ever have imagined.

Lobbying for the Digital Millennium Copyright Act took place in a world of technology we barely remember: VHS tapes, CD-ROMs, earnest manifestos about the potential of "cyberspace." For better and worse, however, this law created today's "Web 2.0" world of YouTube, Myspace, and ubiquitous broadband. Online piracy not only flourished; it became the "killer app" that generated demand for broadband online access. (There are no reliable statistics on how important this was, but the amount of data traffic that consists of pirated content suggests it must have been a major factor, especially before the rise of legitimate online entertainment services like Netflix and Hulu.) Tim Wu, a Columbia Law School professor who writes about copyright and telecommunications policy, said that the law was so important to "user-generated" content sites like YouTube that it was "the Magna Carta for Web 2.0."[27]

Some copyright holders—especially those from industries that don't use copy-protection systems, like music and photography—didn't get that much out of the deal. The safe harbor provision that freed online companies from worrying about copyright infringement meant creators and content companies had to monitor the Internet for unauthorized copies of their work. This is expensive for any company: Viacom has said it spends $100,000 a month policing online infringement of its copyrights.[28] For independent artists—photographers, small bands, and writers who own rights to their work—it's practically impossible. Since they don't have lobbyists, their voices are rarely heard.

YouTube is now considered a respectable business, the go-to Web site for viral videos, independent art, and even presidential speeches. But the site became famous—and attracted enough viewers to be sold to Google for $1.65 billion in November 2006—partly for hosting copyrighted clips like music videos and the famous "Lazy Sunday" skit from *Saturday Night Live*. Although YouTube's motto is "Broadcast Yourself," the site used to show plenty of content to which it didn't have rights. And the company has been sued for copyright infringement by Viacom, as well as several other companies.

"I don't think anyone anticipated something like YouTube," says Verizon's Sarah Deutsch, whose company obviously also benefited from the law. "But where the DMCA didn't work, Google developed its own filtering technology." The company now takes voluntary steps to block infringing content, presumably to advance its negotiations with media conglomerates.

Several movie studio lawyers say they're fairly satisfied, if not totally happy, with the steps YouTube now takes to reduce piracy. (Viacom's suit is over YouTube's actions prior to early 2008.) But what about other companies? Scribd, a site that lets users post documents the way YouTube lets them display videos, can be used to make public information easily available, but it draws considerable traffic for hosting an array of pirated books. Pirated television shows and sports events are a major draw for live-streaming sites like Justin.tv and Ustream, which allow users to stream live video the way YouTube lets them upload short clips. All of these sites have plenty of legitimate uses, but the fact that almost all of them try to strike distribution deals with entertainment companies suggests they need professional content to build a viable business. Since they essentially have the content already—and, depending on the outcome of Viacom's lawsuit, little incentive to remove it—they can negotiate at a substantial advantage.

As telecom lobbyists argued a decade ago, it seems unreasonable to hold Internet service providers liable for any copyright infringement that occurs on their networks. But the interpretation of the law used in the summary judgment in favor of YouTube—correct or not—gives Web sites no incentive to remove copyrighted material before they receive a request. So they leave it online, especially since it helps them draw an audience. And while copyrighted content makes up a small amount of what these sites make available, it can account for a significant amount of views or downloads. YouTube's own employees believed that more than three-quarters of the site's views came from copyrighted content, according to internal e-mails that came out in the course of the Viacom lawsuit.[29] (YouTube does not reveal this kind of information.) Much of the site's most popular video is programming other companies paid to create.

The safe harbor even creates a perverse incentive for sites to do as little as possible to limit copyright infringement. Let's say the founders of an online company see a *South Park* clip on their site. If they remove it, they could reveal their knowledge of infringement, and arguably lose the safe harbor that protects them from other lawsuits. If they do nothing, they can say—with whatever degree of plausibility—that they didn't know it was there or that, for all they know, it may have been uploaded by the copyright holder. (Part of YouTube's argument in Viacom's case against it is that since Viacom uploaded some clips, it had no way of knowing what the company had authorized.)

The Digital Millennium Copyright Act also makes other kinds of enforcement difficult. "Were it not for safe harbor, the record companies would have been able to go to the ISPs and take Napster off the networks," Lehman says. "You would have still had file sharing, but I don't think it would have been as big."

Since part of the Digital Millennium Copyright Act came out of the WIPO Copyright Treaty, other countries adopted similar laws. In May 2001, the European Union passed the Copyright Directive, which required member states to pass anti-circumvention regulations into law (but left them some flexibility in how to do so).[30] Most countries in Europe also have safe harbor, as well as a system for filing a takedown notice. In practice, some foreign companies respond to Digital Millennium Copyright Act takedown notices, even though they're not subject to U.S. law.

The law also affects what kinds of businesses entrepreneurs start. "Every business since the DMCA has been designed to take advantage of the DMCA, which means it's about aggregating user-generated content and relying on the DMCA as a vehicle to take things down," says the Associated Press's general counsel, Srinandan Kasi. The law should make it possible to start such sites, which have become an important part of the Internet. But it makes it all too easy for them to boost their audience with professional content. Not only do those aggregators draw viewers (or readers or listeners) away from sites that pay to provide programming; they drive down the price for advertising because their costs are so low.

This "user-generated" business model has such significant advantages that it's soaking up investment capital that might have gone to companies that produce the content they present. In the 1990s, investors funded companies like CNET and *Slate*, which produced original journalism. But it's hard for them to compete with sites like the *Huffington Post*, which pay to create only some of the content they sell ads against. Given the choice, why invest in creating anything at all?

At McGill University's 2007 copyright conference, most of the academics in attendance disdained the way the Digital Millennium Copyright Act had allowed entertainment companies to lock up their content with technology. But Bruce Lehman was more upset that the act hasn't protected the interests of artists. He pointed out that labels were having so much trouble making money selling albums that they were asking musicians to sign over some rights to their revenue from songwriting, merchandise sales, and live performances. And he worried that music was entering a "post-copyright era" in which labels would be unable to invest in career development and artists would be left to compete for the patronage of wealthy supporters the way Mozart and Salieri vied for the favor of the Viennese court.

"Our intention," he said, "was not that the music business would be flat on its back and many of the other industries we wanted to promote would be in trouble."

CHAPTER 2

FACING THE MUSIC

HOW THE INTERNET DEVASTATED
THE MUSIC BUSINESS

On the morning of May 3, 2000, in front of an unremarkable San Mateo, California, office building with a bank on the ground floor, the music industry collided with the technology business head-on. At 10:30 a.m., a chauffeured Chevy Blazer pulled up carrying Metallica's drummer, Lars Ulrich, the band's lawyer, Howard King, and two men to help them deliver thirteen document boxes to Napster's fifth-floor headquarters. The boxes held a list of 335,000 people who had downloaded Metallica songs from the first file-sharing service that made such widespread piracy possible.

The delivery of the boxes was intended to be theatrical, and the band had tipped off reporters to hear Ulrich speak about how musicians had to stand up to technology companies trying to profit from their work. But Napster staged a rival performance. The fledgling company produced its own supporters, who shouted down Ulrich and called him a greedy rock star; one even smashed his Metallica CDs with a sledgehammer. Most wore matching T-shirts with the Napster logo, and some seemed to know company staffers.[1] But journalists saw the chauffeured Blazer opposite the upset fans and concluded that Metallica was on the wrong side of a new generation gap.

To Napster's users, the real rock star that day was Shawn Fanning, the nineteen-year-old hacker who had written a revolutionary file-sharing program in his Northeastern University dorm room. He had formed a company with his uncle, John Fanning, who had secured initial funding and moved the operation to California in September 1999. By then, the service, which let music fans copy files from one another's computers, had more than 100,000 users. When the RIAA sued Napster three months later, the resulting publicity only made it more popular. By the time Ulrich delivered his boxes of documents, three-quarters of U.S. college students had used the program.[2] The sheer breadth of music available, combined with the opposition of major corporations, made Napster seem less like a technology company than a youth movement, complete with slogans and T-shirts.

Metallica tried to tell the other side of the story. This wasn't about the money—they had plenty already—and, unlike most bands, they had allowed fans to record and trade their performances for years. What upset them was the leak of an unfinished version of "I Disappear," a song they had recorded for that summer's *Mission: Impossible II*.[3] The previous month Metallica had sued Napster for copyright infringement and racketeering. The company might look like the underdog, Ulrich said of Napster at the time, but "they're looking at [the business] like one day there'll be a major IPO or an AOL-type company is going to come and buy Napster out for a gazillion dollars."[4] (As it happened, about a month later Napster received a venture capital investment.)

Metallica was also counting on promised backup that never appeared—a fact that has never been reported. "We thought it made sense to put an artist's face on the litigation—Metallica didn't want to do it alone, and there were commitments from three or four other major artists to do this, including a major country act," King says. But they dropped out when they saw fans threatening to boycott Metallica. King only managed to bring in his client Dr. Dre, who, like most hip-hop artists, isn't exactly sheepish about wanting to make money. No other major artists came forward. "The band knew there would be a negative reaction," King says, "but they were surprised at how big it was."

Ask most people what humbled the mighty major labels and you'll hear the same answers: they failed to negotiate with Napster, missed their chance to turn file sharing into a legitimate business, and got saved by Apple's iTunes Store when Steve Jobs dragged them, kicking and screaming, into the digital age. This makes for a compelling narrative about how a college student revolutionized a calcified business that didn't give consumers what they wanted. But while the labels certainly moved too slowly, the real story is far more complex.

The labels did negotiate with Napster, even as they fought in public, and each side walked away from talks at different times. Even if they had made a deal, a legal version of Napster would have faced competition from second-generation file-sharing services like Grokster and Kazaa, which would have offered for free what Napster charged for. And while Apple gave the labels a workable digital business model, its iTunes Store also replaced sales of $15 albums with ninety-nine-cent songs.

The real story is that for-profit technology companies deliberately set out to make money from piracy and never came up with a workable plan to pay artists. Although Shawn Fanning sincerely wanted to find a better way to distribute music and Napster negotiated with labels, Grokster and Kazaa—based in the offshore tax havens of Nevis and Vanuatu, respectively—didn't really try. Even with the growth in online distribution, sales of recorded music in the United States were worth $6.3 billion in 2009—less than half their 1999 value of $14.6 billion.[5] The music business became trapped in a downward spiral: starved for revenue, major and indie labels alike have laid off thousands of staffers, dropped hundreds of artists, and cut investment in recording, marketing, and tour support. Emerging artists face a choice between signing new contracts that give labels revenue from live performances and merchandise sales or trying to fund their own careers in a touring market dominated by superstars.

In 2000, Napster had no problem presenting itself as the underdog. Over the previous decade the recorded music business had grown and consolidated into five corporate behemoths—Universal Music Group, Warner Music Group, Sony Music Entertainment, Bertelsmann Music Group, and EMI Music—that among them controlled more than three-quarters of the U.S. market. All of them generated enough cash to run as independent fiefdoms within conglomerates that seemed to barely understand how they operated. One key to their success was the rise of the CD, which spurred consumers to replace their old records and cassettes. Labels also phased out singles, which meant that novelty hits like "Thong Song" and "Who Let the Dogs Out?" drove sales of $15 CDs. And as the cost of manufacturing CDs declined, labels didn't lower prices—a decision that came back to haunt them as music buyers began to see whole packages of blank discs on sale for a few bucks.

By the time Fanning released Napster in June 1999, the major labels had been dealing with online piracy for years on a smaller scale. When ordinary consumers started accessing the Web, full audio files were too big to download easily. But hackers embraced the MP3 format, which compresses songs by leaving out sounds unnoticeable to most human ears. At first record labels viewed sites that featured pirated MP3s the way they saw bootleg record-pressing plants: a problem that could be contained with the right combination of lawsuits and lobbying prowess. But technology advanced faster than they expected. "There was a perfect storm around 1999 when manufacturers started putting CD burners in computers, blank discs went down to under a buck, and MP3 came along," remembers Ted Cohen, a technologically savvy executive who shaped the digital strategy at EMI Music.

Like other students in his dorm, Fanning liked downloading MP3s, but it took time to find the ones he wanted. So he decided to write a program that would index the MP3 files on every computer running it. As users logged in to the system, the songs on their computers would become available to everyone else signed in to the network. Fanning's main innovation was that the central server which ran the program wouldn't store the files themselves—just the list of where they were located. He called the program Napster, after a high school nickname inspired by his hair.

The RIAA had been dealing with pirated MP3s by sending Digital Millennium Copyright Act takedown notices to the sites that hosted them. But that wouldn't work with Napster. Since the music could come from any computer on the network, labels had to either contact individual users or deal with Napster directly. But the company, then run by the former venture capitalist Eileen Richardson, was in no hurry to talk. On December 7, 1999, the RIAA sued, seeking $100,000 in damages per song infringed.[6]

Napster's reluctance to negotiate may have been deliberate. A company strategy document written around that time said, "We will use the hook of our existing approach to grow our user base, and then use this user base coupled with advanced technology to leverage the record companies into a deal," according to Joseph Menn's *All the Rave: The Rise and Fall of Shawn Fanning's Napster*, the definitive book on the subject.[7] Essentially, Napster was using free music to assemble an audience big enough to give it a negotiating advantage. It was a strategy that seemed to inspire scores of other start-ups, including—Viacom would later argue in its lawsuit—YouTube.

Before starting at EMI, Cohen had consulted for Napster, and he remembers bringing Napster's vice president Bill Bales to meet EMI's executive vice president Jay Samit at the Capitol Records Building in Hollywood. "Bill laid out what Napster was all about, and Jay said, 'Let's figure out an experiment,'" Cohen remembers. As he walked Bales out of the office, Cohen asked when they would get back to Samit with a proposal for how the two companies could work together. "And Bales said, 'We're not—we just need to stall for a while.' He said, 'I don't think we're going to have to make deals with the labels—we think there's going to be enough people using Napster that they'll change copyright law.'"

In public, Richardson emphasized Napster's legitimate uses, such as downloading tracks by emerging bands that wanted to offer their music for free. At the same time, the site advertised that "you can forget wading through page after page of unknown artists."[8] The company also sought out endorsements from established acts. Public Enemy rapper Chuck D defended Napster on television and in a *New York Times* opinion piece—and received a payment from the company for another project, according to *All the Rave*—while Limp Bizkit got the company to sponsor a tour of free concerts.[9]

Record companies have a well-earned reputation for not dealing fairly with performers, of course. But by the 1990s, the most exploitative contracts were behind them, thanks to corporate image concerns, savvier artist managers, and lawsuits over past behavior. But standard contracts still worked in favor of labels, which used byzantine accounting to pay out as little in royalties as possible. For years, to cite one example, companies deducted money from artist royalties for "breakage"—a holdover from the vinyl business that wasn't much of an issue for more durable CDs.

When the RIAA sued Napster, tensions between artists and labels had just been exacerbated by the passage of a 1999 bill with an obscure amendment that classified music recordings as "works made for hire."[10] That wording change—which *Billboard* reported was quietly made by Mitch Glazier, majority chief counsel to the House Judiciary Subcommittee on Intellectual Property[11]—would have prevented artists from ever filing to regain their copyrights after a certain number of years.[12] ("Nothing can actually be 'snuck' into an IP bill," says Glazier, who points out that another office held the final copy of the bill.) Although that amendment was repealed, musicians and managers were outraged when the RIAA then hired Glazier as a lobbyist.[13] "On the one hand, RIAA creates all this flap about Napster and copyright infringement," Eagles frontman Don Henley said at the time, "while with the other hand, they've taken away artists' copyrights."[14] This didn't exactly inspire artists to speak out on behalf of labels.

At the end of May 2000, about a month after Metallica delivered its boxes, Hummer Winblad Venture Partners invested $13 million in return for 20 percent of Napster and installed one of its partners, Hank Barry, as interim chief executive, a position he ended up keeping for a year and a half. An intellectual property lawyer who had done work for A&M Records as well as numerous Silicon Valley start-ups, Barry understood both businesses and had an easy time talking with label executives, many of whom shared his professional background. Within a week of starting at Napster, he met with the Universal Music digital executives Albhy Galuten and Lawrence Kenswil at the Palo Alto office of Wilson Sonsini Goodrich & Rosati, the law firm where he worked before going to Hummer. "The thing I was really trying to communicate to them was, I want to try to have an industry-supported model," Barry remembers. He believed Napster was legal, but it was far from certain that courts would agree; he knew a case like this had never been decided before. And since a hearing that could shut down the site until a trial started was scheduled for July 26, he knew he might have less than two months to strike a deal.

Napster and the labels put more effort into negotiating a deal to make the service legal than most people realized at the time. The week after Barry spoke with Galuten and Kenswil, he flew out to New York to meet Edgar Bronfman Jr., then the chief executive of the Seagram Company, which owned Universal Studios and its music operation, the industry's largest. In public Bronfman took an aggressive stance toward online piracy, saying he would defend intellectual property with "a Roman legion or two of Wall Street lawyers."[15] In private he was willing to make a deal, though, and both he and Barry remember their meetings as cordial. During one meeting, Kenswil says, Barry showed him a draft Napster press release attacking the labels for suing the company, and Kenswil jokingly corrected the grammar. "There was no ideology," Kenswil recalls. Like almost everyone on both sides of the debate, Barry mostly just wanted to make money for his company.

Bronfman and Barry met twice more, and their discussions went well enough that Bronfman arranged for a larger meeting the following week—at Herb Allen's annual Sun Valley, Idaho, media business summit—with chief executives from the other media companies that owned labels. Ironically, just when the labels and Napster were closest to making a deal, they squared off in public at a July 11 Senate Judiciary Committee hearing about online music.[16] Label executives pointed out that Napster was building a business based on their music, while Barry said studies showed consumers used the service to sample music they then bought on CD.

Both sides were under pressure at the Sun Valley summit—but they also saw opportunity. Each side faced pressure. The labels had a fighting chance to get file sharing under control, and Barry was waiting for a court decision to establish whether he was running an illegal operation or the fastest-growing technology business in the country. "In order to assume they had a lot of value, they had to wait for the judge's decision," Bronfman says. "But I said, 'I don't think you want to risk that, because the odds are overwhelming that you'll lose.'"

Two days after the Senate hearing, in a conference room at the Knob Hill Inn in Sun Valley, Barry and his boss, John Hummer, met with Bronfman; Bertelsmann's chief executive, Thomas Middelhoff; Sony's chief executive, Nobuyuki Idei; and Sony's U.S. chief, Howard Stringer. They discussed a deal that would give the companies that owned labels a two-thirds stake in Napster, as well as greater control of the company, in exchange for settling their lawsuit. Idei and Middelhoff gave Bronfman permission to negotiate for them, with the idea of organizing a potential deal to present to Time Warner and EMI, then in merger talks. "We would have ended up somewhere where we probably could have gotten a deal done," Bronfman says. Middelhoff remembers the meeting differently: he says he left the room thinking the two sides were too far apart to make a deal.

After this, accounts of the negotiations diverge. Bronfman says Hummer "went radio silent for a week," then called six days before the court hearing to tell him that another company wanted to buy Napster. Hummer gave Bronfman the opportunity to match an offer of $2 billion—a startling sum for a company that had no revenue, let alone profit. "I said I don't need to think about this, I'm not going to buy Napster for $2 billion," Bronfman remembers. "If you can get this deal, you should lock the door and take hostage whomever is going to write you this check." An executive who worked with Bronfman at the time confirmed that Hummer tried to sell Napster for a very high price.

A few hours later Bronfman says he got a call from Yahoo!'s co-founder Jerry Yang, who told him his company might buy Napster to forestall a bid from America Online, which Hummer had told him was interested. Bronfman told Yang he thought Hummer was bluffing: America Online wouldn't risk its pending merger with Time Warner with another complex transaction. Yahoo! passed, and an America Online bid never materialized. "I think John [Hummer] just miscalculated," Bronfman says. "If you remember 2000, those were the headiest days of the technology boom, and I think people just got stars in their eyes."

Barry and Hummer say this didn't happen. But they did have a very different idea of what Napster was worth. "Napster was the fastest-growing application in the history of the world, and there was every reason to believe that its value would have been in the billions of dollars," Hummer says. The record companies believed that the secret to this growth was the fact that it was giving away something people usually paid for—and, that obviously played a major role in its success.

Less than two weeks after the Sun Valley meeting, on July 26, the U.S. district court judge Marilyn Patel handed down a preliminary injunction that ordered Napster to stop users from trading copyrighted works, even if that meant the service had to shut down entirely.[17] As for negotiation, Bronfman remembers, "it was kind of done."

Middelhoff, who was fired from Bertelsmann in 2002, thinks both sides overplayed their hands. As venture capitalists during the dot-com boom, Barry and Hummer thought they could turn Napster into an online empire. But Middelhoff thinks the labels fundamentally failed to understand that they were entering a new world where they could no longer control distribution. "In the past, they had the production of CDs; they had all the value chain," he says. "My position was, when the Internet came up, this is the end of this behavior—you cannot control the Internet."

It's tempting to believe that a deal with Napster could have saved the major labels, and many technology executives see the labels' inability to reach one as their undoing. In the thoroughly reported *Appetite for Self-Destruction: The Spectacular Crash of the Record Industry in the Digital Age*, author Steve Knopper suggests that a legitimate version of Napster could have convinced half its 26.4 million monthly users to spend $10 per month—to bring in $1.58 billion a year.[18] But it's hard to see how Napster would have been able to bring in that much revenue. Few consumers buy $10 worth of music per month at the iTunes Store, which has sold an average of fewer than a hundred songs over the life of each iTunes account.[19] Napster also discussed selling subscription access, but services that do so now have struggled to find a paying audience. Most businesses that entice consumers with free products set a goal of converting 5 percent of them into paying customers. That's a little less than the free-to-paid conversion rate of the online music service Spotify, which at the end of 2010 had about 10 million users and 750,000 subscribers.

"The only way [a Napster deal] would have worked is if you had free-to-paid conversion rates that were unheard of," remembers Bertelsmann Music Group's chief executive, Strauss Zelnick, who understood such business models from overseeing the company's old five-albums-for-a-penny music club. And Napster had several other substantial disadvantages: Not all of its users had credit cards, and at least some of those who did would have been reluctant to use them for online purchases in 1999. More important, Napster would have had to change the expectations of an audience it had conditioned to expect free music, and it would have had to do so while competing with illegal services that were still free—and free to offer copyrighted movies and unreleased music when it couldn't.

That hasn't kept technology pundits from insisting the music business missed its big chance. In *The Perfect Thing: How the iPod Shuffles Commerce, Culture, and Coolness*, the former *Newsweek* technology correspondent Steven Levy blames the labels for not making their content free online the way newspapers did, although that didn't work out very well for them (or for *Newsweek*, for that matter).[20] Levy writes that when he interviewed Barry, he saw a look in his eyes that said, *"Why didn't they work with us?"*[21] But Barry is hardly as naive as Levy makes him sound, and even *he* doesn't think the labels were as clueless as some people say.

"To this day it bugs me when people say, 'They're so backward,'" Barry says. "They're not backward at all. They've got a physical model that's a high-margin, high-revenue model. So it's a perfectly rational business decision for them to stay in the physical world as long as they possibly can." The labels wasted time they should have spent setting up legal online services, and they made plenty of other mistakes. But why would any company *rush* to turn $15 transactions into ninety-nine-cent sales, let alone ones worth nothing at all? Hummer says a music business lawyer told him that he worried the record industry could shrink to $1 billion a year and that his job was to delay that for as long as possible, which sounds depressing but might well make sense from a financial perspective. If you really believed music would inevitably be free, the logical thing to do would be to sell what you could for as long as you could, and use the time and cash flow to sign new contracts with artists that let you make money on live performances or merchandise sales.

Labels that wanted to cooperate with Napster also faced a potentially serious legal problem: they didn't have all the rights they needed to operate a file-sharing service. Older artist contracts didn't include permission to sell music online, and labels worried that working with Napster while it still ran its original service would make them vulnerable to lawsuits from performers or other companies. Technology executives tended to dismiss this. As it turned out, however, when one media company did make a deal with Napster, it found out the hard way that this was more than an idle concern.

As Bronfman and Barry were negotiating politely, almost everyone else in the music and technology businesses was issuing angry pronouncements about the future of artistic creativity, technical innovation, or civilization itself. Even as the RIAA's chief executive, Hilary Rosen, privately urged label chiefs to prepare for a digital future, she played the music industry's bad cop in television interviews. John Hummer told *Fortune*, "I am the record companies' worst nightmare."[22]

"Napster upped the PR ante, so we upped the PR ante, and there was a very hostile environment created," Rosen says. "I had bodyguards at one point, from death threats."[23] That was years before the major labels sued individuals, so this intense ill will stemmed only from the RIAA's lawsuit against Napster.

By that point it had become clear that, whatever the company's intentions, Napster was essentially building a business on piracy. The labels presented a study that looked at more than a thousand users and found they were all trading copyrighted files, although not all of the files they shared were copyrighted.[24] The legal discovery process also found that Napster's co-founder Sean Parker —the Facebook executive portrayed by Justin Timberlake in *The Social Network*—had sent an e-mail to Shawn Fanning about convincing the RIAA that Napster was "not just making pirated music available."[25]

Barry hired the superlawyer David Boies, who had just represented the government in its antitrust case against Microsoft and would soon work for the Democrats in *Bush v. Gore*. Boies argued forcefully that Napster should be legal as long as it was "capable of substantial non-infringing uses," the standard the Supreme Court established in the Betamax case. He said the labels were holding back innovation by refusing to license their content for sale online. And in July 2001, he convinced the U.S. Court of Appeals for the Ninth Circuit to stay Patel's injunction.[26]

As Boies shaped Napster's defense, anti-copyright activists weighed in separately to support the service. The free culture activist Lawrence Lessig, then teaching law at Stanford University, submitted an "expert report" to Judge Patel that argued Napster would have legitimate uses, even if they hadn't emerged yet.[27] John Perry Barlow, who had written "A Declaration of the Independence of Cyberspace," contributed a manifesto to *Wired* claiming that Judge Patel's injunction had turned "millions of politically apathetic youngsters into electronic Hezbollah."[28] Barlow said he thought Napster should have been "Napster.org"—a nonprofit— even though everyone at the company but Shawn Fanning was motivated by monetary gain.[29] In Barlow's view, the future would involve voluntary payments to artists "without the barbaric *inconvenience*"—italics his—"currently imposed by the entertainment industry."[30]

Other pundits simply decided the law didn't matter. In her book *Digital Copyright*, the law professor Jessica Litman asserts that "if forty million people refuse to obey a law, then what the law says doesn't matter."[31] But most of those people didn't have a philosophical objection to the law; they just violated it because they knew they wouldn't get caught.

About forty million speeding tickets are issued every year, according to some estimates, and few drivers would argue that traffic regulations are irrelevant.[32] Like copyright laws, they are often inconvenient, occasionally annoying, and plainly necessary for the greater good.

On Halloween 2000, Napster finally got what it wanted: a lifeline from an old-media executive who believed that file sharing was the future. At a press conference in Manhattan's Essex hotel, Thomas Middelhoff announced that Bertelsmann had made its own deal to lend Napster $60 million, convertible into equity, in order to create a legitimate version of the service. Bertelsmann had a reputation as a risk-averse company with roots in the book-club business and a headquarters in sleepy Gütersloh, Germany, but Middelhoff had made his reputation with an extremely profitable investment in America Online, and he wanted to make another bold move. But he didn't share his plan with Zelnick, who ran Bertelsmann's music business, until just before he announced the deal.

"I was recovering from oral surgery, and I got a phone call" from Bertelsmann's digital chief, Andreas Schmidt, Zelnick remembers. "I said, 'No, listen, we can't do it this way.'" Zelnick, who has a background in technology as well as a law degree, worried that Bertelsmann could share liability for Napster's copyright infringement. "Thomas felt that there was only one path forward, which was digital, and he was right about that," Zelnick remembers. "He felt that it was taking a long time to develop anything and that we were losing ground in the meantime, and that was true. In many ways his vision was apt. The problem was that his answer to that vision was not a good answer." Zelnick wrote Middelhoff a memo with ten things that could go wrong—which, he says, more or less predicted the course of events—but his concerns were dismissed. "He said, 'I invested in America Online because I had a certain feeling about where it would go and I have the same feeling now,'" Zelnick says. "I'm not a believer in prayer as a business plan." Zelnick resigned within a week, although he says he didn't make the move because of Napster.

Middelhoff says legal liability shouldn't have been a problem. "What we did was give money to Napster to develop a legitimate service," he says. That was the only thing the company was allowed to do with the money. "It was for nothing else: not to run their business, not to buy new servers, it was just about that." As Middelhoff took meetings with the other labels, though, he found them less receptive to the idea of a legitimate Napster service than he thought—perhaps because the parent company of one label group would end up with power over the others. Middelhoff says the chief executives of the media conglomerates that owned labels understood that the world was changing, but the record executives beneath them wanted to hold on to what they had, and missed an opportunity as a result. "Napster could have been the early iTunes," he says.

On February 12, 2001, the U.S. Court of Appeals for the Ninth Circuit mostly upheld Patel's injunction, on the grounds that, unlike the makers of the VCR, Napster had an ongoing role in copyright infringement.[33] A week later, Barry and Middelhoff called a press conference to offer the other labels $1 billion over five years from future Napster subscription revenue in exchange for settling the suit. It was a grand gesture but a paltry sum, especially considering how much the service would have cut into CD sales. On July 2, Napster went off-line, unable to filter out copyrighted content as well as Patel wanted.

As Napster ran out of legal maneuvering room and operating capital, it was every venture capitalist for himself. Negotiations for an outright Bertelsmann acquisition stalled as John Fanning argued with Hummer Winblad over who would get the proceeds or receive protection from liability.[34] And when Bertelsmann tried to buy the company out of bankruptcy, a judge ruled against the sale on the grounds that Konrad Hilbers, a former Bertelsmann executive and friend of Middelhoff's who had replaced Barry as Napster's chief executive, had a conflict of interest in making the deal. Napster was eventually sold to the software company Roxio and then to Best Buy, both of which operated it as a legal music site without much success.

As for Bertelsmann, because of its role in helping Napster stay afloat, it was sued for copyright infringement in February 2003 by songwriters and the publishing companies that control their copyrights, much as Zelnick warned.[35] During the course of the bankruptcy proceeding, evidence emerged that Bertelsmann exercised some degree of control over Napster and its loan had been used for everyday operating expenses. The other major labels sued too, and settling all the cases may have eventually cost Bertelsmann more than €390 million.[36] Middelhoff, who was fired in 2002 amid disagreements over the direction of Bertelsmann, points out the company was never found liable for any wrongdoing and says it would have prevailed in court. "There is no way I would have settled this," he says.

The only way the major labels could have invested in Napster without taking a legal risk would have been to shut down the company's illegal service *before* launching a legitimate one. In the meantime, though, illegal competitors would have taken many of Napster's users. But problems like this would soon come to seem quaint. The next generation of file-sharing services decided that free online content represented the future of the music business—whether the music business liked it or not.

Silicon Valley executives have always seen the music business as a mess of inefficiency. As music became cheaper to record and distribute, labels spent most of their money generating demand—marketing and promoting performers they wanted to make into stars. Aside from Apple, the technology world has never placed a high value on consumer marketing, and most entrepreneurs saw it as inefficient. Why couldn't artists record on a computer, give away their music online, and then find something else to sell?

From the outside, this makes sense, since—as technology executives kept pointing out—most performers don't make much money on album sales anyway. After a major-label artist receives an advance for signing a contract that assigns copyright of his recordings to the record company, he doesn't receive any further royalties until he's "recouped"— earned back—the money spent on recording, promotion, and other label expenses. Due to high spending and what might charitably be called imaginative accounting, most acts never see any additional money, while those that do make $1.25 to $1.50 an album in royalties—a pittance compared with the retail price. Major-label recording contracts have been compared to mortgages that leave the bank owning the house after it's paid off.

While record-label contracts leave some artists feeling exploited, however, file-sharing services don't replace record companies; they just replace the trucks that deliver CDs to stores. For all their faults, labels advance artists money to live on, pair them with songwriters and producers, and help find audiences for their albums. At their best, they also serve as creative partners, such as when the Atlantic Records executive Jerry Wexler brought a modestly successful gospel and rhythm-and-blues singer named Aretha Franklin to FAME Studios in Muscle Shoals, Alabama, and helped reinvent her as a soul powerhouse. At their worst, labels ignore projects that aren't priorities and throw money around as recklessly as the hip-hop stars in their videos. But although some artists regret signing with labels, the choice is theirs, and they can sue if they feel they've been wronged. File-sharing services give them no such options.

To understand why the music industry has had so much trouble operating online, it helps to understand that "the music industry" is only a general term for several interrelated businesses that coexist in the same world but run very differently. When a label releases an album, it only controls the right to the recording. Separate copyrights cover the songs as compositions, which are usually owned or administered by publishers; they collect money when songs are played on the radio, recorded on albums, or licensed to movies or television. And the concert and merchandise businesses have their own approaches to making money, and hence their own priorities.

The modern music business evolved during the 1960s, when more artists began to write their own songs and albums started to replace singles as the dominant format. Both shifts gave labels the money and power to organize every aspect of an artist's career around new releases—concerts would promote albums, instead of the other way around. "Historically, record companies were the marketing engine for all of this—your live career, your songwriting career, and your merchandise career," says Danny Goldberg, president of the talent agency Gold Village Entertainment and a former chief executive of Warner Records. "They had the publicity and the promotion and the people who would get you onto the soundtrack."

So far, the acts that have most successfully used free music to promote major tours—Radiohead and Nine Inch Nails—have benefited from millions of dollars' worth of marketing from their respective major labels. "Almost never does an artist establish a national or global career without a lot of money being spent—six or seven figures—with a team of experienced professionals," says Ron Shapiro, a former president of Atlantic Records, who now manages Regina Spektor and other acts. "And I do not see that changing."

Although young artists like Lily Allen and the Arctic Monkeys found fans on Myspace, they quickly signed with labels to advance their careers. So did Hollywood Undead, which had 400,000 Myspace friends but chose to release their album on A&M Octone. "It's great to have Web visibility, but the things that have helped to break this band are the old-school things—radio, retail, and that stuff," says Mike Renault, their manager. Like most bands, Hollywood Undead also needed "tour support," money provided by labels to help with touring expenses. Before performing live becomes a source of revenue, it can be a considerable expense.

Consider an actual budget provided by the manager of a developing rock act that released its first album on a major label in the fall of 2009.[37] For its first proper tour, the band played the East Coast and the Midwest—sixteen shows in nineteen days at small venues with a capacity of two hundred to five hundred. It would take in $1,000 to $2,000 a night, or around $24,000 for the whole tour—not bad for less than a month's work.

That's before costs, though. This band has six members; it's a big group, but that means they don't have to pay a roadie or a driver. The budget calls for them to share rooms with an average cost of $100 per night and spend $25 a day each on food; $3,000 is allocated for insurance and replacement equipment, while transportation should only cost $1,500, since the group has its own van. That's more than $12,000 worth of expenses.

That leaves the band with $12,000 for three weeks of work. Assuming the manager makes a 15 percent commission, each member will take home about $1,700 before taxes. That's not a great living—especially because it's hard to play the same cities more than a few times a year. But it could be a wise investment. If the band uses these shows to build a following and gets popular enough to play venues that hold a thousand people, it could make a nice living.

But that could take some time; it's not easy to build a following. And while the Internet creates opportunities for bands to get their music to a mass audience, that doesn't mean people will listen. Even in online music stores, with their impressive selection, 5 percent of songs account for 80 percent of downloads.[38] This may have less to do with major-label marketing than with the fact that people gravitate toward experiences they can share. This may not be a bad thing. The Beatles sold hundreds of times as many albums as Gerry and the Pacemakers—contemporaries who also worked with the manager Brian Epstein and the producer George Martin—but few music fans would call that an injustice.

Can musicians make money without reaching a big audience? Some technology pundits predict a world of niche culture, but underestimate how tough that could be for artists. In 2008, the former *Wired* editor Kevin Kelly wrote a blog post titled "1,000 True Fans."[39] Assuming each dedicated fan spent $100 per year on an artist's work, he could bring in $100,000 a year, Kelly wrote, "which minus some modest expenses, is a living for most folks." But the products Kelly believes acts should sell, such as vinyl records and T-shirts, cost money to produce, so an artist might only keep half of that $100 after expenses. After setting aside $10,000 for instruments, recording equipment, and a van in which to tour, the artist might end up with $40,000—less if he has a manager, lawyer, or booking agent.

Then there's the issue of how to find those fans in the first place. Some bands get inexpensive exposure by encouraging fans to freely share their music or live performances, like Phish and the Grateful Dead did. But that takes a while, and most acts need income in the meantime. (Early in their career, before they signed to Warner Records, the Grateful Dead were funded by the LSD chemist Owsley Stanley.[40]) And artists who offer their music for free online still need to control their intellectual property rights—much as the Dead did—in order to sell vinyl records, T-shirts, and other merchandise.[41]

Many of the acts using innovative strategies to make money without selling recordings also rely on the old music business in one way or another. In his blog, Kelly cites the example of the singer-songwriter Jill Sobule, who raised $75,000 to make an album by selling various items, from $10 downloads to a $10,000 guest vocalist spot. But many of Sobule's fans first heard her music over a decade ago, when Atlantic Records gave her money to make a funny video with Fabio and helped get one of her songs on the soundtrack to the movie *Clueless*. The most expensive work—getting an artist enough exposure so some listeners become fans—had already been done.

The Internet offers plenty of inexpensive ways to promote music, from Myspace to Twitter. The problem is that those platforms have become so full of musicians that it's hard to stand out from the crowd—and harder to convert an online following into a career. The rapper Soulja Boy started as a YouTube phenomenon, then had a radio hit with "Crank That (Soulja Boy)," which sold 4.6 million copies to become the fourteenth most popular digital download ever.[42] He gradually amassed 2.5 million Twitter followers. But when he released his third album in November 2010, it sold a disappointing 13,000 copies its first week in stores.[43] All that online activity didn't make up for the lack of a hit single.[44]

Even by the end of 2001, most record label executives didn't realize how profoundly file sharing would affect their business. They had vanquished Napster, and CD sales had dropped less than 4 percent compared with 2000—and in a weakening economy at that. Perhaps consumers really were downloading music to decide what CDs to buy.

If that was the case, it was the second generation of file-sharing services that decisively shifted the listening habits of teenagers and twentysomethings. Gnutella launched in 2000, with a design that let users download files from one another's computers without relying on a central directory, as Napster did. Other services further refined that model.[45] That meant the precedent set in the Napster case might not apply, and the fact that some new services were based outside the United States further complicated matters. In October 2001, twenty-eight major labels and movie studios sued the companies that owned Grokster, Kazaa, and Morpheus.[46] In the technology world, the move was viewed as a direct attack on the precedent set by the Supreme Court in the Betamax case.

As the case proceeded, the conflict moved to Washington, where film companies started to flex their muscle. Since DVD players were built with copy-protection technology, studios started to ask why computers couldn't include it as well. In February 2002, Michael Eisner, the chief executive of Disney, testified in front of the Senate Commerce Committee that "there are people in the tech industry who believe that piracy is the killer app for their business."[47] Eisner was mocked for this comment, with some justification. But Napster certainly believed that piracy fueled its growth; it said so in its own strategy document.

The movie business is bigger than the music industry, and it received more sympathy in Washington, where the then-recent controversy over gangsta rap hadn't won labels any fans. But the technology business commanded respect as well, and companies like Intel argued that mandating content protection would interfere with innovation.[48] (Intel apparently changed its philosophy, since it later developed copy-protection systems of its own.) And Silicon Valley had an easier time appealing to consumers, who liked getting content for free online. "The entire theme of the copyright community is that downloading off the Web is both illegal and immoral," said the Consumer Electronics Association's chief executive, Gary Shapiro, at a technology conference in September. "It is neither."[49]

With a nod toward the Home Recording Rights Coalition, the venture capitalists Joe Kraus and Graham Spencer started the organization DigitalConsumer.org to promote a "Consumer Technology Bill of Rights"—which would also help protect their investments. Public Knowledge, an advocacy group that receives funding from technology and electronics companies, started to criticize lawsuits against file sharing as well. "It became a consumer movement," says the RIAA's Hilary Rosen.

Both sides dug in for the Grokster lawsuit. This time, though, there was no sympathetic young inventor in the mold of Shawn Fanning. Kazaa installed "malware" that served up advertising on users' computers.[50] It also complained that Kazaa Lite, a modification of its program that removed the malware, violated its copyright.[51] *Wired* said the Vanuatu-based company, which was eventually dropped from the case, had such a byzantine financial structure that it resembled a "corporate nesting doll."[52]

Like Napster, the file-sharing companies argued that their services had legitimate uses, such as distributing free software or music that was no longer covered by copyright. If so, those uses never caught on. The entertainment companies presented evidence that 97 percent of all files downloaded from Grokster infringed copyright.[53] So far, no reputable study has found a popular file-sharing network where more than 10 percent of downloads are legitimate, and most show that fewer than 5 percent are. (The percentage of available files that infringe copyright can be very different; it was 90 percent in a study presented in the Grokster case.) Many of these studies have been criticized for bias. But a 2010 study by a Princeton student also found that 85 to 99 percent of files distributed on the BitTorrent file-sharing network infringed copyright, and his work was supervised by Ed Felten, a computer science professor, who has criticized copyright laws.[54]

In April 2003, a U.S. district court ruled in favor of the file-sharing services, in part because they were set up differently from Napster. In a summary judgment, the U.S. district court judge Stephen Wilson held that "Grokster and StreamCast are not significantly different from companies that sell home video recorders or copy machines, both of which can be and are used to infringe copyrights."[55] Although the services were covered by the Betamax precedent, Wilson ruled, their users were still liable for copyright infringement. In August 2004, after the U.S. Court of Appeals for the Ninth Circuit mostly upheld the decision, the media companies appealed to the Supreme Court.[56]

By then, the RIAA had started suing individuals. In September 2003, a few months after it lost the Grokster case in district court, the RIAA filed 261 lawsuits against users who distributed copyrighted music on file-sharing services. (The RIAA's lawsuits against individuals depended mostly on illegal sharing, not downloading.)[57] The organization had considered this for some time, but Rosen and Warner Music Group's chief executive, Roger Ames, stopped the suits from moving ahead until Apple's iTunes Store provided a convenient way to buy music online. "I think we had sued almost every service around that was a real threat," says Rosen, who had left the RIAA by the time the suits against individuals were filed. But when the courts ruled in favor of the services, the labels felt they had no choice but to sue individuals.

From a public relations standpoint, the lawsuits were a disaster. U.S. copyright law sets statutory damages for infringement at $750 to $30,000 per work—or up to $150,000 if "infringement was committed willfully"[58]—but that penalty was devised with moneymaking pirate operations in mind. Although the RIAA offered to settle for pennies on the dollar—the lawsuits, however ill-advised they may have been, were never intended to generate profit—the potential damages still shocked most observers. And as the RIAA continued to file lawsuits based on Internet protocol addresses—a standard but not reliably accurate way of identifying Internet users—the public relations hits just kept on coming. Among others, it sued a grandmother who didn't know how to download and someone who had died.[59]

Almost every individual accused of illegally sharing copyrighted songs settled with the RIAA, although some challenged the lawsuits on various grounds. The first case to reach a jury involved Jammie Thomas, a single mother from Brainerd, Minnesota, who said she hadn't downloaded the songs in question.[60] Journalists portrayed her as a victim of media conglomerates, but the jury didn't take long to find her liable for willful copyright infringement and awarded statutory damages of $222,000 for sharing twenty-four songs—more than $9,000 a track.[61] In a retrial, ordered because of an error in jury instruction, Thomas was found liable for damages of $1.92 million, presumably because the jury didn't believe her account of events. (The law sets a range of damages that's absurdly high, but both juries awarded well over the minimum; this indicates that either Thomas didn't come across well in court or ordinary Americans don't see file sharing as a victimless crime—or, probably, both.) The judge reduced this award to $54,000, and the RIAA offered to settle for $25,000 if Thomas would ask the judge to vacate that decision, so it wouldn't set a precedent.[62] Thomas declined this offer, and the labels rejected the judge's remittitur. In November 2010, a third trial solely to determine damages found Thomas liable for $1.5 million—a verdict she has said she will appeal. In December 2010, Thomas made a motion to set aside that verdict as unconstitutionally high, and the RIAA plans to respond. The labels don't want to jeopardize their ability to ask for high damages, and Thomas seems to be fighting on principle.

Did all of these legal fees and publicity missteps actually accomplish anything? The lawsuits alienated fans, tied up the legal system, and arguably made it harder for the RIAA to push antipiracy legislation that might have been more effective. Meanwhile, the number of tracks downloaded illegally continued to rise. But at least some of that increase is the result of faster connections and larger hard drives. Between 2006 and 2009, the percent of Internet users who downloaded music illegally declined slightly, according to the research company NPD Group, no small thing given how fast it had been rising.[63] It's almost impossible to stop committed pirates, but the RIAA's lawsuits probably kept their numbers from growing—although at too high a price.

In a few years, the major labels managed to destroy the cultural cachet they had spent decades building. In the late 1960s, CBS Records used to advertise its counterculture acts with the tagline "The man can't bust our music." Now most teenagers believe the major labels were trying to do just that.

Some of the negative publicity came down to poor planning and bad luck. "By putting Metallica out there, it became a farce," says Bob Mould, the former Hüsker Dü frontman and solo artist, who thinks the band members' hearts were in the right place. It might have been different "had it been a newer artist who said, 'I think it's great that you're sharing my music, but I have to get paid or I can't do this full-time like you want me to.'"

Some younger fans tend to sneer at musicians who want to get paid, partly because one of rock's defining myths is that no one is in it for the money. This is unique to rock: country performers value material success, and rappers go to absurd lengths to show it off. But it was never in anyone's interest to discuss the details of the music business, which weren't very glamorous anyway. "Artists don't like to talk publicly about getting paid," says Danny Goldberg of Gold Village Entertainment. "Rock and roll is a rebellious art form, dealing with a teenage sensibility, and through the lens of that attitude it's easy to look at record company executives as uncool and shallow."

The labels tried to project a simple message: file sharing copyrighted music was theft. But as technology business lawyers rushed to point out, they're not the same thing at all: different laws cover copyright infringement and stealing, and copying a file doesn't deprive its original owner of anything. The implication was that theft was wrong, copyright infringement less so.

It makes more sense to compare copyright infringement to a theft of service—sneaking into a movie or jumping a subway turnstile. (In the case of uploading files, it's more like breaking a door or turnstile so others can do so.) In all of these cases, nothing is literally taken; as is the case with music, enough other people pay that it seems like a minor infraction. But both are still illegal, because if everyone stopped paying, we would no longer have movies or public transportation of the same quality. And while file sharing isn't theft, it's not exactly "sharing" either.

After CD sales fell 10.7 percent in 2002, labels heard a "geek chorus" of suggestions on how to reinvent their business. While it's hard to know for certain if they could have prevented their decline, the labels' biggest failing was not organizing a legitimate, convenient online retailer before Apple launched its iTunes Store in April 2003. Such a store would have struggled to compete with Napster, but it would have appealed to consumers troubled about taking songs without paying for them and put the labels in a better position to lobby for laws that encouraged legal commerce online. When the five major labels finally introduced two online stores among them—Universal and Sony launched Pressplay, while EMI, Warner Music Group, and Bertelsmann Music Group started Music-Net—they were plagued by confusing prices, confusing copy protection, and compatibility problems.

The music industry's own online stores were such disasters that Napster postponed its demise by getting Judge Patel's permission to gather evidence of whether the labels had colluded to suppress competition. The record companies certainly wanted to gain more control over how their product was sold, but they may have quarreled more than they cooperated. "They mistakenly thought this was an opportunity to change the equation," Rosen says of the labels. "Maybe they wouldn't just invest, record, promote, and market—maybe they could even sell." But disagreements between labels, publishers, and artists made it hard to put together offers that interested consumers, Rosen says. "Everybody was fighting among themselves for a couple of years rather than coming together."

The labels also missed an opportunity in the late 1990s to replace the CD with a secure music format they could control. Any copy-protection system will eventually be cracked, but they didn't need to make piracy impossible—just inconvenient. The labels tried to do this in 1998, when they gathered scores of electronics, software, and technology companies to form the Secure Digital Music Initiative. The idea was to give music files protection like that on DVDs. But the organization's work stalled as labels argued for more security and electronics companies pushed for convenience—rightly so, since a legal format has to be as convenient as piracy. When unprotected MP3s became the de facto standard, though, negotiations broke down as electronics companies realized they could make more money selling gadgets that would play pirated music; they had nothing to gain by cooperating. Technology and consumer electronics companies maintain that consumers hate copy protection, but that may depend on whether it gets in their way; it doesn't seem to have held back Apple's iTunes Store.

Once the labels realized they couldn't establish a secure music format, they should have eliminated copy protection entirely. This isn't a contradiction—just an acknowledgment of reality. As long as labels released CDs with unprotected music, it didn't make sense to protect the same songs just because they happened to be sold online. In 2005, Sony BMG Music Entertainment released CDs that, unbeknownst to users, installed rootkit software on Windows PCs that limited copying but also made the computers vulnerable to viruses. The public outcry was immediate: copy protection had gone too far. Sony BMG was forced to recall the affected CDs and settle several class-action lawsuits. More important, bad publicity over the incident angered consumers who hadn't known much about copy protection until then. The labels never made another serious attempt to protect CDs.

The labels could have also tried to postpone their decline in other ways, including cutting wholesale prices, although Universal Music tried this in 2003, without success. In retrospect, though, it's hard to know if any of these ideas would have worked. As other media businesses began to face the same problems, executives talked confidently about their plans to avoid making the same mistakes as the major labels. But they didn't even agree on what those mistakes were. It's not as easy as it looks to run a business based on giving away what you once sold, especially in a medium where ads can be stripped out.

"There were plenty of stupid record executives, there was plenty of short-term thinking, and there were some incredibly awkward PR moments," Goldberg says. "But even if they had done everything right, the end result would have been basically the same. Because how about the newspaper business, how about all these other content businesses that didn't sue their customers? They're just as screwed up."

For about two months in the summer of 2002, the University of Texas economics professor Stan Liebowitz became a hero to everyone who hated record labels—by then a large enough group to win him some media attention. That spring, he published a paper with the libertarian Cato Institute suggesting file sharing would hurt the recording industry.[64] But he started questioning his conclusion once he saw sales weren't actually falling much.

Liebowitz stepped back from his earlier beliefs and suggested the recession could have caused the slight decline and that music fans might be sampling songs online and then buying the ones they liked—just as Napster had argued in court. He pointed out that labels had also worried about piracy in the early days of the audiocassette, although the format eventually expanded the market: some consumers taped albums rather than buying them, but others bought new cassettes for their cars. "I try to let data tell me what's actually happening in the world," Liebowitz told Salon.[65] "And when the theory says one thing and things don't work that way, then I say something's missing in the theory."

Liebowitz, already respected among academics for his work on the economics of copyright and software, suddenly had a wider audience. Music Web sites linked to his paper. The Dallas Observer called him "the journalist's go-to guy on the issue of online music distribution."[66] And Lawrence Lessig praised his work in an opinion piece for the Financial Times. "When the data say something different from the party line," Lessig wrote, "the academic should do as Prof Liebowitz did: speak the truth even if that means changing your mind."[67]

And then Liebowitz changed his mind again, because the data started saying something else entirely.

In July he saw that the midyear numbers for music sales had dropped 9.7 percent from the previous year. Examining three decades of music sales, Liebowitz found that previous recessions hadn't caused such significant declines and concluded the falloff probably did come from illegal downloading, even though he didn't think every pirated copy of a song represented a lost sale. In a second *Salon* interview, a little more than two months after the first, Liebowitz predicted that file sharing would lead to a 20 percent drop in music sales.[68]

At that point, "I stopped getting calls from reporters," Liebowitz remembers. "People liked the story that [file sharing] wasn't causing harm. People don't like big companies, they don't like the recording industry, and they liked the idea that they could get something for free."

This wasn't the first time Liebowitz had researched the economic effects of copyright—or caused controversy with his findings. Before 2002, most of his studies had concluded that unauthorized duplication actually *helped* copyright holders, and he believes he was among the first economists to suggest this.[69] He came up with a theory called "indirect appropriability," which said the ability to make copies of a work could raise its value to a consumer. The example he used was the way photocopy machines allowed libraries to get more value out of scholarly journals. "Needless to say, I was not very popular with organizations representing copyright holders," Liebowitz wrote on his Web site.[70] (He has since done some research for the International Federation of the Phonographic Industry, the global recording business trade organization.) "In those days there was not an army of copyright critics to embrace my work and make me a hero."

Since the Napster lawsuit, any evidence that file sharing doesn't hurt the music business has found an eager audience. In March 2004, when a paper by the economists Felix Oberholzer-Gee and Koleman Strumpf concluded that file sharing had little or no effect on music sales, journalists found the counterintuitive take as irresistible as they had found Liebowitz's.[71] The economists analyzed the relationship between album sales and file sharing and found that uploading increased during school vacations in Germany, which at the time supplied a substantial amount of the music downloaded by file-sharing service users worldwide. This surge prompted U.S. Internet users to download more songs, but album sales didn't decline accordingly when they did.

Liebowitz questioned Oberholzer-Gee and Strumpf's research, pointing out that German students would upload a lot of music that wouldn't interest Americans and that, contrary to what Oberholzer-Gee and Strumpf said, genres that were more popular on file-sharing services saw larger sales declines and sales were falling around the world.[72] ("We were studying file sharing in 2002," Strumpf says. "We're now in 2011, and it's a very different world.") In May 2007, Industry Canada released a study by the economists Birgitte Andersen and Marion Frenz that found that file sharing actually *helps* sales.[73] Liebowitz challenged that paper as well, and Andersen and Frenz later concluded there wasn't a strong relationship between piracy and CD sales after all. Asked about the study, Andersen says the Pirate Bay file-sharing service doesn't offer much copyrighted music from major-label acts—although even a cursory glance at its Web site shows that isn't true.

Many factors have hurt music sales, including the closing of so many record stores. But almost every other study has concluded that file sharing played a role,[74] and anyone who believes otherwise is running out of alternative explanations. Several studies have shown that individuals who download music illegally also buy it, but that only proves correlation, not causation. Some suggested CD sales fell because music fans are no longer replacing their old records, but "catalog" sales of older releases declined less than overall sales from 2004 to 2009.[75] Others speculated that DVD sales cut into the CD market, but now they're declining as well.

Music sales have also declined disproportionately in countries where file sharing is more common. In Spain, where fully 45 percent of Internet users get media from pirate services—about twice the average rate in Europe[76]—CD sales declined 77 percent since 2001, compared with a continent-wide average decline of 54 percent.[77] And Japan is now the No. 1 market for CDs, despite having one-third the population of the United States, partly because many people there access the Internet with mobile phones that don't run file-sharing programs.[78]

In June 2010, with U.S. music sales less than half what they were a decade earlier, Oberholzer-Gee and Strumpf published another paper which conceded that file sharing *had* affected sales, but not that much and in a way that helped society.[79] They said that 60 percent of online traffic consisted of file trading—an astonishing statistic that implies illegal downloading accounts for more than half of all Internet use—but that all this piracy accounted for 20 percent or less of the decline in music sales. And they pointed out that despite weaker copyright protection, artists were creating more work than ever: the number of new albums issued each year had doubled since 2000, and book and movie releases rose substantially as well. "Artists often enjoy what they do, suggesting they might continue being creative even when the monetary incentives to do so become weaker," they wrote. "In addition, artists receive a significant portion of their remuneration not in monetary form—many of them enjoy fame, admiration, social status, and free beer in bars."

Essentially, two respected economists argued that people will work for beer. (This may be literally true, of course, but that doesn't mean they'll work as hard as they otherwise might have.) Oberholzer-Gee and Strumpf also pointed out that the music business has grown over the last decade if you count iPod sales. Since in the United States none of this revenue goes to anyone who makes music, this is like saying the clothing business is booming if you count the installation of customized closets—both technically accurate and entirely beside the point.

What Oberholzer-Gee and Strumpf really proved was that more music than ever is available for sale in a way that can be measured. They got their numbers on new album releases from Nielsen Sound-Scan, which tracks new titles, whether or not they contain new music, which means they counted reissues, new compilations of old material, and foreign releases available only online. (Probably because there's only so much more old music to sell online, 2010 saw a 22 percent decline in album releases.) They also counted thousands of digital-only releases on iTunes from bar bands, who a decade ago might only have sold their albums at concerts, where SoundScan couldn't count them. And much of the increase over the past decade seems to have come from hobbyists: the number of U.S. residents employed as musicians has declined 19 percent since 2001.[80]

That's important because the purpose of copyright is to "promote the Progress" of the arts, not simply encourage participation. It's hard to see any relationship between the quantity and the quality of work produced. It's even harder to argue, as Oberholzer-Gee and Strumpf do, that society benefits much from all this new music, given that so few people hear it. Of the seventy-five thousand albums released in the United States in 2010, sixty thousand sold fewer than a hundred copies, and many of those sold fewer than ten.[81] If a band makes an album and no one is there to hear it, does it still make a sound?

In the grand narrative of the music business collapse, the labels were rescued from their own incompetence by Steve Jobs's iTunes music store, which made piracy a marginal problem. Apple certainly pushed the labels into doing something they were unable to do themselves, and its iTunes Store has become the biggest music retailer in the United States. But legitimate online music stores like Apple's have hardly stopped piracy: more music is downloaded illegally than legally, according to the NPD Group.[82] (Not all of those songs represent lost sales, of course, but surely some must.) And, like the industry's attempts to turn file sharing into a legitimate business, the real story of Apple's effect on the music business is more complicated than most people realize.

In October 2001, Apple was a second-tier technology company that controlled about 3 percent of the personal computer market and was slowly regaining its relevance with high-design candy-colored Macs.[83] When it introduced the $400 iPod just as the economy slowed, consumers didn't exactly line up in front of Apple stores (of which there were only a few at the time anyway). Record labels were even less enthusiastic. In October 1998 the RIAA had sued Diamond Multimedia to stop the sale of the Rio, one of the first MP3 players. The organization argued that the device didn't comply with the 1992 Audio Home Recording Act, which mandated that digital recording devices incorporate copy-protection technology and pay a royalty that would go to labels, performers, publishers, and songwriters. After a court ruled the law didn't apply since the Rio didn't record songs, other companies followed Diamond into the MP3 player market, including Apple.

Later that year, following the introduction of the iPod, Jobs called America Online's chief executive, Barry Schuler, to ask about selling music from the company's Warner Music Group. "He had the device, but devices without content don't sell well," remembers Paul Vidich, a Warner Music executive vice president at the time. So Vidich went to Cupertino, California, where he initially spoke with Jobs about DMX, a proposed secure music format. "I had someone giving a PowerPoint presentation and Steve was rocking back and forth in his chair, obviously agitated, and he basically said, 'I don't want to talk about this—I want to talk about this other thing,'" Vidich remembers. "And he launched into a tirade against the music industry. The room went dead silent. And I looked at him and said, 'Steve, you're absolutely right, but that's why we're here. We're here because we think you—Apple—can help us solve this problem.' And that sort of broke the ice."

Over the next six months, Vidich met with Apple executives as they designed the iTunes Store. By then he knew consumers wanted an easy experience, and Warner agreed to a copy-protection system that allowed buyers to burn songs on CD. Jobs insisted on selling individual songs for one set price, and Vidich suggested ninety-nine cents. Jobs next approached the Universal Music Group, where the chief executive, Doug Morris, and Interscope Records' chairman, Jimmy Iovine, loved the store's elegant simplicity. Approval from the other majors and most big indies soon followed. Since the deals to sell music ran for a year and only applied to the Macintosh, executives figured they could always renegotiate later. "If this was really successful," Vidich remembers thinking, "we'd find a way to differentiate the prices and charge more."

Ironically, the one decision the labels usually get credit for making correctly may have been among their worst. Their eagerness to find a decent digital rights management system led them to accept one they didn't control, which allowed Apple to dominate the market. They successfully pressed Apple to get seventy cents out of every ninety-nine-cent sale, which doesn't leave Apple with much of a profit after the costs of processing credit card transactions and running the iTunes Store. The company makes so much on the iPod and related products that it essentially runs its online retailer to market them. Like Walmart, it sells music to promote more profitable goods, which means it has the leverage to sell music however it wants.

"We pushed hard to make sure all the constituencies around the table grabbed a lot of margin, which meant there wasn't enough left for the retailer," says Strauss Zelnick, who believes this was one of the industry's biggest mistakes. (By then, he had left Bertelsmann.) "We would have been vastly better served to allow someone to grab ten points of net margin to have a bigger business than what we have today." Allowing retailers to make more money could have created more competition.

In September 2005, Bronfman, by then chief executive of Warner Music Group, gave a speech saying that the price of a song should vary according to its newness and popularity, much like that of a DVD. "We are the arms supplier in the device wars," he said.[84] To some extent, this was true. The labels had given Apple a powerful weapon—its digital rights management system, FairPlay, which it refused to license to other companies. The iPod would only play MP3s and songs purchased from the iTunes Store, and songs from the iTunes Store would not play on other digital music players. That discouraged iPod owners from using other online music stores, and they couldn't switch to another kind of digital music player without losing the songs they bought from iTunes. It also let Apple sell the iPod for a premium. Eventually, it helped Apple use the iTunes Store to develop the App Store that helped it lead the smartphone market, introduce the first successful tablet computer, and ultimately become one of the most valuable companies in the world.

By the end of 2004, the iTunes Store had sold 200 million songs. Until 2009, sales of digital downloads grew dramatically every year. But iTunes also encouraged fans to buy ninety-nine-cent songs instead of $10 or $15 albums.

Even if they continue to grow, those ninety-nine-cent-song sales won't come close to making up for the corresponding decline in CD sales. "When they let Steve Jobs roll over us, that was the end," says

Peter Mensch, co-founder of Q Prime Management, who works with Metallica, the Red Hot Chili Peppers, and other acts. "They thought, 'It's another way to sell music.' But now I'm selling singles when I should be selling albums." Mensch dismisses the idea that labels had to make the deal to compete with file-sharing services. "The 40 or whatever percent of people who steal music—they're gone and they're never coming back."

This goes against the conventional wisdom of the technology world, which has pushed labels to cut prices in order to turn pirates into consumers (and, in the process, help their own businesses). But trying to compete with free in this particular way might not have been a smart move. In January 2009, Apple announced that labels had agreed to eliminate copy protection from iTunes songs in exchange for more power to set song prices, which would range from sixty-nine cents to $1.29 in the United States. Technology executives predicted sales would decline, which they did. At the same time, though, revenue *increased*. In the following six weeks, the revenue generated by most of the $1.29 songs increased, according to a *Billboard* study, and the online store's overall revenue went up 12 percent.[85] Since label studies say between 10 and 15 percent of music fans are dedicated pirates, in most cases it makes sense to ignore them and concentrate on consumers who are willing to spend money.

More surprisingly, some of the most successful acts of the last few years aren't on iTunes at all, and one reason for their success may be that they sell more entire albums. Most technology writers have a hard time believing this: in November 2010, when the Beatles finally made a deal to sell their music on iTunes, the *Washington Post* wrote that by holding out, they had "proved themselves to be lousy capitalists."[86] But in the first decade of the new century, the Beatles sold more albums in the United States than any act besides Eminem; their hits collection, *1*, was the best-selling album of the decade.[87] And although the *Post* suggested that the Beatles had ceded the market to pirates, illegal downloads of the band's songs actually *increased* after their iTunes debut.[88]

The Beatles are an exception to almost every rule. But other acts may also have received a sales boost by staying off of iTunes. In 2008, when iTunes was already the largest music retailer in the United States, the country's No. 4 and No. 5 best-selling albums were by Kid Rock and AC/DC, neither of which sells music on Apple's store in the United States.[89] (Kid Rock sells music on iTunes in Europe and in online stores that don't break up his albums; AC/DC doesn't currently sell any music online.) The success of that Kid Rock album, *Rock n Roll Jesus*, was driven by the anthemic radio hit "All Summer Long." Since it wasn't sold as a single, some people downloaded it illegally, but many others apparently decided to spring for the album.

To some extent, Kid Rock just found a new take on a time-tested strategy. In the 1970s, when the music business was still based around singles, some rock acts deliberately didn't release them, in order to stimulate album sales. The most famous example is Led Zeppelin, which never put out "Stairway to Heaven" as a single in the United States; fans who wanted the song had to buy the band's fourth album. Other hard rock bands, like Metallica and AC/DC, never even put out greatest-hits albums.

AC/DC's attitude toward their music might be best summarized as "Have it our way." The hard rock group doesn't authorize samples and rarely licenses songs to advertisers. As CD sales have plummeted, AC/DC albums do as well as or better than ever, and the group sells more catalog albums than any other act but the Beatles.[90] "They felt like they made albums and they wanted them dealt with in that way," says Steve Barnett, chairman of Columbia Records, the band's label. "My opinion is you just have to look at the numbers—that should tell you what they do is working." Even though AC/DC's music isn't legally available online, it was actually downloaded illegally less than that of Led Zeppelin in 2007.[91]

"Popularity on file-sharing networks really only correlates to one thing, and that's popularity," says Eric Garland, founder of the media measurement company BigChampagne. "Is there more Kid Rock file sharing because he's not on iTunes? Maybe. But we'll probably never know, because a much larger factor is what's going on with Kid Rock in general: Does he have a new album, is he on tour, did he perform at the VMAs [the MTV Video Music Awards]?"

All the performers who succeed without iTunes are "album acts," with followings interested in more than their latest hit. Pop singers— "singles acts"—wouldn't succeed with this strategy. And online sales are becoming more important: Data provided by Nielsen SoundScan showed that Def Leppard, another iTunes holdout, would almost certainly be better off selling its music online. At some point—soon, if not already—it will be impractical for any band not to sell music on iTunes.

But several studies suggest that "unbundling" albums—the selling of individual songs—contributed significantly to the decline in music sales. A 2007 study by the consulting company Capgemini funded by the U.K. music industry found that 18 percent of the labels' 2004–2007 revenue loss stemmed from piracy, while the rest was the result of selling music by the track.[92] And a May 2010 study by the Harvard Business School professor Anita Elberse found "strong evidence of the negative consequences" of unbundling and estimates that it caused about a third of the revenue decline during the period of her study.[93]

Media companies have always relied on bundling to sell products for a price that can cover their fixed costs, and they're not alone. Many businesses bundle goods in some way, like clothing stores that don't break apart suits to sell jackets and trousers separately. Although some consumers take their business elsewhere, this can be an effective strategy. Just ask Apple, which doesn't sell separate replacement batteries for the iPod.

By the end of 2004, when the U.S. Supreme Court agreed to hear the Grokster case, it was obvious to everyone that the recorded music business was hurting, and the people who ran it knew things would get worse. That year $12.3 billion of music was shipped, up slightly from 2003 but down 16 percent from 1999.[94] The companies that owned the labels were preparing for the worst as it became clear that legal action alone couldn't stop online piracy from seriously cutting into sales. Sony and the Bertelsmann Music Group combined their operations in a joint venture. Time Warner sold its music business to a group of investors led by Bronfman. And all the labels laid off employees in what became a grim annual ritual.

The Supreme Court started hearing oral arguments in the Grokster case at the end of March 2005, and the stakes were high. If the Supreme Court turned a blind eye to businesses that essentially encouraged illegal behavior, it would render copyright meaningless in the digital age. But if it outlawed certain kinds of technologies, it would give the entertainment industry veto power over inventions like the iPod.

The justices didn't want to do that, but they also seemed uncomfortable with the idea that Grokster depended on illegal activity. "I know perfectly well that I can buy a CD and put it on my iPod," Justice David Souter said at one point. "But I also know if I can get music without buying it, I'm going to do so."[95]

On June 27, 2005, the Supreme Court handed down a unanimous decision that Grokster and Morpheus were liable for "inducing" copyright infringement. After two successive defeats, media companies had added to their case a new argument based on "active inducement," a concept from patent law. The Court allowed the Betamax precedent to stand, but its decision outlined a doctrine that would hold companies liable for promoting infringement. "One who distributes a device with the object of promoting its use to infringe copyright, as shown by clear expression or other affirmative steps taken to foster infringement, is liable for the resulting acts of infringement by third parties," Souter wrote in the majority opinion.[96] The decision sketched out how companies could be found liable for inducing infringement if they promoted illegal uses of a product, made no effort to reduce these uses, and depended on them for profit.

Many legal scholars praised the decision for its fairness, since the justices seemed to find a way to protect copyright without jeopardizing technological innovation. But anti-copyright activists resented any limits at all. The Electronic Frontier Foundation issued a white paper, "What Peer-to-Peer Developers Need to Know About Copyright Law," which basically outlined how file-sharing services could stay on the right side of the law.[97] And while technology groups predicted the Grokster ruling would "chill technology innovation," one could just as easily argue that the continued operation of file-sharing services would prevent the development of legitimate new businesses.[98] It's hard to imagine Apple would have spent the money to build its iTunes Store if the Napster case had made it legal to give away music online. The same goes for Spotify and almost every other online music service.

For all the anger on the other side, the Grokster case didn't exactly save the entertainment business. As the decade went on, the value of U.S. music sales went from bad to worse, dropping 9 percent in 2007, 18 percent in 2008, and 12 percent in 2009. (These numbers include digital sales.) As record stores closed and big-box retailers cut shelf space for music, sales of CDs continued to fall at least partly because there was nowhere to buy them.

"I call it the death spiral," says Russ Crupnick, an analyst at NPD Group. "While everyone was so focused on price, what people wanted was a shopping experience—flipping through the racks, looking for stuff." Crupnick sees the same spiral in the way labels operate: less revenue leads to less spending, less promotion, and, ultimately, even less revenue. As much as the music business has changed, you still have to spend money to make money—look at Lady Gaga or Taylor Swift.

"I don't know what will happen to the record labels, and I don't think they'll look anything like they do now," says Charlie Walk, who was president of Epic Records from late 2005 to 2008. "But a funny thing happens when you don't promote a project: nothing."

The major labels are no longer the only companies that can promote projects effectively. For the last couple of decades, they had three key advantages indies couldn't match: marketing budgets, efficient distribution, and access to radio. None of those are exclusive to them anymore, although this has less to do with the Internet than with other changes: start-ups have money, the majors now distribute music from other companies, and layoffs have created a pool of industry veterans who can be hired on a freelance basis. Established acts can now strike deals directly with retailers—as the Eagles and Journey did with Walmart—that can spend more on promotion than most labels.

"Record labels, at a time when they should be expanding their personnel, they've gone in the other direction," Peter Mensch says. "So there's less and less reason to be with them." Mensch's Q Prime started its own label, as have several other management companies with the staff and cash flow to provide the services only labels once could. As management companies start releasing albums, major labels are acting more like managers. Labels now sign most artists to "multi-rights deals" that let them share in revenue from songwriting copyrights, merchandise sales, and even concert performances. The British pop star Robbie Williams signed a contract like this with EMI in 2002, and Paramore and Lady Gaga have similar arrangements with Atlantic Records and Interscope Records, respectively. These deals give labels an incentive to emphasize career development over quick hits, but some acts worry that these contracts will leave them with less money in the long run.

In the half decade since the Grokster decision, all four major labels have spent significant money and resources diversifying their businesses—with multi-rights deals, merchandise businesses, and strategic investments in technology companies. But they've also seen their share of chaos. Warner Music Group, which went public under Bronfman in 2005, has seen its stock price lag. In 2007, EMI was sold to a private equity firm, which has since lost it to Citigroup. In August 2008, Bertelsmann sold its half of Sony BMG Music Entertainment to Sony and got out of the recorded music business entirely. Only the Universal Music Group has had a relatively smooth run, thanks to dominant market share, but it has come under pressure to cut spending.

The major labels also made some difficult decisions about how to sell music online, with varying degrees of success. Start-ups say they asked for advance fees that were too high, and perhaps they did. But those payments kept start-ups from giving away music in order to gain market share, and destabilizing the rest of the market as they did. Once the labels identified iTunes as a steady source of cash, they had an interest in not undercutting it. And so far at least, no label of any size has found a way to make much money giving away music. Online streaming services like imeem never sold enough advertising to meet their expenses, although Vevo, a joint venture in which three of the four major labels share ad revenue with Google, shows promise.

A decade after Napster, labels of all sizes are still struggling to reinvent their businesses, with consequences for the culture business as a whole. "Years ago, if you were really talented, you didn't have to work a normal job—you were a full-time musician," Mensch says. "We live in fear that the next Kurt Cobain is sitting around saying, 'Fuck this, the music business is over—I'm going to join my dad at the printing plant.'"

Jack White is adjusting to the new music business about as well as any artist out there. The former White Stripes frontman owns his own label, Third Man Records, which releases his albums through a distribution deal with Warner Music Group. He runs a subscription service called the Vault, which sells rare songs and concert recordings for up to $20 per month. He also records and releases material from other acts, both online and on vinyl records that appeal to fans and collectors; recent products include limited-edition multicolored vinyl, "Texas-size" thirteen-inch LPs, and Halloween singles that glow in the dark.

White has the clout to follow Radiohead and Nine Inch Nails and distribute his music online instead of relying on Warner. But he says he's had better experiences with major labels than with indies, and he worries that the same technology which makes it easy for him to run his own label could hurt other artists. He also loves records as tactile objects.

As White sees it, music has become so easy to copy that listeners forget how hard it is to create in the first place. "I think a lot of people think that because of digital technology things happen in two seconds and you don't go into the studio and spend six months working," he says. "I did a lot of interviews with the Dead Weather, and people kept saying, 'Shouldn't music be free?' I was giving it right back to them: 'Food should be free, movies should be free, so should paintings.' I really just don't understand that mentality—it's an insult to the artist."

White isn't personally concerned about losing money to illegal downloads, but he worries about how piracy has devastated labels. "It's one of those things where people think it's no big deal because they don't see the drastic effects," he says. These days a band like the Dead Weather might get a $5,000 budget from its label to make a video, he says, while a half decade ago the White Stripes might have been able to play with $300,000. It's easy to scoff at such a budget now that artists get fans to make their videos for free. But the White Stripes got a big boost in popularity from the clip for "Fell in Love with a Girl"—one of the last truly iconic music videos—for which Michel Gondry (*Eternal Sunshine of the Spotless Mind*, *The Science of Sleep*) simulated animation with Lego bricks. Working with a director like Gondry costs money, but the investment paid off. "What I'm worried about," White says, "is that ten years from now there will be no videos and you won't be able to record in a studio if you want to because you can't afford it."

The idea that artists will give away their music assumes they'll create it cheaply—at home, on a computer, by themselves. But making an album can take time and outside expertise, neither of which has fallen in cost the way the price of equipment has. Even if a computer can replicate the equipment at Abbey Road Studios, it cannot replace Producer George Martin, whom the Beatles relied on for musical arrangements that brought their vision to life. And how would a music business based on performances and merchandise sales compensate songwriters like Jimmy Webb, or Jerry Leiber and Mike Stoller?

Artists also need time to focus on their work. Many musicians begin their careers performing for admiration and beer, much as Oberholzer-Gee and Strumpf suggest. Some record albums without much hope of getting paid, even indirectly. But artists who create great work usually do so after a few years, and musicians who can't make money might not keep at it that long.

"How is the up-and-coming band going to quit their jobs and focus on music if they're not signed?" White asks. "If the music is free and no one's buying the record, who's paying for it to be made? Who's paying for it to be recorded? Who's paying so that artist doesn't have to have a day job anymore and can dedicate himself and go out on tour?" Right now, many artists signed to labels will never make a dime beyond their signing bonuses, but they'll get the recording budget and tour support that could help them build an audience. And if their labels drop them, that audience won't.

The idea that recorded music is little more than a way to promote concerts will also inevitably affect the quality of albums that get made. Since the mid-1960s, recording has been its own art form—hence the term "recording artist." "I realize that now a record is nothing more than a postcard to get people to buy a ticket," says Bob Mould. "Albums are still everything to me, but I've had to cut corners—I don't make money on them anymore. I hear a lot of great music, but not a lot of great *records*, where you listen to it and say, 'What a great production.' A lot of that is because of budgets and home recording."

Artists who don't sign with labels have to decide what to charge for, what to give away, and how to keep Internet companies from turning the first into the second. "Today, I would have to say that I find the huge Internet companies to be more of a threat," says Eagles frontman Don Henley. "I'm still not a fan of the large record companies, but on this issue of copyright and protection of creative works I find myself on the same side of the table with them."

Proponents of file sharing often point out that the overall music business is fairly healthy if one counts marketing deals, publishing income, and concert ticket sales. But much of that business is generated, indirectly, by the major-label marketing of the past. Endorsement deals work best for stars, and publishing revenue depends partly on licensing hits from the past. And the concert business depends disproportionately on higher ticket prices from older stars.

Digital song sales by themselves won't save record labels, and many executives believe they represent a transitional business model that will soon seem as outdated as CDs. "I believe that music will evolve from a product-only business—meaning you buy a CD, a video, or some combination of the above—to a product and service business," Bronfman says. He means some consumers will continue to buy CDs or vinyl, while others will buy music subscriptions the way they now pay for cable television. "In order to have access to music—to be able to playlist, to share, to do things that the community wants to do—you'll pay X amount per month or year."

It's a promising vision—the ability to hear any song from a store like iTunes for a single monthly fee. So far, though, the services that offer these subscriptions haven't caught on with consumers. The largest in the United States, Rhapsody, has about 750,000 paying subscribers.

The one subscription service that has caught the imagination of consumers is Spotify, a well-designed online streaming service that's available in the U.K., France, and several Scandinavian countries. Spotify announced that it would launch in the United States before the end of 2010—after planning and postponing a 2009 debut—but couldn't arrange deals with the major labels in time. The company uses a "freemium" model: users in the U.K. can hear a limited amount of music with ads for nothing, pay £4.99 a month to eliminate the restrictions and commercials, or pay £9.99 to use it on a mobile device. The major labels like the company's subscription business—it has been reported that they own shares in the company[99]—but they're concerned that its free service is good enough that consumers won't feel they need to pay for it. "Our perspective is that you really need to restrict free, so that it's basically a customer acquisition vehicle and not a service alternative," says a major-label executive who deals with digital services. "If the free service is really good, what's the incentive to convert?"

It's a more important question than most observers realize. As of the end of 2010, Spotify had sold subscriptions to 7.5 percent of its users, and label executives say the company wants to get to 10 percent by promoting its mobile subscriptions. But a service like Spotify could hurt labels if users who don't subscribe choose to buy fewer CDs. As an example, let's imagine a million music fans who spend $60 a year on CDs and iTunes songs—representing $60 million in retail revenue—but might cut that amount by a third once they start using Spotify. If the company can sell subscriptions to 10 percent of its users for $10 a month, it would generate $12 million in fees; those 100,000 customers would spend another $4 million a year buying music, for a total of $16 million. But the other 900,000 consumers using the service for free will only spend another $36 million. That adds up to $52 million—only $8 million less than before—except that the first users of Spotify will be the consumers who now spend the most on music.

The problem with Spotify is all too common in the online world. In order to compete with pirate sites, legitimate services have to aggressively cut prices or offer some media for free. But this can hamper the growth of companies with the potential to generate more revenue. It's the new-media catch-22: you have to give away content to attract an audience that turns out to be worth less than you thought because they're attracted to free content.

"I just think it's very hard to compete with free—the reason people pay $50 or $100 for a concert ticket and won't pay $10 for their CD is because you can't get into the concert for free," says Danny Goldberg. "What happened is this extraordinarily powerful financial juggernaut entered society and changed the rules about intellectual property. But that was not necessarily inevitable, and it wasn't driven by all of these consumers—it was driven by people who made billions of dollars changing the rules."

CHAPTER 3

GEEKS BEARING GIFTS

GOOGLE'S WAR ON COPYRIGHT

On March 13, 2007, Viacom sued YouTube for copyright infringement, seeking more than $1 billion in damages. The media conglomerate charged that "YouTube appropriates the value of creative content on a massive scale" by ignoring copyright infringement and profiting from pirated work.[1] YouTube has always maintained that it's covered by the safe harbor of the Digital Millennium Copyright Act, since the content it offers is uploaded by users. In June 2010 a district court judge agreed, granting the video service a summary judgment.[2] Viacom appealed and hired the former U.S. solicitor general Theodore Olson to help make its case.[3] The suit could go to the Supreme Court, and its outcome will define the future of the Digital Millennium Copyright Act, and perhaps the Internet itself.

Like all online disputes, the case has also been tried in public. Five days after Viacom filed its suit, the law professor Lawrence Lessig argued in the opinion pages of the *New York Times* that Viacom was trying to get a court to overturn the Digital Millennium Copyright Act and darkly warned that such a decision would stifle innovation. "The Internet will now face years of uncertainty before this fundamental question about the meaning of a decade-old legislative deal gets resolved," Lessig wrote, in an essay that mostly took YouTube's point of view.[4] He did not mention that Google, which had just bought YouTube, had recently given $2 million to the Stanford Center for Internet and Society, which Lessig founded and ran when the donation was made.[5]

Google announced its gift to the Stanford Center on November 28,

2006, two weeks after closing its deal to buy YouTube. (Lessig says he didn't disclose the donation since the money didn't directly benefit him and he had no role in raising money at Stanford.) The company knew its acquisition of the video-sharing site could draw litigation: it set aside $200 million to deal with lawsuits.[6] But Google also apparently wanted some academic firepower on its side. Although the center's policy only allows unrestricted gifts that can be used for any purpose, it announced that Google's donation would be used to "establish a balance between the right to access and use information and the ownership of information"—presumably by the center's Fair Use Project.[7] While the center says it "avoids litigation" involving Google, much of its work involves challenging copyright laws in ways that would benefit the company.[8] This could, in turn, help Stanford: the company has given stock to the university.

Ever since the late-1990s debate over the Digital Millennium Copyright Act, technology companies have funded anti-copyright activists in ways that are rarely reported. Over the past few years, as Google has clashed with media companies, the search giant and its executives have brought this giving to another level, funding academic institutions like Stanford's Center for Internet and Society advocacy groups like Public Knowledge, and even the New America Foundation, a think tank where Google's executive chairman and former chief executive, Eric Schmidt, serves as chairman of the board of directors.

Few organizations benefit more from the generosity of Google and its executives than Creative Commons, a nonprofit Lessig helped found that makes it easy for creators to share their work freely online by renouncing some of their rights. In 2008 Google gave the organization $1.5 million. (Lessig, who no longer works with Creative Commons, says this amount exaggerates the group's dependence on Google, since the gift is a pledge to be fulfilled over the course of several years.) In 2009 the company's co-founder Sergey Brin and his wife, Anne Wojcicki, donated $500,000— more than a fifth of the money contributed that year. It was something of a family gift, since Wojcicki's mother, Esther Wojcicki, of the organization's board of directors.

All of these organizations do legitimate work, and some present compelling ideas for copyright reform alongside ideas that would amount to handouts to Google. (The Electronic Frontier Foundation also pushes for weaker copyright laws, but it has a broader purview and has not been afraid to challenge technology companies, especially on the privacy issues that these other groups ignore.) But they have framed the debate over intellectual property as one that pits the public interest against that of big companies, even as they promote policies that would help Google, a corporation that in 2009 booked almost twice as much revenue in the United States as the entire recorded music business.[9]

Most observers see technology companies as the underdogs in their disputes with major labels and movie studios, since the RIAA and the MPAA have so much power in Washington. In reality, the big money comes from telecom companies: Disney spent about $3.8 million on lobbying in 2010, while Verizon spent $16.8 million, according to the Center for Responsive Politics. Although Google is still a newcomer to Washington, it spent $5.2 million in 2010, compared with $5.5 million from the RIAA and $1.7 million from the MPAA. (Direct spending on lobbying is only one measure of influnce, but it is one of the most important.) Despite its reputation, Hollywood's trade association spent less on lobbying than Intel ($3.7 million), Amazon ($2 million), and the Consumer Electronics Association ($1.9 million).

There are plenty of good reasons to reform copyright: the term is too long, statutory damages for infringement are too high, and the concept of fair use creates too much uncertainty for creators and entrepreneurs alike. But the single biggest problem is that the protection the law offers has become purely theoretical. Music and movies are available on pirate sites within hours of their release—if not before. Although the groups backed by Google have some smart ideas for reforming copyright, they also want to make the current laws impossible to enforce. And while they point out that Hollywood has a track record of writing laws to its liking, we should be equally suspicious of letting Silicon Valley do the same.

No one has brought more attention to the movement for copyright reform than Lessig, whose name recognition and plainspoken style have made an abstract issue accessible to a mass audience. He has the academic recognition to go from Harvard to Stanford and back, as well as enough pop culture star power to promote his books on Comedy Central's *Colbert Report*. Like many copyright critics, he's outraged that Congress keeps extending the length of copyright, angered by the potential legal damages for file sharing, and—he takes pains to say—against piracy. At the same time, he has accused the media business of waging a war against our children and trying to "break" the Internet.[10] Lessig says he uses that term technically, in that media companies would like to replace a system that makes it easy to share content with one that favors protecting it.

Like many academics, Lessig got into what he calls the "copyfight" because he thought the Digital Millennium Copyright Act and the Copyright Term Extension Act gave media companies too much control over culture. "In the space of one year you have two major copyright bills pass and they were both radical in different ways," says Public Knowledge's president, Gigi Sohn. "It set off a backlash." At that point Sohn was at the Ford Foundation, working to preserve media diversity at a time of consolidation. But she thought these laws posed a larger threat to culture and helped found Public Knowledge three years later.

At the same time, Lessig's ideas about the structure of the online world were gaining prominence in legal and academic circles. In his seminal 1999 book, *Code and Other Laws of Cyberspace*, Lessig famously argued that "code is law" and warned that bad software—to enforce censorship, for example—could have the same consequences as repressive laws. He worried that the Digital Millennium Copyright Act's anti-circumvention provision would restrict access to knowledge, even though copyright only covers the expression of ideas, rather than ideas themselves. More reasonably, he argued that the Copyright Term Extension Act was inconsistent with the purpose of U.S. copyright law: giving artists an incentive to create. In this case, although living artists might want to know that their heirs would benefit from their work, Congress retroactively extended more protection to works from deceased creators, who couldn't very well keep working no matter what incentive they were given.

In January 1999, Lessig filed a case challenging the Copyright Term Extension Act on the grounds that such a retroactive copyright extension interfered with free speech. The plaintiff was Eric Eldred, a publisher who distributes public domain works online. Lessig lost twice in lower courts, then argued the case before the Supreme Court in October 2002.[11] By then, as the debate over file sharing made copyright a more visible issue, Lessig's case became a cause célèbre in technology circles. If the Supreme Court overturned the law, all the work that would enter the public domain—from *The Great Gatsby* to early Disney cartoons—would become legitimate fodder for file-sharing networks. "I'm quite confident they'll see that a free culture is a free speech issue," Lessig said of the Supreme Court.[12]

They didn't. In a 7–2 ruling, the Supreme Court held that, however inadvisable the law might be, it didn't represent an unconstitutional limit on free speech. "The First Amendment securely protects the freedom to make—or decline to make—one's own speech," wrote Justice Ruth Bader Ginsburg in the majority decision. "It bears less heavily when speakers assert the right to make other people's speeches."[13]

As his challenge to the Copyright Term Extension Act moved through the legal system, Lessig started speaking out in favor of Napster and file-sharing services, which he idealized as a democratizing force. He always says creators need to be compensated, but he takes a dim view of their attempts to block unauthorized distribution of their work. He favors a statutory license for recorded music that would allow anyone to distribute recordings as long as they pay rights holders, not unlike the way radio stations pay songwriters now. "Ten or twelve years ago, if we had embraced alternative compensation [like this], where would the world be today?" Lessig asks. It's a compelling vision. Until then, however, he wants creators to have a right they can't enforce—which is no right at all.

Lessig points out that he has never taken any money from technology companies, and he spells out his conflict of interest policy on his blog. But Google supports almost every organization he's ever been involved with, and few of them have taken issue with the company. Ironically, Lessig has been aggressive in calling out politicians for their dependence on fund-raising, and in 2007 he announced that he would devote most of his attention to reducing corruption in public life. He explored a congressional run, then launched Change Congress, a project aimed at reducing the influence of money on Capitol Hill. (Lessig, who taught with President Barack Obama at the University of Chicago, was also mentioned as a candidate for the Federal Communications Commission [FCC] commissioner.[14]) In December 2008, Lessig announced he would return to Harvard, where he would teach at the law school and run the Edmond J. Safra Foundation Center for Ethics. As an example of what he might study, Lessig mentioned "legal academics receiving money to provide public policy advice from the very institutions affected by that advice."[15]

It isn't out of idealism that Google spends millions of dollars to influence public policy. For starters, looser copyright laws would make it easier for the company to make money from YouTube. In general, more free professional content online would draw more consumers away from TVs and movie theaters to the Internet, where Google dominates the market for advertising. Most of all, Google knows that its search engine works best when content is free—both of cost and of restrictions. Copyright can get in the way of Google's mission: "to organize the world's information and make it universally accessible and useful"—since it lets creators limit access to their work, even if only by charging for it.

Although Hollywood has always had strong relationships with Democrats, Google has bought its own influence with the Obama administration. Google employees donated $803,000 to Obama's 2008 campaign, more than those of any company except Goldman Sachs and Microsoft.[16] Eric Schmidt, who publicly supported Obama, served on the Transition Economic Advisory Board and took a place on the president's Council of Advisors on Science and Technology. (He and five

other company executives each donated $25,000 to Obama's inaugura-
tion.[17]) And the White House hired several former Google employees,
including Andrew McLaughlin, the company's former head of public
policy. In May 2010, McLaughlin, the administration's deputy chief
technology officer, received an official reprimand for using his personal
e-mail address to communicate with a Google lobbyist about issues that
affect the company.[18] (McLaughlin left the administration in December
2010 to return to found two technology ventures.) In the e-mails,
revealed in a Freedom of Information Act request, McLaughlin's
successor, Alan Davidson, tells him that the Open Internet Coalition, an
online industry organization that includes Google, would "have your
back" after he made a controversial comment about online policy.[19]

In February 2008, Schmidt became chairman of the board of the New
America Foundation, an established and respected think tank. (He was
already serving on the board.) He also donated $1 million.[20] The founda-
tion does important work on more than a dozen issues, from energy to
health policy. But its "Open Technology Initiative" champions the kinds of
open systems that would help Google. The week Apple released the iPad,
Slate and the New America Foundation presented a panel titled "Why
Your Cell Phone Is So Terrible," at which a Slate columnist and three people connected with the foundation praised the kind of open access wireless
policies that Google pushes for.[21] (A spokesperson for the New America
Foundation says that Schmidt has little involvement with policy projects
and that the board also includes the wife of Steve Jobs, Laurene Powell
Jobs, whose interests often run counter to those of Google.)

Google also donates money to the Berkman Center for Internet
and Society, a Harvard Law School project founded in 1997 that has
since become its own division of the university. Like its sister institution at Stanford, Harvard's Berkman Center does important work,
such as studying how young people use technology. But most professors
there express hostility toward enforcement of copyright law, and few
do any work on privacy, a hot-button issue for Google. The company
has given the center donations of $500,000 and $280,000, relatively
modest amounts given the size of Berkman's budget. But some of that

money was earmarked to fund the Chilling Effects Web site, which tracks DMCA takedown notices. The site presents lawful requests from creators to stop unauthorized distribution of their work as a threat to free speech, an idea courts have generally dismissed. Since a substantial share of the notices come from Google itself, the implication is clear: asking Google to abide by the DMCA as it currently exists somehow threatens free speech.

Along with other technology companies, Google also gives money to Public Knowledge, a consumer advocacy group that promotes looser copyright laws. The organization receives more than three-quarters of its money from various foundations and most of the rest from Google, Microsoft, eBay, the Consumer Electronics Association, and other private donors.[22] (These companies, among others, sponsor the organization's annual awards.) In February 2010, Public Knowledge drafted a copyright reform act that would streamline music licensing and expand fair use to include incidental uses, "non-consumptive uses" like Google Books, and "personal and noncommercial uses"—a category that could be interpreted to include anything from recording cable television shows to using online file-sharing services.[23] The "incidental" change is obvious and overdue; it would allow documentary filmmakers to capture television clips in the background of shots without worrying about their legality. The "non-consumptive" change would make it easier to index information—a huge boon for Google, which was sued by authors and publishers over its project to scan the world's books so anyone could search them. The last change would essentially legalize file-sharing services, which could then become as convenient and efficient as the iTunes Store, and free besides. While that would certainly help individual consumers, it's hard to see how it would be in the public interest.

Groups like Public Knowledge also give legitimacy to projects that wouldn't otherwise have much. In October 2006, when the Consumer Electronics Association launched the Digital Freedom campaign to promote looser copyright laws that would help gadget manufacturers, Public Knowledge and the New America Foundation signed on as partners.[24] In January 2010, when Public Knowledge held World's Fair Use Day, Google and the Consumer Electronics Association sponsored the event. (While exceptions to copyright are important worldwide, fair use is a U.S. legal doctrine, so this was like having a global celebration of the First Amendment as opposed to free speech—conceptually valid but legally nonsensical.) McLaughlin spoke, offering the perspective of a former lobbyist for Google, at an event sponsored by Google, which was run by an organization that receives funding from Google.

Public Knowledge discloses its funding, and it wasn't afraid to challenge the Google Books settlement, for example. "We try to build alliances with companies because they've got the kind of resources and the kind of backing in political places that we'll never have," says Sohn, who points out that Google's donations represent a small part of her budget. But the alliance of public advocacy groups with technology companies promotes the idea that what's good for Google helps the United States as a whole.

Technology companies hardly have a monopoly on funding scholars whose work might help them. (Most of these academics held their views before they benefited from Google's generosity, but the company's money helps their voices get heard.) Major labels and movie studios contribute to the Institute for Policy Innovation, the Progress and Freedom Foundation, and Arts + Labs, which tend to exaggerate the negative effects of piracy, using what might charitably be called "Hollywood accounting." While piracy is bad for the economy many studies overstate the damage.

So far, Google hasn't had much success in changing copyright law. But organizations the company funds may influence the American public. In October 2008, the Berkman Center's co-founder Charles Nesson and a class of his law students volunteered to represent Joel Tenenbaum, a Boston University graduate student who had been sued by the major labels for illegally sharing music on a file-sharing service.[25] Nesson ran Tenenbaum's defense like a show, having his client admit to sharing songs after denying it in a deposition, claiming that all file sharing could be considered fair use, and saying that his client's behavior was typical of a generation of "digital natives." He lost the case—a

jury awarded the labels $675,000, after which the judge lowered the
amount to a tenth of that on the grounds that statutory damages that
high were unconstitutional. (Both Nesson and the RIAA appealed.) But
he may have been more interested in making a point. "Law in the court
of public opinion," Nesson said, "is what shapes law in the courts and
in the real world."[26]

Although statutory damages are absurdly high, the digital natives
may be getting restless with rhetoric like Nesson's. In December 2010,
the student-run *Harvard Crimson* ran an editorial saying, "The MPAA's
recent approach to illegal downloading is refreshing."[27] It praised the
organization's reminders that universities have an obligation to fight illegal file sharing under the Higher Education Opportunity Act of 2008,
as well as Harvard's "three strikes and you're out" policy on infringement—the kind of idea Nesson and other Berkman professors argue that
young people find foolish. "We believe that intellectual property rights
are important," the editorial said, "and the unauthorized downloading
of copyrighted music, movies, and television programs is wrong."

The first real copyright law was Britain's 1710 Statute of Anne,
which granted a fourteen-year term of protection that could be renewed
for another fourteen years. As reformers like Lessig tell it, the act grew
out of the Stationers' Company, a printing monopoly that controlled
who could publish what, in order both to protect authors' rights and to
censor sedition. Formally known as "An Act for the Encouragement of
Learning, by Vesting the Copies of Printed Books in the Authors or Pur-
chasers of such Copies, during the Times therein mentioned," the Statute
of Anne balanced the rights of publishers with those of the public. The
former got a limited monopoly, the latter an assurance of less expensive
books once the twenty-eight-year term passed. Authors didn't get much
at all: the law was "for the Encouragement of Learning," not writing.

Copyright in the United States followed similar logic. As presented
in the Constitution, it was intended to "promote the Progress of Science
and useful Arts, by securing for limited Times to Authors and Inventors

the exclusive Right to their respective Writings and Discoveries." From this perspective, copyright is a relatively recent invention, with roots in a censorship system, that gives authors a temporary economic monopoly for the good of the public.

Steeped in the technology world, Lessig and other copyright reformers were inspired by the marvels of online mass collaboration, from *Wikipedia* to the Linux operating system. Such projects represent a new style of creativity, which technology makes possible and the Internet can turn into a business. In these open-source projects, today's finished work becomes tomorrow's raw material. Everyone works for the benefit of all, and individual rights mostly just get in the way.

This fits with the trend toward deconstruction, which has made academics ever more skeptical of the Romantic ideal of individual genius. All artists build on the work of others, just as programmers combine existing bits of code. By locking up today's art, the argument goes, copyright interferes with tomorrow's. Examples of such building are especially easy to find in pop music, from hip-hop hits to the lyrical tropes Led Zeppelin pinched from old blues singers. Eventually, originality itself becomes suspect. In his book on intellectual property, *Common as Air: Revolution, Art, and Ownership*, the Harvard creative writing professor Lewis Hyde—also a faculty associate at the Berkman Center—argues, "All that we make and do is shaped by the communities and traditions that contain us, not to mention by money, power, politics, and luck."[28] If we all create culture, why should one person own it?

In his 2005 book, *Free Culture: The Nature and Future of Creativity*, Lessig talks about what he calls "Walt Disney creativity."[29] Although Disney's animated films represent Hollywood at its best, Lessig says, they aren't really original in the way most people use the word. The stories for *Snow White* and *Cinderella* came from old folktales that had entered the public domain, and Disney's genius lay in giving them a new spin with the technology of the time. Even Mickey Mouse—*the very symbol of corporate copyright itself*—isn't as original as most Americans believe. Lessig says the iconic early Disney cartoon *Steamboat Willie* is a parody of the Buster Keaton movie *Steamboat Bill Jr.*, which in turn drew inspiration from the song "Steamboat Bill." The problem with today's copyright laws is that they no longer allow this kind of borrowing, he argues. To strengthen creativity, it follows, we need to weaken copyright.

But this argument is based on a very selective reading of history.

Although the Statute of Anne is considered the first copyright *law*, the idea that unauthorized copying of artistic work is wrong goes back much further, and in many other countries. European "printing privileges" date back to fifteenth-century Venice,[30] and Chinese law prohibited the unauthorized reproduction of some books as early as 1068.[31] The earliest and deadliest conflict over intellectual property appears to be the A.D. 561 battle of Cooldrumman in what is now Ireland, where about three thousand people died. Now *that* was a "copyfight."

The dispute began over a Vulgate, the definitive fifth-century translation of the Bible into Latin by Saint Jerome. Saint Finnian came to have the only copy in Ireland, and he showed it to Colmcille, formerly his student but now an ambitious priest who copied the book by night without permission.[32] When Finnian discovered this, he objected and demanded the duplicate. The men brought their dispute to King Diarmaid, where they made arguments that wouldn't sound out of place in a modern courtroom, according to a paper by Ray Corrigan. "My friend's claim seeks to apply a worn out law to a new reality," said Colmcille. King Diarmaid saw the issue differently. "I don't know where you get your fancy new ideas about people's property," he said. "To every cow its calf, to every book its child-book."[33]

Continental European copyright differs significantly from that in the United States, since it focuses more on the rights of artists to their creations. In 1586, the lawyer Simon Marion established the French idea of intellectual property by arguing that "by a common instinct, each man recognizes every other to be the master of what he makes, invents, or creates."[34] Even in the United States, Congress is charged with "securing" the rights of creators; it doesn't grant them.

In this view, copyright still represents a temporary monopoly, but one that encourages more creativity than it stifles. It's not a limit on free speech so much as "the engine of free expression," in Justice O'Connor's words.[35] Most important, the public interest lies not only in enabling faster, less expensive access to work but also in giving artists an incentive to create more of it.

In his eagerness to cast copyright law as a barrier to creativity, Lessig misrepresents Disney's work, as the writer Stephen Manes noted in a review of Lessig's book *Free Culture*.[36] Although Disney's *Steamboat Willie* shares a title and setting with *Steamboat Bill Jr.* and the song "Steamboat Bill," they have little else in common. The song is about a boat race that ends in tragedy, the Keaton movie follows a college boy trying to bond with his working-class father, and the cartoon shows a mouse using other animals as musical instruments.[37] *Steamboat Willie* has no race and no rival; if it's a parody, it's an extremely subtle one. All Disney did was nod to a popular phenomenon of the time by licensing part of the song "Steamboat Bill" and coming up with a takeoff on its name (a matter for trademark law, not copyright).

"There's specific intent on the part of Disney to evoke *Steamboat Bill* in the context of creating *Steamboat Willie*," Lessig says. "The argument that I'm trying to make is that the sensibility of the creator that Walt Disney was is inconsistent with the sensibility of the creator that Walt Disney Corporation wants to be, or enforces the world to be—or at least did for a period of time."

That may be true. But today's copyright laws wouldn't have prevented Disney from making any of his classic films. (Disney's lawyers may bully independent remix artists, but that has less to do with specific statutes than with the litigious nature of large corporations.) Lessig rarely mentions that Disney paid to license the works he adapted into *Dumbo*, *Lady and the Tramp*, *101 Dalmatians*, *Bambi*, *Peter Pan*, and *Song of the South*.[38] To the extent that Disney was a remix artist, he was one who was happy to play—*and pay*—by the rules. And as Manes points out, the Brothers Grimm fairy tales would have passed into the public domain in time for Disney even under today's extended copyright terms.[39]

Lessig objects to what he calls copyright's "permission culture," which can get in the way of remixes.[40] But many media companies stand up for a liberal definition of fair use, since they rely on it themselves, to use the television news clips mocked on *The Daily Show*, for example. The kinds of commercial parodies that have become so common on You-Tube were established as fair use when Luther Campbell—a.k.a. Luke Skyywalker of the rap group 2 Live Crew—won a 1994 Supreme Court case against Acuff-Rose Music that involved the Roy Orbison song "Oh, Pretty Woman."[41] Ironically, Campbell was later successfully sued by the Silicon Valley icon George Lucas for using the name of a *Star Wars* character.

And what about those cases when the objection to a remix comes from an artist rather than from a corporate copyright holder? In August 2010, Don Henley and his songwriting collaborators Mike Campbell and Danny Kortchmar settled a lawsuit they brought against the Republican Senate candidate Chuck DeVore, whose campaign made a YouTube ad that used takeoffs on "The Boys of Summer" and "All She Wants to Do Is Dance" with new lyrics to attack his opponent, Senator Barbara Boxer (D-Calif.).[42] "My opposition is less about lost revenue and more about the integrity of an original work," Henley says.[43] "It's highly offensive when somebody comes along and treats that work like a plaything or an interactive game of some kind. I vehemently disagree with people like Larry Lessig and the defenders of 'remix culture.'"

Other artists have a more positive view of remixing—until one of their songs is used in a way they find objectionable. David Byrne, who is more interested in remix culture, sued the governor of Florida, Charlie Crist, for using the Talking Heads song "Road to Nowhere" in a campaign ad distributed on YouTube.[44] "I'm a bit of a throwback that way," Byrne wrote online, "as I still believe songs occasionally mean something to people."[45]

The dangerous leap in Lessig's logic is that respecting remix culture means tolerating mass piracy. In the first case, artists use existing works to create something new, whether that infringes copyright (like DeVore's campaign ad) or not (like 2 Live Crew's "Pretty Woman"). In the second, consumers simply make an unauthorized copy of a work to enjoy it themselves. The first could be called "creative infringement," suggested the legal blogger Terry Hart, the second "consumptive infringement."[46]

The first clearly involves free speech, and the issues need to be weighed accordingly. Whether or not you believe that DeVore should have faced liability for using Henley's song, any political commentary is a First Amendment issue. But that's not true of consumptive infringement: there's no free speech argument to be made when someone distributes an unaltered copy of "Boys of Summer" online.

Activists assume that encouraging a vital remix culture means tolerating piracy, since works need to be freely available in order to serve as building blocks for future art. But one could just as easily argue that piracy damages remix culture, by endangering its raw material. One of the funniest shows on YouTube is *Chad Vader: Day Shift Manager*, an absurdist comedy about Darth's underachieving brother. Copyright law allows this kind of parody, as it should. But widespread piracy could jeopardize the kinds of blockbusters tomorrow's parodists might want to spoof. *Chad Vader* depends on fair use, but it also depends on *Star Wars*: Chad wouldn't be funny without Darth.

Like many copyright reformers, Lessig idealizes the past as a time when more participatory art flourished in the absence of large media corporations. Traditionally, folk musicians often borrowed words and melodies from each other—although many jumped at the chance to copyright their work once they could—and Lessig seems to believe that YouTube can bring back this kind of organic culture. The idea is that the rise of modern media companies is merely an interregnum between the folk culture of the early twentieth century and the online remix culture of the twenty-first. Technology has finally freed us to create, not simply consume. And the riches of this collective culture should be in "the commons," a repository of art and intellectual knowledge that all can use freely.

To drive home this point about participatory culture, Lessig tells a story about the composer and bandleader John Philip Sousa, who testified in front of Congress in 1906 about what he later called "the menace of mechanical music."[47] Once, Sousa told Congress, "in front of every house in the summer evenings you would find young people together singing the songs of the day or the old songs. Today you hear these infernal machines going night and day. We will not have a vocal cord left."[48]

As Lessig tells it, Sousa was warning that recording technology would lead Americans away from the participatory culture that they had grown up on—one Lessig believes user-generated content can bring back. "He was a professional concerned with the amateur, and I think that's an interesting balance," Lessig says.

But this misrepresents Sousa's views on the subject, according to a paper by the University of Maryland professor Patrick Warfield, who generally agrees with Lessig's take on copyright.[49] The composer disliked the phonograph partly because at the time labels didn't pay composers when artists recorded their songs, and Sousa, who helped build the performance rights society ASCAP, was fighting to change that. He also made money selling songbooks, and "the rise of mechanical music threatened to transform these ticket buyers from active performers into passive listeners."[50] Sousa overcame his hostility to recordings as he started earning money from his own.[51] Ironically, some critics cast Sousa as the Metallica of his day, out of touch with new ways to deliver entertainment.[52] If Lessig had been around at the time, he might have accused Sousa of trying to break the phonograph.

When YouTube launched in 2005, it seemed like the kind of site free culture advocates were waiting for. It made it easy for anyone to distribute "user-generated content," from home movies to the homemade remixes Lessig loves. The company presented itself accordingly: its motto is "Broadcast Yourself," and two of the three founders, Chad Hurley and Steve Chen, told reporters they came up with the idea in order to share their videos from a dinner party. When Google bought the site for $1.65 billion in November 2006, it seemed like a vote of confidence in a future where everyone would make their pets famous for fifteen minutes.

There's also another side to the story. In YouTube's early days, Chen and YouTube's product manager, Maryrose Dunton, both estimated that three-quarters or more of the site's views came from copyrighted material.[53] The Google managers who ran a competing service before their company bought YouTube, had the same view.[54] And using the existence of this piracy to negotiate with content owners has been part of the site's strategy, according to both Viacom and a presumptive class-action suit filed by the Premier League as well as several music publishers and other media companies.[55] (As of early 2011, the suit had not been certified as a class action.)

YouTube turned a blind eye to this piracy, according to internal e-mails released during the course of the Viacom case. At various times, employees discussed creating a system to detect videos with titles like "Family Guy" or building a tool to let users flag videos that contained copyrighted content, but the company didn't make these projects a priority.[56] For months, YouTube did little more than take down individual videos about which it received DMCA takedown notices, ignoring obviously unauthorized material on the grounds that it might have been posted by the owner— even when it had no reason to believe that was the case.

Right now, all of this is in the past: Viacom's suit only covers the period before May 2008. YouTube now filters uploaded videos using its own system, which movie studios are fairly happy with. The outcome of Viacom's lawsuit could determine whether or not this is required by law. And while YouTube has implied that it's impossible to run a user-generated content site that screens out copyrighted material, it now does exactly that.

From a business perspective, the behavior attributed to YouTube makes perfect sense. Copyrighted content helped the site draw an audience—YouTube's court filings say the informal estimates by its own employees were speculative, but it surely played some role[57]—so why do more to remove it than the law requires? If it's up to content creators to monitor the Internet for infringement, why not leave that tough task to them and benefit from their work in the meantime? The question— the $1 billion question at the center of Viacom's lawsuit—is what the law requires.

Empires are built on such dry distinctions. Before Google bought

YouTube, its competing Google Video service took some basic steps to screen out copyrighted content, and some executives there believed it didn't draw as many viewers because YouTube's tolerance for copyright infringement gave it an edge, according to an internal presentation Viacom quoted in its court documents.[58] In June 2006 one Google executive suggested that Google Video could "threaten a change in copyright policy" and "use threat to get deal sign-up," but another wondered if this tactic was "Googley"—representative of the company's values.[59] It's hard to know what some of the other executives thought: Hurley lost his e-mail from that time (this happened before Google purchased YouTube), Eric Schmidt testified that he deletes his unless specifically asked to do otherwise, and Google's co-founder Larry Page, who became the company's chief executive in April 2011, said in a deposition that he couldn't remember whether or not he favored buying YouTube—a $1.6 billion acquisition that was the largest in the company's history.[60] "I don't remember being upset about it," he said, "so my guess is I was more positive than negative."[61]

In March 2010, documents unsealed by the court revealed that Viacom employees had posted clips of the company's shows on YouTube, and that the conglomerate had explored buying the video site in the summer of 2006. At the time, Viacom's general counsel, Michael Fricklas, sent an e-mail to a co-worker saying, "User generated content appears to be what's driving [YouTube] right now," although Viacom's case makes the opposite point.[62] Although the release of these e-mails embarrassed Viacom—especially because it showed the company's top executives jousting over who would run YouTube—it shouldn't affect the issues at the center of its case. "Everyone on earth took a look at YouTube," Fricklas says. "We never made an offer."

Another point of contention is whether YouTube offered its filtering technology only to companies with which it had licensing deals. Viacom had been talking to YouTube about licensing its content in 2006, when Google's acquisition of the company suddenly made negotiations more serious. The two companies had agreed on the outline of a deal when negotiations suddenly fell apart. On February 2, 2007, Viacom announced that it had sent YouTube takedown notices for 100,000 clips at once. (YouTube removed the videos promptly.) Hurley told the *New York Times* that YouTube would discuss filtering unauthorized Viacom content from its site as part of a deal to show the company's programming.[63]

"We were holding the complaint in our hand, and that's what made us decide to file it," Fricklas says. "We said, 'We'll set up a mechanism so we can tell you what's authorized,' and they said, 'We're not doing that for anybody but our business partners.'" YouTube says it never made filtering conditional on distribution deals.

In order to qualify for protection under the Digital Millennium Copyright Act, a company cannot get "a financial benefit directly attributable to the infringing activity" or be "aware of facts or circumstances from which infringing activity is apparent." Viacom argued that YouTube's offer to filter content for companies that made deals with it, as well as some of its other behavior, implies both. "Clearly they knew there was infringement going on," Fricklas says. Among other causes of action, Viacom also argues that YouTube's behavior qualifies as inducement under the precedent set by the Supreme Court in *MGM v. Grokster*. A Google spokesperson declined to address this but pointed out that YouTube now "has partnership deals with thousands of large content providers who share ad revenue," including CBS, the BBC, and Universal's and Sony's record labels.

YouTube argued that in order to lose the protection of the Digital Millennium Copyright Act, it would need to receive a financial benefit from specific clips or know of particular videos with infringing content. But it says it couldn't know which clips Viacom wanted it to remove because the media company had posted videos on YouTube in order to promote its own shows.[64] In some cases, Viacom even hired outside promotion companies to upload footage that looked as if it had been leaked.[65] How could YouTube know which clips Viacom considered infringing and which the company wanted to put online as promotion?

Viacom's strategy of posting its own clips online makes it a less sympathetic litigant, but it doesn't change the underlying issue, which affects independent artists as well as large companies. The first creator to sue YouTube was Robert Tur, the Los Angeles television journalist who shot the famous footage of a mob attacking Reginald Denny after the acquittal of the four police officers who beat Rodney King.[66] He was more interested in the principle than in a payday: he sued You-Tube before Google acquired it and has gone to court to protect his intellectual property in the past. Much to the relief of Viacom, which feared Tur did not have the budget to prevail against a defendant with such deep pockets, he joined the presumptive class-action lawsuit filed by the Premier League and others.[67]

The presumptive class-action lawsuit also accuses YouTube of reserving filtering for companies that agreed to distribution deals. "When a license fee sought by a copyright holder is low enough to be deemed satisfactory to Defendants," the presumptive class-action complaint charges, "Defendants find themselves able to shed their blinders and employ technology to safeguard the rights of their new 'partners.'"[68]

In June 2010, the court handed down a summary judgment for You-Tube in both cases. (Appeals are pending.) Based on a close reading of the Digital Millennium Copyright Act, the judge concluded that You-Tube was entitled to safe harbor protection as long as it didn't know that specific clips infringed copyright. No matter how much of YouTube's traffic came from unauthorized videos, "mere knowledge of such activity in general is not enough."[69]

Viacom's appeal will largely hinge on the interpretation of the Digital Millennium Copyright Act. On the most general level, every site that features user-generated content "is aware of facts or circumstances from which infringing activity is apparent." As YouTube points out, however, it's hard to be absolutely sure about the status of any given file. Both extremes seem impractical: the first would create a massive liability problem, while the second essentially offers online companies a license to infringe.

Outside the courtroom, YouTube argues that requiring it to take responsibility for the video on its site would effectively doom user-generated content, since companies that faced liability for every infringing work couldn't afford to stay in business. But YouTube filters content now, and the site still attracts viewers. And giving such sites some responsibility would put them on a more equal footing with old media. If Comedy Central has to hire lawyers to make sure that parodies on *The Daily Show* adhere to fair use, shouldn't YouTube, which competes for the same ad dollars, have the same responsibility?

YouTube generates Google's most visible copyright issues, but by no means its only ones. The search giant makes almost all its money on two businesses—the AdWords ads that appear as "sponsored links" on search results pages and the AdSense ads it sells on other sites—so it takes issues that involve them extremely seriously. As with YouTube, however, copyright infringement is always someone else's responsibility, even if the money goes to Google.

The independent filmmaker Ellen Seidler found out how Google ends up making money on piracy after she and Megan Siler directed and produced *And Then Came Lola*, a lesbian romantic comedy. The very existence of the movie is a testament to the power of technology: the two filmmakers funded a high-definition digital video shoot with about $250,000 scraped together from credit cards, retirement accounts, and family members. Based on what they knew about similar movies, they figured they could break even or make a small profit without a theatrical release by selling DVDs, Blu-ray discs, and digital downloads. "The lesbian audience is a very loyal audience, and there's not a lot of decent material out there," Seidler says. This was the promise of the Internet—that falling costs and more efficient distribution would allow independent creators to make quality media for niche audiences.

As Seidler discovered, it hasn't quite worked out that way. A few days after the movie's April 2010 DVD release, Seidler found hundreds of illegal copies of *Lola* online. She expected to find her film on file-sharing services and shady-looking Russian pirate Web stores, but it surprised her to find it on sites with slick ads for companies like Netflix and

RadioShack. "It's one thing to get hooker ads or ones for illegal gambling, but these were ads for legitimate companies," she says. So Seidler, who used to work in television news and now teaches video journalism at the University of California, Berkeley, decided to look into the piracy of her movie the way she'd report a story, then write about her experience on a blog. And she soon realized that many of the corporate ads on pirate sites came from Google AdSense, the biggest of the online networks that sell space on small Web sites.

By the fall, Seidler had found more than thirty thousand links to illegal copies of her movie, many presumably generated automatically, including some with foreign-language subtitles that had been added by pirates. Individually, no site was that big a deal: some said her film had been downloaded between ten and four hundred times. She figures that a considerable amount of this interest came from men who mistook her film for pornography. And she knows not every illegal download of her movie represents a lost sale. But her count of online copies only includes sites she could easily find, and all those downloads must have some effect. "Let's say that 5 percent [of those downloaders] might have bought it," she says. "If we got a dollar for each sale, we'd be all set."

Lola is widely available from legitimate online retailers, including iTunes and Amazon. "But you can click on this Spanish Web site and see it for nothing, so who's going to pay?" Seidler asks. "If we had released this movie four years ago, we would have broken even," she says. "Now if we make $100,000 [in revenue] we'll be lucky."

Many of the sites on which Seidler found links to her movie didn't use AdSense; some charged a flat fee to stream movies, while others ran ads from other networks. And it's important to note that only a small fraction of AdSense sites benefit from copyright infringement, and Google has always officially barred pirate sites from the program. At the same time, however, the company doesn't do much to screen the sites it sells ads for, even those with suspicious addresses like movies4stars.net and onlinefilmshow.com. From at least December 2010 to March 2011, both ran AdSense ads and offered movies that were only playing in theaters.

In some cases, pirate sites also attract traffic with AdWords ads that run in Google's search results. In a 2005 lawsuit filed by the major movie studios against easydownloadcenter.com and thedownloadplace. com, the founders of the sites gave depositions saying Google assigned them account representatives and offered them credit to buy more than $800,000 worth of AdWords placements against searches like "bootleg movie download," according to the *Wall Street Journal*.[70] Although Google wasn't named in the suit, it told the journal, "We are continually improving our systems to screen out ads that violate these policies" and stopped selling AdWords ads against certain search terms.

Seidler says she likes it when fans post clips from her film on YouTube: "That's the kind of stuff that helps you because it gets people to see the film." What makes her mad is that online companies are making money from her movie and she isn't. So she started spending a couple of hours a day sending Digital Millennium Copyright Act takedown notices to pirate sites, one of which had the chutzpah to respond by lecturing her on the need to find a new business model for the digital age. Then she tried contacting the AdSense advertisers directly, without much success. Finally she realized that she could send takedown notices directly to Google, which says it removes AdSense ads from pages with pirated content, although it is unclear whether or not it has a legal obligation to do so.[71]

In response to several of Seidler's notices, Google forwarded her emails in other languages that employees referred to as "counter-notifications" – statements, provided for in the DMCA, that contest incorrect or improper takedown notices. Google employees said that, in light of these counter-notifications, Seidler would have to file a court order to get copies of her movie removed. But in three cases, *the e-mail Google described as a counter-notification was actually an apology or admission of guilt from the site in question*.[72] (Ironically, Seidler read the e-mails with Google Translate, but she then checked with native speakers to be sure she was right.) Although the sites removed Seidler's movie, Google didn't remove its AdSense ads, even from pages that contained nothing but scores of links to pirated movies. Every time Seidler tried to contact Google by phone, the voice mail for the number advertised for this purpose was full.

It's hard to know whether Google could face legal liability for selling these ads, since the safe harbor provision of the Digital Millennium Copyright Act doesn't seem to apply to ad networks. But Hollywood wants to find out for sure. In August 2010, Disney and Warner Bros. Entertainment sued Triton Media for providing advertising services for pirate sites in what looked like an attempt to set a legal precedent against a company that lacks Google's resources; the studios obtained a $400,000 consent judgment that didn't set a precedent. [73]

Major movie studios have an easier time getting Google's attention, or at least a better number to call. But Seidler is still trying to figure out how she can make another film. Having seen stories about independent artists soliciting donations for their work online, Seidler posted a link so anyone who saw an illegal copy of the movie could make a donation for "good karma." After more than a month she had received less than $100.

"It has really put a damper on any incentive I have to make another movie, and we've had offers," Seidler says. "A lot of artists make things out of passion and not because they see a pot of gold at the end of the rainbow, but I don't think it's unrealistic to think that at least if there's some money to be made that you might be the one making some of it."

Over the course of 2010, Google started cooperating more with entertainment companies on piracy issues, presumably because it wants licensed content for YouTube and other projects. In December, it announced four changes in its copyright policy: it would act on takedown notices within twenty-four hours, experiment with making authorized content come up higher in search results, do more to review AdSense sites, and prevent common pirate sites from appearing in autocomplete—the feature that finishes words users start typing. It's a significant step forward for a company that made some copyright holders send in takedown notices by fax until 2007. In May 2006, RIAA's president, Cary Sherman, complained about this in a speech he gave to a few hundred Google employees at one of the town hall meetings the company hosts. The audience applauded. "That's when I realized the kind of culture we're dealing with," Sherman says. "They just see copyright as something that gets in the way of what they want to do."

When bloggers tell artists like Seidler to try new business models, they often bring up Creative Commons. In 2001, after Lessig unsuccessfully challenged the Copyright Term Extension Act in the court of appeals, he, the plaintiff, Eric Eldred, and the MIT professor Hal Abelson formed the San Francisco organization as a nonprofit group that lets creators renounce some rights to their work while keeping others. The idea is to give artists a way to say "some rights reserved."

Various Creative Commons licenses allow artists to give away the right to distribute their work, use it for commercial or noncommercial purposes, or even remix it. An Attribution Noncommercial No Derivatives license, for example, allows Internet users to share an artist's work as long as they credit him and don't use it for commercial purposes or alter it. The looser Attribution license lets users distribute, remix, and use a work for any purpose, as long as they identify the artist. While some detractors describe Creative Commons as an alternative to copyright, this isn't true. The organization's licenses *depend* on copyright law; they just give creators a standard legal structure to sign away certain rights.

Before Creative Commons, artists who wanted to allow remixes had to publicize that fact, and anyone who wanted to do a remix had to ask permission or risk a lawsuit. Creative Commons licenses make it easier for artists who want their work distributed freely to communicate that, and they've been used by Wikipedia, Nine Inch Nails, and thousands of other organizations and artists. By helping to identify hundreds of millions of songs, photographs, and videos that can be shared freely, Creative Commons also helps technology companies. More content free from restrictions means more content to build businesses around. That's one reason the group's contributors include Google, Microsoft, eBay, Best Buy, and the Consumer Electronics Association.

Several of the fourteen members of Creative Commons' board of directors have ties to businesses that would benefit from having more work free from copyright restrictions online. Glenn Otis Brown is the music business development manager at YouTube, and Caterina Fake and the chief executive, Joi Ito, were, respectively, a co-founder and an investor in Flickr, a photo-sharing start-up that used Creative Commons licenses. Esther Wojcicki, Sergey Brin's mother-in-law, who served as the board's chair for a year and a half before becoming vice-chair in September 2010, may not benefit directly from Google's success, but her relative lack of experience in law and nonprofit management makes her an odd choice. (Previous chairs include Lessig and James Boyle, another academic who favors copyright reform.) Strikingly, for an organization ostensibly dedicated to creativity, the board includes only one artist: the documentary filmmaker Davis Guggenheim. That doesn't mean Creative Commons licenses don't help artists; they can be valuable tools. It just means that, even more than a record company or a movie studio, the organization may not have the best interests of artists at heart.

Ito points out that Creative Commons has a code of conduct that includes a conflict-of-interest policy, and that it has no obligation to use money Google donates for any specific projects. "We haven't found this problematic," he says of the board's composition. As for Wojcicki, "her primary role is to bring the perspective of a teacher to the CC board and to explain CC to teachers, education being one of our main areas of focus." [74]

Creative Commons says it doesn't lobby to change copyright law, but many of the board members do so in other capacities. Three members are also on the eleven-person board of Public Knowledge, while several others have worked at Stanford Law School, the Berkman Center, or both. [75] "It's not about how do we change the law," Lessig says. "It's just about how do you make existing copyright work more efficiently for people who want to waive some of their rights while retaining others."

Of course, artists haven't had many problems having their work distributed online—sometimes whether they like it or not.

While Creative Commons promotes the way its licenses give artists more control over the distribution of their work, the organization filed an amicus brief with the Supreme Court on behalf of Grokster, which made a business of taking that control away. "What we said was that Grokster is deploying a technology, which, at least at the time, seemed crucial to the spread of amateur creativity," says Lessig, who wrote the brief and doesn't condone piracy. "If you're a documentary filmmaker and you want to make your film available, [Grokster is] a pretty cheap way to do it." Of course, there are plenty of other ways to do it as well, some of which would also allow filmmakers to make money. If Grokster had prevailed in court, Lessig says, lawmakers would have been under pressure to fund a way to compensate artists for this distribution of their work—perhaps with a statutory rate like the one paid by artists to record songs by other composers. But a lawyer like Lessig would know that this hasn't worked in the past: Hollywood couldn't get a law passed to collect money from sales of blank videotapes after the Supreme Court's Betamax decision. And artists would have less income until such a situation was fixed.

To understand how Creative Commons helps the companies that fund it, consider the photo site Flickr, which offers online photo storage and the ability to look at images posted by others. Flickr encourages users to post photos with a Creative Commons license, which makes it a good source of free photos for blogs as well as a virtual photo album. Traffic, and income from advertising, rose accordingly. In March 2005, when Flickr was acquired by Yahoo!, reportedly for more than $30 million, the photographers received nothing.[76] Most of them didn't mind: they got free photo storage and a chance to show off their work. But it's worth noting that Joi Ito, who runs Creative Commons, sometimes seems more excited about the investment opportunities provided by free content than about helping artists.

"I think that Creative Commons will also mark an explosion of innovation that will happen on the content level," he said in July 2010. "As an investor, for instance, I can't invest in many of the music companies because of the risk of copyright litigation."[77] This is true enough. But Creative Commons' fund-raising pitches rarely mention the work it does providing litigation-free investment opportunities for venture capitalists.

June 28, 2010, was a busy day at Eric Schmidt's New America Foundation. In the think tank's sleek Washington, D.C., headquarters, a block from K Street's lobbyist offices, the White House economic policy adviser Lawrence Summers announced an Obama administration plan to auction off spectrum to wireless broadband companies. It will free up space for more mobile Internet traffic, which Summers said would spur economic growth and generate employment opportunities. It will also help Google, which sees the smartphone market as a crucial source of growth.

Six hours later, at a New America Foundation event hosted by Public Knowledge and CopyNight DC, the activist and science fiction novelist Cory Doctorow gave a speech titled "How Copyright Threatens Democracy."[78] The foundation offered Doctorow a serious forum, with a uniformed elevator operator to take guests to the fourth-floor conference room, where a spread of fresh fruit and cheese awaited. The tone of the presentation was less stately. Introducing Doctorow, the foundation's program associate James Losey compared the way the summer 2010 World Cup games were not available to Americans without cable television to censorship under despotic regimes. "The Internet is hailed as a democratizing force, and countries like China, Iran, and Burma are criticized for blocking Web sites like Facebook and otherwise restricting access," Losey said. "Earlier this year, Secretary of State Hillary Clinton said that new technology does not take sides. Yet ironically, American Web users are faced with restricted access to Web sites here at home to watch a sporting event shared by the world."

Doctorow didn't mince words either. He compared the entertainment industry's agenda to that of "the most repressive governments in the world." The stakes, he said, were high. "The major problem of the copyright wars isn't what they're doing to culture," Doctorow declared, "it's what they're doing to every other part of human endeavor, from civic engagement to education to family life."[79] (He neglected to mention the viewing of soccer games.) In his opinion, any effort to restrict the free flow of information would be dangerous for free speech and consumer rights. Creators will just have to give up their rights and get out of the way.

It would be hard to find a judge who agrees with this kind of thinking, which ignores the Supreme Court precedent that copyright also encourages free speech. Listening to Doctorow, you'd never know that the world's healthiest democracies also have the strongest copyright systems. The latter is probably the result of the former, rather than the other way around, but it's hard to think of a country without intellectual property laws where free expression really thrives. And whatever one thinks about copyright law, a speech by a science fiction author claiming that it endangers democracy is not the type of scholarship the New America Foundation is known for.

Gradually, the New America Foundation and the other copyright "reform" groups allied by Google have changed the terms of the debate about intellectual property—as well as the discussion about the role of professional creators in society. Artists discuss the merits of Creative Commons licenses that let them give up their rights and get nothing in return. Journalism schools now receive grants to study how—not if— user-generated content can replace newspaper reporting. And it's rare to see a conflict of interest disclosed clearly.

Tim Wu, a Columbia Law School professor who was a New America Foundation Bernard Schwartz fellow for much of 2009 and 2010, has written pieces for *Slate* arguing that YouTube's foray into film rental "could radically change the way Hollywood does business" and criticizing Apple's iPad as a sellout of the company's original values of openness.[80] Although Wu was identified as a New America Foundation fellow, Schmidt's involvement with the organization wasn't mentioned in either case. (In February 2011, Wu joined the Federal Trade

Commission's Office of Policy Planning.) Wu says "it never occurred to me as necessary to disclose that Mr. Schmidt is one of [the foundation's] many individual donors when speaking or writing."[81] But while there are many donors, Schmidt is the only chairman of the foundation's board.

Another writer with some influence on the debate over copyright is William Patry, a prolific scholar who now works for Google as a senior copyright lawyer. In *Moral Panics and the Copyright Wars*, Patry argues that the media business has deceptively framed copyright as a moral issue by using words like "piracy" and "theft." (That may be true, but the use of the word "piracy" in this context predates the Statute of Anne, and "file sharing" isn't exactly neutral language either.) It makes more sense to look at copyright as an economic issue, but Patry doesn't seem to understand the businesses involved. He says labels are selling more music than ever by using numbers for individual track sales (which is like saying someone who receives nineteen pennies in return for a quarter has more money).[82] He overstates the success of the video game industry (by saying *Grand Theft Auto IV* sold ninety-five million copies in its first year of release when it actually sold about seventeen million copies in its first two).[83] And he concludes that media companies need to abandon outmoded business models and embrace ones like that of his employer, even though Google's business model depends to some extent on those same media companies. Patry tells readers that the opinions in the book are his, not Google's. But his job at Google involves lobbying on its behalf about copyright law; in an e-mail to Andrew McLaughlin that came out in a Freedom of Information Act request, he wrote, "98 percent of my time is spent in policy."

The main idea behind much of this thinking is that there are other ways to create the kind of artistic work we enjoy now without laws to protect it, either by funding it in ways that don't involve the media business or by using the reach of the Internet to harness volunteerism. Could art be "crowdsourced," created by scattered people working together online, much as *Wikipedia* is? While online collaboration has intriguing possibilities, it seems to work better as a way of creating tools—like software or encyclopedias—rather than art. As ambitious as it is,

Wikipedia depends on facts that can be sourced from other expensively produced publications, and experiments with crowdsourced original reporting have been underwhelming compared with professional work. A system based on these arrangements would also create a new generation of media gatekeepers.

In the meantime, free culture advocates take any chance they get to argue that the media business can adjust to a world in which laws against illegal copying are not enforced. Even if listeners aren't convinced, the flurry of studies, op-eds, and panel events create an atmosphere of uncertainty that makes it hard to pass laws that would be more effective in tackling piracy. In April 2010, the U.S. Government Accountability Office, which has a reputation for producing neutral studies, issued a report concluding that "it is difficult, if not impossible, to quantify the net effect of counterfeiting and piracy on the economy as a whole."[84] A few days later, the Electronic Frontier Foundation, Public Knowledge, the Consumer Electronics Association, and the Computer and Communications Industry Association bought ads in *Politico* and *Roll Call* that said, "Content industry piracy claims are bogus." In smaller type, the ads said that claims about the damaging effects of piracy were "completely baseless."

The implication was that piracy wasn't a problem, but the report didn't say that—just that its effects were hard to measure. "In general," it said, "literature and experts indicate the negative effects of counterfeiting and piracy on the U.S. economy outweigh the positive effects."

Google doesn't like to frame the issue that way. In October 2010, the company co-hosted Internet at Liberty 2010: The Promise and Peril of Online Free Expression, a three-day conference of activists and politicians. In a blog post on the subject, Google lobbyist Bob Boorstin extolled the event's lofty aims: "helping individuals protect themselves online; promoting corporate and government transparency; finding the right balance between privacy and free expression." Right alongside those, Boorstin mentioned one of the company's less charitable goals— "making sure that platforms like Google aren't held liable for content they host."

CHAPTER 4

THE SIREN SONG OF "FREE"

WHY NEWSPAPERS STRUGGLED ONLINE

No newspaper editor has devoted more thought to the Internet's potential than Alan Rusbridger, who runs the London-based *Guardian*. In 1996, when most newspapers were still figuring out how to put stories online, Rusbridger, who had been named top editor the previous year, started the Guardian Online as a separate division. During the dot-com bust, as other newspapers cut online staff, he kept investing in digital journalism. More recently, he delivered some of the smartest coverage of the U.S. diplomatic cables from WikiLeaks, dealing with Julian Assange to get the information and asking readers what was worth searching for in the trove of documents.

Although more news outlets have started charging for content, Rusbridger believes Internet "paywalls" could hurt journalism itself. "That might be the right direction in *business terms*, while simultaneously reducing access and influence in *editorial terms*," Rusbridger said in a January 2010 speech at the London College of Communication. "It removes you from the way people the world over now connect with each other. You cannot control distribution or create scarcity without becoming isolated from this new networked world."[1]

Rusbridger pointed out that the *Guardian* was only the ninth or tenth most popular newspaper in the U.K. Online, he said, it's the second-biggest English-language publication in the world, after the *New York Times*, with thirty-seven million readers per month.[2] Rusbridger himself—a rumpled intellectual with Harry Potter–esque glasses and a sideline writing children's books—has become a major player in the media business. In 2008 he moved the *Guardian* from its cramped headquarters on Farringdon Road, where the print and online departments were separated, to a museum-like glass office building with a theater that overlooks the Regent's Canal near King's Cross.

As Rusbridger extolled the possibilities of digital journalism, however, a message flashed behind him on a screen he was using to display slides: "You are running on reserve battery power."[3] For all his optimism, Guardian News and Media—which includes the *Guardian* and the *Observer* and their respective Web sites—has not made money since 2003. A few months before Rusbridger's speech, the company, which is owned by a charitable trust, disclosed that the paper was losing £100,000 per day.[4] It had two rounds of layoffs in 2009 and reported a pretax loss of £57.9 million ($92.6 million) in its 2009–2010 fiscal year. (The *Guardian* declined to comment.) A rival British newspaper, the *Independent*, wrote of Rusbridger, "His editorial ambition and The Guardian's revenue have travelled in opposite directions."[5]

In the United States, newspapers have never been more popular—or less profitable. Even amid considerable competition from blogs and online start-ups, newspaper Web sites reach about seventy-five million readers a month, more than a third of all U.S. Internet users.[6] That actually undercounts the impact of newspaper reporting, which is packaged by online aggregators, repeated on Twitter, and discussed on blogs. Old-media companies published 99 percent of the stories linked to on blogs, according to one study, and four of the biggest—the BBC, CNN, the *New York Times*, and the *Washington Post*—accounted for 80 percent of those links.[7]

All this online activity isn't generating much income, though. Between 2006 and 2009, newspaper ad revenue fell almost 45 percent.[8] Since 2007, newspapers have cut about 13,500 newsroom jobs—almost 25 percent of the old total[9]—and around two hundred newspapers have either folded or stopped publishing print editions.[10] Even big-city dailies are shrinking: Seattle's *Post-Intelligencer* now only publishes online; Detroit's *Free Press* has limited home delivery to three days a week; and the Tribune Company, which owns the *Chicago Tribune* and the *Los Angeles Times*, entered bankruptcy in late 2008.

This downsizing inevitably affects what stories get reported. One in five news executives say they don't have the resources to deliver more than a minimum level of coverage.[11] International and investigative reporting is mostly limited to the *New York Times*, the *Wall Street Journal*, the *Washington Post*, and the *Los Angeles Times*. Many city and even state government issues now go uncovered.

Understanding why newspapers are going broke reaching so many readers requires understanding that they've never actually been in the business of selling news—at least not directly. Newspapers make money by assembling an audience and selling it to advertisers. The news is there—along with columns, crosswords, and comics—to attract readers. The price for one copy of a newspaper rarely even covers the costs of printing and distributing it. The real money—traditionally about 80 percent of revenue for most U.S. newspaper companies—always came from advertising. The bigger the audience, the more money that advertising brought in.

Like Rusbridger, American newspaper executives looked at the Internet as a way to get what they always wanted: a larger audience for advertising and, truth be told, a larger stage on which to play. With online distribution practically free, millions of readers were only a click away, so they figured ad dollars would be theirs for the taking. But they ignored the basic facts of supply and demand.

For decades, local newspaper publishers had set ad prices in a print world where the supply of space was limited and few media markets had much competition. For most of the last two decades, they enjoyed easy double-digit profit margins, even as they cut newsroom staff. Online, the amount of ad space has no obvious limit. Back in the 1990s, online ads sold for a fairly low CPM, or cost per thousand, the most popular measure of advertising cost. Publishers expected prices to rise as advertisers adjusted to marketing on the Internet. But to the surprise of old-media and online executives alike, they never really did. Faced with theoretically unlimited ad space—and, later, the ability of sites like Facebook to generate more at almost no cost—demand couldn't keep up. Since overall ad spending rarely grows much faster than the economy in general, it probably never will.

These days, a major metro paper might have an average CPM of between $80 and $100, while its Web site could charge a tenth of that.[12] According to statistics from the Newspaper Association of America, a print reader is worth an average of about $539 in advertising alone, while an average online reader is worth $26.[13] The money saved on printing and distribution doesn't come close to covering the difference.

Logically, then, the dumbest move for newspapers would have been to convince their readers to abandon the print edition in favor of their Web site, where they're worth between a tenth and a twentieth as much. Yet this is exactly what most of them have done. They've poured resources into free sites full of extra blogs, video reporting, and data-driven presentations. By improving their online offerings—and often raising the price of the print edition to fund them—newspapers essentially encouraged readers to stop buying physical copies.

The conventional wisdom of the technology world was a seductive force, says Rob Grimshaw, managing director of FT.com at the *Financial Times*, which has thrived by charging for content. Rather than reassess their strategies for the digital age, publishers created online divisions, staffed them with inexperienced executives, and gave them a free hand. "They said, 'We've spoken to all our friends in the Internet community, and they tell us we should be giving it away and putting advertising on it,'" Grimshaw says. "Publishers swallowed everything they told them and said, 'Okay, great, stick everything on the Web for free.'" As much as anything else, charging for online content was considered extremely uncool.

It's hard to know how much of the decline in CPM at online news sites is simply a result of the Great Recession. Some of it is certainly due to the rise of "remnant ad networks," which Web sites use to sell extra inventory. Online, most advertisers pay to reach a certain number of consumers, measured in either views or clicks. If publishers draw more traffic than they have ads to sell, networks can fill the space with low-cost ads—usually for the kinds of products consigned to the backs of magazines. While this gives publishers a way to collect a little extra revenue, it drags down their average CPM and, more important, further erodes their pricing power.

Newspaper publishers "had no idea how much the Internet would change ad spending, and they didn't realize that ad inventory on the Internet was infinite," says Ken Doctor, a former vice president at Knight Ridder Digital who now works as an industry analyst. When the recession hit in 2008, newspapers lost much of their automobile and real estate advertising. By then, Web sites like Craigslist and Monster.com had already taken most of the classifieds that generated as much as half of all ad revenue at some publications. Due to bad decisions that had nothing to do with technology, many newspaper chains were saddled with enormous debt run up by parent companies that overspent to buy publications and gain market share. And they faced a post-boomer generation of readers who have not picked up the habits of paying for news or reading it on a printed page.

Conventional wisdom says that newspaper journalism must be reinvented for a changing world—blogged, Twittered, or somehow crowdsourced. It's a tempting prescription—innovative, optimistic, and forward-looking—but it doesn't get to the heart of the problem. Despite complaints about the media, newspaper journalism now reaches a larger audience than ever before, both directly and on various sites that summarize it. How dissatisfied can readers really be?

The product isn't the problem. Online publications that Twitter on a 24-7 schedule face the same difficulties, and even the inventive start-up *Politico* has said it makes most of its revenue on the print edition it distributes in Washington, D.C.[14] At most online start-ups, any interest in journalistic innovation seems to come from the desire to cut costs, which is why more of them are experimenting with "citizen journalism" than, say, professionally shot video.

For all the talk about how people now consume information differently, the real online revolution is in advertising. For more than a century, marketers funded content without caring much about it; they just needed a way to reach consumers. (Advertising without content was called junk mail and generally ignored.) Now they can reach potential customers directly—on search results pages, through social networks, and on their own sites. The car companies that used to advertise in newspapers now spend part of their ad budgets creating Web sites that offer potential customers more information about vehicles than print ads ever could.

Newspapers that believe in the potential of ad-supported Web sites promote the concept of the "Rusbridger Cross"—the idea that rising online ad revenue will equal, then surpass, falling print spending. But that doesn't mean those online ad dollars will go to newspaper Web sites. The sheer scale of the Internet means that less revenue will go to any individual publication, and the changing nature of advertising means most of it won't go to any publication at all. About half of all online marketing spending goes to search sites, and that percentage is rising.[15] This is just a matter of efficiency. Traditionally, appliance stores bought ads in newspaper sections aimed at readers who might be looking for a new TV—the Sunday sports pages, for example. It was inexpensive to reach each reader but pricey overall, since advertisers paid to put their message in front of millions of people who had little interest in it. By advertising on search pages with Google's AdWords program, those same appliance stores can target Internet users who enter a specific search query, such as "new TV." Newspapers can't offer that kind of efficiency.

This fundamentally changes the dynamics of the advertising market. In the print world, newspapers competed with niche publications that charge premium ad prices to reach a more desirable audience. Online, the sites that get the highest ad rates are the ones that have the most information about readers. The airline ad budget doesn't go to the publication with the most appropriate content—whether that's *Condé Nast Traveler* or a local newspaper travel section—it goes to the site where users are searching for "flights to Paris." The incentive to produce compelling journalism has been replaced by one to track readers.

Newspapers have an informational disadvantage, since online giants like Google and Facebook have access to data they can only dream about. From its various products, Google might know what users watch (You-Tube), how they communicate (Gmail), and even where they go in the real world (its Android mobile phone operating system). Facebook can track users' behavior on its own service, as well as any Web site they sign in to using Facebook Connect. Both companies have not only sophisticated ad targeting but the scale to collect information from all over the Internet. Many newspapers only track where users go on their particular sites (and how much does a lively interest in state politics really reveal about a reader anyway?).

As readers and advertisers move online, newspapers need to either increase revenue or cut costs. So far, almost all of them have chosen to do the latter, which usually means laying off reporters, since it's hard to make incremental cuts in printing or distribution. But this makes it even harder to compete with the online journalism start-ups courting their readers. If newspapers want to keep putting out the kind of journalism they do now, they're going to have to find a way to get into the business of selling news.

Just outside his sleek glass office in News Corporation's east London headquarters, James Murdoch keeps a life-size statue of Darth Vader. The unusual trophy comes from Lucasfilm, whose *Star Wars* movies were distributed by the company's Fox Studios. It could be taken as an inside joke: this is how a sizable portion of the public sees Murdoch and his father, Rupert, whose News Corp. owns *The Times* and the *Sun* in the U.K., the *Wall Street Journal* and the *New York Post* in the United States, and scores of other newspapers, as well as an array of cable television assets around the world. Newspaper reporters, many of whom resent the politics and tabloid sensibility of some of the Murdoch family's properties, are probably even more likely to hold that opinion. That's why the Murdochs make such unlikely candidates to become saviors of journalism.

Polished and pragmatic, James Murdoch—who works standing up

behind a high desk because it helps him stay focused—is the opposite of the *Guardian*'s Rusbridger in almost every way. Unsurprisingly, he has a very different vision for journalism, which involves charging readers and making money. Although News Corp. earns most of its money in the cable television business, Murdoch shares his father's passion for newspapers. "I love the business of journalism," says Murdoch, now chief executive of News Corp. in Europe and Asia. "It was our first business in Adelaide in the fifties and it's the heart of this company in many ways."

Along with his father, James Murdoch, who ran the online operations for News Corp. in the late 1990s, has come to believe that newspapers are killing themselves with free content. He has challenged Google's right to excerpt his papers' stories without compensation. And he has no kind words for Rusbridger, who took aim at the News Corp. plan to start charging for *The Times Online* in his January 2010 speech but four months later said on a radio show that it would be "crazy to be fundamentalist" about the issue.[16]

"The problem with the *Guardian* is that they become orthodox about something very faddish and then they assert it as a principle," Murdoch says. "So free news online has been orthodoxy for a while and then, when it looks like we start to make some headway, he goes on the radio and says, 'Well, if it works, we might do it.'" (There's little love lost between the Murdochs and the *Guardian* for a variety of reasons.) The *Guardian* can afford to lose money, since it's owned by a trust. But Murdoch places more trust in the market.

To him, that means charging for content. "If you're going to monetize something, you should probably not give it away for free," he declared in November 2010, at the Monaco Media Forum.[17] The *Wall Street Journal*, which News Corp. owns, has had an easy time selling content on the Internet, and it now has 400,000 online subscribers. But it won't be as easy to convince readers of the unique value of the *Post* or the *Sun*. In July 2010, *The Times* started charging readers who don't subscribe to the paper £1 per day or £2 per week, and it attracted just 100,000 consumers; another 100,000 get free access with their print subscriptions.[18] The Web site's traffic plummeted by almost 90 percent, and much of the U.K. media declared the idea of charging a failure, especially after some public relations companies said they were less eager to get clients in the paper.[19] But the economics of online journalism means the company could actually be making more money; it's impossible to tell until it releases more numbers. Perhaps most important, *The Times* could have a smoother transition to a digital business if it can make about as much revenue from an online subscriber as it does, after distribution costs, from a reader who buys the print edition.

As News Corp.'s heir apparent, James Murdoch takes a much broader view of the online media business than most newspaper publishers. The company is involved in almost every aspect of the media business, including movies and television through Fox and book publishing through HarperCollins, and Murdoch began his career at the company running the Australian music label Festival Records. (Before that, he had helped to found the independent hip-hop label Rawkus Records.) All of these businesses are now plagued by piracy. "You have what everybody agrees is illegal activity going on," he says, "but you're accused of not being either bright enough or innovative enough or modern enough if you can't figure out how to make a return when everyone's stealing or indexing your stuff."

Both James and Rupert Murdoch have made the case—aggressively and publicly—that News Corp. should get paid when Google indexes or excerpts its journalism. Google has always said that both its search engine and Google News are covered by fair use, but that only applies in the United States—the U.K. has similar laws, but other countries don't—and Murdoch points out the company has wavered from its stance that it should never have to pay for content it indexes. In May 2010, Eric Schmidt mentioned that the two companies were in talks about the issue, which Murdoch sees as progress.[20] "When [Schmidt] disclosed that we were in negotiations with them, I think Google ceded the ground they had from the standpoint of righteousness," Murdoch says.

To get a sense of how Murdoch sees Google, consider that he named News Corp.'s most ambitious online journalism venture Project Alesia, after a 52 B.C. battle in which Julius Caesar conquered the barbarians of Gaul. The plan, postponed indefinitely in October 2010, called for News Corp. to build an online system that would make it easier to sell content from all of its newspapers, as well as other publications that signed on. The company bought rights to the Skiff digital reading device to provide the hardware, and made a substantial investment in new technology.

Just as Rupert Murdoch has his roots in tabloids, James Murdoch is a creature of the cable television business. He made his reputation fixing Star TV, News Corp.'s Asian satellite television service, then ran the British pay-television company BSkyB (in which News Corp. owns a stake). Like cable companies, Project Alesia would have signed up content companies, bundled their products, and established a monthly billing relationship with consumers—in order to sell something that used to be free. But News Corp. couldn't convince enough other newspapers to join the project.[21] Murdoch says News Corp. will bring back another version of the project, and that much of the staff, thinking, and technology behind it went into the *Daily*, the iPad newspaper News Corp. launched in February 2011.

"We saw a situation that was frustratingly lacking leaders, so we got out there and we started talking about it," Murdoch says. "Basically, nearly all the CEOs and publishers are saying, 'I'm with you, win or tie.' We may be wrong, but at least we're out there trying to make change happen."

Despite the nervousness at newspapers about charging for content, the *Wall Street Journal* is not the only visible success. The *Financial Times* had 200,000 digital subscribers by the end of 2010, and it predicts that by 2013 it will get as much revenue from selling content as it does from advertising. "This is not about some mission to spread liberal journalism or some conquest of the U.S. media marketplace," says FT.com's Grimshaw, in what might be interpreted as a reference to Rusbridger. "This is about generating profit for our shareholders—that's what we're here to do." But this decidedly unsentimental view can result in better journalism. While sites that rely on advertising have to attract as many readers as possible, the *Financial Times* can focus on what it does best: European news, international economics, and market analysis.

Although many publishers believe paywalls will cut into their online advertising revenue, Grimshaw says that isn't necessarily so. Since FT.com gets some data on users who buy subscriptions, it can get higher CPMs—between £30 and £40. "For very precise targets—let's say senior managers in particular industries—you can get to £60 or £70 CPM," he says. "The difference comes in terms of what you know about the reader."

In many ways, the *Financial Times* is more forward-looking than other newspaper companies. In June 2010 it became the first newspaper to win a "Best iPad App" award from Apple, which has a reputation for being a finicky critic of design. It gives staffers £300 toward the purchase of an iPad at a time when benefits of any kind are disappearing from newsrooms. And it has started to sell subscription licenses directly to corporate clients, rather than going through database companies like LexisNexis.

At the same time, most of the newspaper's online success comes out of the fact that it produces a product readers are willing to pay for, in part because the staff hasn't been decimated by layoffs. "You've got major publishers all over the world wringing their hands, saying how could they ever produce something compelling enough to pay for," Grimshaw says. "I look at these organizations, with hundreds of journalists, and, frankly, if they're not producing anything worth paying for, it's time to go down to the newsroom and have a quiet word."

It's the third day of the April 2010 NewsNow Ideas Summit, the annual conference of the American Society of News Editors (ASNE), and the publisher of the *Arkansas Democrat-Gazette*, Walter Hussman Jr., is talking about how he keeps his paper profitable. A voluble sixty-three-year-old with a tan jacket, a southern accent, and a passing resemblance to James Carville, Hussman is speaking on a panel in the basement of the Washington, D.C., JW Marriott about whether charging for content is "fix or folly?" He's arguing for the former.

In 2001, when Hussman started charging for most of the content on the *Democrat-Gazette* Web site, his peers at other papers thought he was nuts. Now, Hussman says, his Little Rock, Arkansas, paper remains profitable, and its weekday circulation is holding steady at about 177,000.[22] (Financial information for the paper is not publicly available, since the company that owns it—as well as some other publications and a few small cable companies—is privately held.) In a business declining as quickly as newspaper publishing, that makes him something of a hero, and the buzz of side conversations quiets when he tells his story.

When Hussman used to offer free access to the online *Democrat-Gazette*, "People kept coming up to me and saying they appreciated me putting up the content for free so they didn't have to subscribe," Hussman says with a sly chuckle. He started charging when he realized the site was taking readers away from his more profitable print business. (The newspaper's entire site is free to print subscribers, and its headlines and Associated Press wire stories are free to anyone.) "The first reaction was outrage," he remembers.

The *Democrat-Gazette* immediately lost about 60 percent of its unique visitors. But the number of Web page views, which determines how many ads a site can show, declined far less. Hussman mostly lost casual readers who might have followed a search engine link to a particular article. Some of them didn't live in the area, which meant they weren't worth much to him anyway.

Even though Hussman charges for content, it turns out he's not all that interested in selling it, and he only has thirty-four hundred online-only subscribers, who pay $9.95 a month each. He mostly just wants to discourage readers from canceling their print subscriptions. Hussman fought hard for those subscribers in a late-1980s newspaper war between his *Arkansas Democrat* and Gannett's *Arkansas Gazette*, which he bought in 1991. "That's probably why I was one of the first people to charge," he says.

Hussman isn't afraid to use free goods as a marketing tool; long before Craig had a list, he gave away classifieds to win readers from the *Gazette*. But he takes a certain amount of pleasure in mocking new-media buzzwords. "I've heard a lot of people say, 'We're platform agnostic,'" Hussman says. "And I think, 'Why would we want to be platform agnostic?' Every Sunday, Best Buy buys a circular, and they pay about $40 per thousand [readers]. When we sell advertising on our site, we're lucky to get $4 per thousand." He says a newspaper like his can generate more than $300 a year in revenue for each print subscriber but only about $10 for each online reader. That could turn any agnostic into a believer.

Putting up a PowerPoint slide that compares his 1998 and 2008 circulation with those of other large dailies in the central-southern United States, Hussman shows that the daily circulation of his *Democrat-Gazette* is up 1.7 percent, while those of almost all the other papers fell, from as little as 2.7 percent in Knoxville, Tennessee, to as much as 29.3 percent in Dallas. (This ignores the Louisiana papers, since the state's population shifted so much in the aftermath of Hurricane Katrina.) Hussman's Sunday circulation fell by 1.1 percent, but that's the smallest decline on the slide.

The newspaper business is full of skeptics, and one editor raises his hand and asks if it's true that Hussman's paper had some layoffs. Hussman replies that his newsroom went from 190 to 170 employees over the past few years, mostly due to the recession. His revenue declined too, by 13.2 percent in 2008 and by another 14.6 percent the following year. But that counts as good news to this crowd: the industry saw average declines of 16.6 percent and 27.2 percent in those years.[23] "At first people thought, 'This guy's a Luddite,'" the *Dallas Morning News*'s chief executive, James Moroney III, says after the conference. "Now he's been vindicated." *Editor & Publisher* named Hussman Publisher of the Year in 2008, and the *Atlantic* chose him as one of its "Brave Thinkers" the following year. Executives from bigger newspaper chains regularly call for advice.

Some technology executives have advised publishers to embrace the

Internet, even if that means losing money. In March 2010, Netscape's co-founder Marc Andreessen, who owns part of the online news recommendation service Digg, suggested that newspapers abandon their print businesses entirely, to "burn the boats," as the Spanish conquistador Hernán Cortés is said to have done to force his expedition forward. More free online news would certainly benefit Digg, but it's hard to see how it would help newspapers. Printing and distribution account for about half a newspaper's costs, but the print editions it produces can generate about 90 percent of its revenue. As their readers go online, newspapers obviously need to prepare for the future. But it's easier to do that with the revenue from a healthy print business and the reporting staff it can support.

Hussman knows he's only putting off the inevitable. "Absolutely, I'm delaying it!" he says with a laugh. "But I'm doing a lot better job of delaying it than most people are by giving their content away for free. If we can delay it long enough, maybe something else will come along." When it does—*if it does*—the *Democrat-Gazette* will still have the staff to produce a product like the one it does now.

Charging for content changes the nature of competition in the news business. Online, if current trends hold, newspapers and start-ups will compete on a more even playing field: both will survive by selling inexpensive ads. Since readership for most publications has some inherent limit—only so many people are interested in Little Rock politics, for example—the journalism business could become a brutal contest to do more and more with less and less. Charging for news would change the game, allowing publications to distinguish themselves by the quality of their coverage—assuming anyone is willing to pay for it.

So far, the results of experiments with paywalls have been mixed and hard to measure, since revenue from a small increase in print circulation can offset money lost from a large decline in online traffic. Most surveys show that between 15 percent and 50 percent of newspaper readers are willing to pay for online access.[24] But New York's *Newsday* only got thirty-five subscribers in three months after it began charging for its

Web site in late 2009, even as the paper's print circulation fell.[25] "From what we've seen," says Ken Doctor, "the paywall strategy tends to work better in local areas with a limited number of alternatives."

Newspapers like Idaho's *Lewiston Tribune* and New Mexico's *Albuquerque Journal* have been charging for online content for years. The *Tribune*'s paywall stabilized its circulation, although its publisher, Nathan Alford, says it faces no local print or television competition. The *Journal* has seen a 10 percent decline in circulation—not as good a record as Hussman's, but better than most papers of its size—and it's now experimenting with selling online access to individual editions of the paper as well as subscriptions. "Charging isn't a panacea that's going to save the industry," says the *Journal*'s assistant managing editor, Donn Friedman. "But not charging is a certain route to failure."

Hussman has some important advantages most newspapers don't: his company has no significant debt, he understands his local audience, and only one blog competes with the paper to cover Arkansas state government. Hussman knows more will follow. When they do, though, they'll face off against a newsroom that hasn't been decimated by layoffs, as so many others have been. "I don't think they'll be able to have a sustainable business," he says of potential online competitors. "If they want to come into this market and generate $3 per thousand [as a CPM] and compete with me when I'm generating $40 per thousand, I'm not too worried about that."

What he should be worried about are the sites that aggregate his journalism and sell ads against it themselves.

For someone who appears on television all the time, Arianna Huffington loves to criticize the mainstream media. True to form, she sits down at the ASNE conference panel called "The 24/7 News Cycle," promotes what she's doing on her *Huffington Post* Web site, and tells a roomful of editors what's wrong with their newspapers. In her view, it has nothing to do with the fact that online readers are worth less than a tenth of their physical counterparts; it's the stories themselves—many of which her site links to and summarizes.

Huffington launches into a critique of newspapers, characterizing their coverage of the 2008 financial crisis as too little, too late, and pointing to a lack of reporting on safety problems that could have played a role in the disaster at Massey Energy's Upper Big Branch coal mine in West Virginia the previous week. Sitting alongside the director of the University of Southern California journalism program, an editor of the *Orlando Sentinel*, and the *New York Times* business columnist David Carr, she says her site can compete to cover these big stories by excerpting and linking to other articles online.

By the time of the ASNE summit, the *Huffington Post* had become one of the ten most popular news sites on the Internet, with an editorial staff of only about a hundred. (In January 2011, the *Huffington Post* drew 27.6 million readers in the United States, second among news sites only to the *New York Times*, which had 34.5 million.[26]) And while the site later poached the *Times* journalists Peter Goodman and Tim O'Brien, with plans to do more ambitious reporting, most of the *Huffington Post* still consists of Associated Press wire stories, summaries of pieces from other publications, and blog posts written by volunteers. "Self-expression is the new entertainment," Huffington says. For a site like hers, which compiles it in bulk and makes sure it scores high in Google's search results, it's also a new business model. In February 2011, the *Huffington Post* was acquired by AOL for $315 million.

The panel starts taking questions, and a woman walks up to the microphone in the audience and introduces herself as Geri Ferrara, editor of the *Dominion Post*, a twenty-two-thousand-circulation daily paper located about two hours away from the site of the mining disaster. "I just want to ask," she says, her voice rising with emotion, "how many reporters you have at that site, Arianna?"

Huffington isn't fazed; she's accustomed to fielding such questions from ink-stained newspaper types who don't share her vision. "We are going to aggregate," she says in her Greek-accented purr, "and we are going to link people to your story." Huffington, who likes to say that the mainstream media suffers from attention-deficit disorder while her site has obsessive-compulsive disorder, said it would continue to follow the story. For the rest of 2010, the *Huffington Post* aggregated many stories about the mine disaster but published few of its own. Most of its original stories consisted of opinion columns, Associated Press pieces with added reporting, and a few calls to revise safety regulations. (Huffington has had a sometimes controversial relationship with originality at times herself: her 1981 biography of Maria Callas drew charges of plagiarism—which eventually resulted in an out-of-court settlement—and an art history professor accused her of borrowing heavily from her thesis on Picasso for a subsequent book, although no legal action was taken.[27] Huffington has denied this.) And while the *Huffington Post* brings attention and online traffic to newspapers like Ferrara's, those drop-in readers have little value.

When the *Huffington Post* runs original material from bloggers, it doesn't exercise the kind of editorial oversight one would find at most newspapers. According to a July 2009 story in *Salon*—an Internet site that does smart original reporting but has had trouble finding a business model to support it—the *Huffington Post*'s health coverage has been dominated by "bogus treatments and crackpot medical theories."[28] It regularly ran stories about the supposed link between vaccinations and autism, which credible scientists say doesn't exist. A blogger promoting a book on colon cleanses recommended them as a way to avoid swine flu. And the site's wellness editor, Patricia Fitzgerald, is a medical doctor, but she has a doctorate in homeopathy. (A *Huffington Post* spokesman said, "The opinions expressed by our bloggers are their own, and encompass many viewpoints about health and wellness issues.") This might be excused as the growing pains of a new form of journalism if Huffington weren't implicitly promoting it by criticizing the mainstream media every chance she gets.

Many online sites produce original journalism that's as good as or better than that in any newspaper: *TechCrunch* regularly breaks Silicon Valley business stories, *Calculated Risk* delivers prescient financial analysis, and *Talking Points Memo* offers smart left-leaning reporting. Competing with them will make newspapers better, or at least keep them on their toes. But aggregators like Google News and the *Huffington Post* excerpt or summarize the work of other publications without adding much to it, besides a link that few readers follow. (Google News, which offers excerpts and links to news stories, is distinct from the search engine.) A 2010 report by the research firm Outsell concluded that fully 44 percent of Google News users don't click through to the original articles it excerpts.[29] (A Google spokesperson has expressed serious doubts about the study's methodology and pointed out that Google News sends publishers a billion clicks a month.) "The vast majority of the value gets captured by aggregators linking and scraping rather than by the news organizations that get linked and scraped," according to Arnon Mishkin of the Mitchell Madison Group, who studied the subject.[30]

Publications have always summarized stories, and they have the right to do so under copyright law, which specifically covers only the expression of an idea rather than the idea itself. *Time* started as a digest of newspaper journalism, radio stations commonly paraphrase news articles, and every newspaper takes information from others in some form. Until recently, this wasn't a problem, because differences in location, frequency, and format limited direct competition: dailies weren't chasing the same audience or advertisers as the radio stations and local newscasts that relied on their reporting. Online, competition is immediate and fierce: the *Huffington Post* pursues some of the same advertisers that newspaper Web sites do. And large aggregators have an inherent advantage, since sites with more links show up higher in Google search results.

Like so many other situations on the Internet as it now exists, this amounts to what economists would call a market failure, since it rewards behavior that will eventually be bad for online journalism in general. Right now companies can make as much money aggregating content as they can creating it. Since aggregators spend less, they can sell ads at prices that producers of original content can't match. Inevitably, this will lead more companies to aggregate and fewer to invest in original reporting. Eventually, when there aren't as many stories to summarize, even the aggregators will suffer.

And *this* is why publishers like Walter Hussman should worry. By offering the same news at the same time as the publications that report it, aggregators make it very difficult to sell content. Discerning readers might seek out the original versions, but many Internet users would settle for summaries, to judge by Outsell's research on Google News. Some bloggers might even take a certain pride in undercutting a storied daily: *Gothamist*'s co-founder Jake Dobkin mocked the *New York Times* for its "slavish devotion to originality."[31]

Over the past few years, as the threat posed by aggregators has become more clear, newspaper executives have searched for a legal precedent that would give them some protection. They may have found it in a 1918 case, *International News Service v. Associated Press*, in which the Supreme Court established what was known as the "hot news misappropriation doctrine."[32] The Court held that the common-law doctrine of unfair competition—as opposed to copyright law—could be used to prevent one news service from immediately taking stories from another, even if it rewrote them. In the years since, news organizations haven't litigated that many hot news cases, but a 1997 case in which the National Basketball Association sued the STATS news service brought the idea into the digital age.[33] Although the NBA's suit was unsuccessful, the U.S. Court of Appeals for the Second Circuit held that hot news claims could be valid if they showed that the plaintiff spends money to gather information; the information is time sensitive; the defendant's use of the information constitutes "free-riding"; the defendant's product competes directly with the plaintiff's; and the ability to free ride would reduce the incentive to produce a product of the same quality.

Some news organizations are already trying to use the hot news doctrine to stop aggregators, or at least slow them down. In 2008, the Associated Press sued All Headline News for rewriting its stories and negotiated a settlement in which the aggregator paid an undisclosed sum and agreed to stop making "competitive use" of the wire service's content.[34] In March 2010, a group of investment banks got an injunction—later stayed—against the Web site flyonthewall.com for collecting and publishing their investment recommendations.[35] (Flyonthewall.com appealed the case.) And in November 2010, Dow Jones settled a case with Briefing.com, which paid an undisclosed sum and admitted to violating the former company's hot news rights.[36] (The Briefing.com case also involved alleged copyright infringement.)

Lawyers, activists, and many journalists have suggested that the hot news doctrine would allow some publications to "own the news" or lead to a wave of lawsuits that could stifle free expression online. It does place some limits on free speech. But it doesn't prevent anyone from discussing or re-reporting stories—just rewriting them without adding anything—and it couldn't be used against hobbyist bloggers. It protects against the deliberate and continuous use of reporting from another company, in an ongoing pattern, and it would protect small blogs from having their reporting taken by larger publications, which have an easier time drawing traffic from Google. If anyone can report news, shouldn't anyone be able to benefit from it?

So far, courts have dismissed cases that don't involve a serious investment in information.[37] "People say the AP is shutting down the Internet," says the Associated Press's general counsel, Srinandan Kasi. "But the truth is that there are very few cases in this area for good reason: the pleading standards are very high. The fact that you took five hundred words once to illustrate something is not a 'systematic taking' that takes away my incentive to remain in the business I'm in. If you're running a competing service and you are essentially free riding on my work, then that is a problem."

The Associated Press is already having trouble continuing to provide reporting of the quality it does now, and it would have a difficult time licensing news that other sites could rewrite for nothing. "It's a battle for survival," says the AP's chief executive, Tom Curley. "We're quite worried, and that's started us on a number of responses."

One of the more interesting initiatives is the Associated Press's plan to launch a new licensing agency that would ensure it and other organizations get paid for the use of their articles online. Rather than allow or forbid other sites to reprint certain content, the News Licensing Group—a separate company that starts operating in 2011—will track the use of articles and try to collect compensation accordingly. In concept, it's not unlike the music collection societies ASCAP and BMI, which pay songwriters for use of their compositions on radio and in restaurants. Technology companies that want to start businesses around Associated Press articles or content from other member companies would have an easy time arranging it, while those that don't pay would have no excuse.

At a May 2009 Senate Commerce Committee hearing on the future of journalism, Arianna Huffington mocked the idea that the *Baltimore Sun* could charge for content that only *Sun* subscribers could read. "That's not how people are consuming news," she said.[38] This is true, of course, but mostly because the *Huffington Post* and other online sites use *Sun* stories to draw in readers. The *Sun*, she implied, would just have to adjust.

Rather than apply regular media economics to online publications, which would involve spending more money on reporting, most technology executives push traditional publications to adapt online economics: inexpensive ads and content that costs as little as possible. Their ideas for the future of journalism include citizen journalism, nonprofit-funded reporting, and various innovations based on publicly available data. But they don't seem to involve many journal*ists*.

Few companies have done more to promote these ideas than Google, which has used the public discussion about the future of journalism to push its own priorities. In April 2010, the Knight Commission on the Information Needs of Communities in a Democracy, a group funded by the John S. and James L. Knight Foundation, issued a report with a series of recommendations, including having the government encourage the spread of high-speed broadband and maintain "open networks."[39] Google, whose vice president Marissa Mayer co-chaired the commission, has lobbied for both policies, and the company gave the Knight

Foundation a $2 million grant in October 2010. And both the Knight Foundation's chief executive officer, Alberto Ibargüen, and its vice president for journalism programs, Eric Newton, promoted the idea of universal broadband access at government hearings about the future of journalism.[40] (Ibargüen says Mayer was only one of fifteen commission members, and that $2 million is a fraction of the foundation's $40 million annual budget.)

The Knight Foundation is absolutely right that broadband access needs to be available and affordable. But while widespread high-speed broadband access would help ensure the *distribution* of journalism, there's no reason to expect it would help with the *creation* of journalism. Funding digital infrastructure won't address that problem any more than building paper mills might have helped a few decades ago. At a time when Americans have faster and easier access to more information than ever before, they don't seem to be any more informed than they were two decades ago. In a November 2010 study, for example, only 14 percent of Americans identified John Boehner as the presumptive Speaker of the House of Representatives.[41] It's hard to believe the other 86 percent couldn't get information about the 2010 election results. Presumably, most of them probably just choose not to. This is definitely a serious problem, but it may not be one technology can solve.

Groups like the Knight Commission are also promoting the idea of public and nonprofit journalism. In today's political environment, increased funding for public media isn't realistic, however desirable it may be. Important investigative work has already been produced by some promising nonprofits, including the *Texas Tribune* and *ProPublica* (which won a 2010 Pulitzer Prize for a story about a New Orleans hospital overwhelmed by Hurricane Katrina). But while those organizations can serve a vital function by devoting resources to expensive stories, they don't have the funding to get people to local zoning board meetings. As the media executive and news business blogger Alan Mutter pointed out, U.S. newspapers now spend $4.4 billion a year on reporting, while nonprofit journalism institutions raised only $144 million over the last *four*.[42]

"The finding about that in general is that the content is great and the funding model is very unstable," says Nicholas Lemann, dean of the Columbia University Graduate School of Journalism. "Then there are these experiments in crowdsourcing and other forms of social production, and my view is that they haven't really delivered the goods."

Although nonprofit groups like the Knight Foundation have become enamored with citizen journalism projects, their track record has been uneven at best. A 2010 study by the Pew Research Center's Project for Excellence in Journalism that examined the news "ecosystem" of Baltimore over the course of a week found that traditional media produced 95 percent of the stories with new information and that newspapers were responsible for most of them.[43] (It also found that 80 percent of all stories contained no new information at all, which is damning for old and new media alike.) "In every community I've ever studied," wrote the Project for Excellence in Journalism's director, Tom Rosenstiel, "the print news organization in that community has more reporters and editors than all of the other news organizations in that community combined."[44]

Newspapers need to find a better way to compete online—ideally one that involves bundling content from different publications under one fee and sharing data to get more money for ads. Journalism Online, a start-up founded by Steven Brill, Leo Hindery Jr., and the former *Wall Street Journal* publisher Gordon Crovitz, provides an e-commerce platform that could eventually allow publishers to do both of those things. They have a similar vision to that of Project Alesia, and in June 2010 News Corp. announced it was investing in the company. As of early 2011, Journalism Online's Press+ allows a dozen publications—including the *Augusta Chronicle* and the Scranton *Times-Tribune*—to charge readers for news and adjust how much content they give away for free. If it attracts enough newspapers, it could let them share information about readers to get the kinds of ad rates that only online giants now command.

To understand how this might work, think about how companies value readers of print papers and online sites. To advertisers, each reader of a print paper is worth the same amount, since it's almost impossible to figure out what sections a reader actually looks at. But the value of online users varies widely according to what they look at—and how often—and publishers should be able to charge advertisers accordingly, without having to depend on another company for data. They also need to use better online tracking to identify and charge regular readers who are dedicated consumers of the paper's unique content. That way they can get some online subscription revenue without losing the less profitable drive-by traffic that comes from blogs and search engines.

By changing the way newspapers generate revenue online, Journalism Online would also change the incentives that make many of them chase the same stories online. As long as advertisers focus on numbers of readers, publications will tend to bring in traffic with general news and celebrity stories. Few readers will pay for this, simply because so many sites run similar fare, but a thin story about a national issue will generate more hits than smart reporting about a local one. If Journalism Online can convince local audiences to pay for content, it would give newspapers an economic incentive to specialize in the state and local news coverage that has disproportionately been lost to layoffs.

"What they'd need to do is have the best, most talked-about coverage of the town zoning board or the mayor's new education plan," Brill says. "You can start thinking like an editor again." His plan assumes that at least one of every ten readers of a particular news site will pay for it—a figure well within the range of most surveys.

Of course, Brill's plan will only work if newspapers retain the staff, and the institutional will, to create journalism locally engaged readers will pay for. In spring 2010, Brill met with an executive at a big-city daily—he won't say which—that's planning to join Journalism Online. "Walking out, the editor says to me, 'This is great, but I don't have anything left in this paper that I think anybody would buy anymore,'" Brill says. "That's tough stuff."

More than ever in the coming years, the way publishing companies make money will determine the kind of journalism they do. Publications that charge for news will need to produce the kinds of stories readers are willing to pay for, while those that give away content will have to cut costs and attract the broadest audience possible. They'll embrace citizen journalism, maximize page views by creating photo galleries, or use "search engine optimization" to choose stories and headlines that will score high in Google's search results.

The city of Seattle is already serving as a makeshift media lab for these two approaches. In March 2009, after the end of a joint operating agreement that allowed the *Seattle Times* and the *Seattle Post-Intelligencer* to run parts of their businesses together in order to save money, the two newspapers took very different paths.[45] The family-owned *Times* maintained its print edition, while the Hearst Corporation's *Post-Intelligencer* became an online-only publication, cut its editorial staff to twenty, recruited two hundred volunteer bloggers, and introduced eye-catching new features to boost Web traffic. Hearst thought this approach might point the way toward a successful model for online journalism.

So far, not much has changed at the *Times*, which picked up some of its rival's subscribers. The paper maintains a newsroom staff of 170, and in 2010 it won a Pulitzer Prize for its coverage of the fatal shooting of four police officers. The company is not net profitable, but it is cash flow positive, according to its publisher, Frank A. Blethen. "We believe there's nothing wrong with the newspaper model," he says.

The *Post-Intelligencer* offers local coverage as well, but its Web site also features photo galleries—of celebrities, fashion, and even "The week in dogs." (On the Internet, cute pets are the new hot girls.) It now has 2.7 million readers a month.[46] It's tempting to think that a major daily could slim down to a fighting weight of twenty journalists and use the power of the Internet to succeed. (Hearst declined to comment on whether the *Post-Intelligencer* is making money.) But, like many online businesses, it lacks a sustainable competitive advantage. Any number of local entrepreneurs could hire twenty reporters, set up a Web site, and fight for traffic—including some of those twenty *Post-Intelligencer* reporters themselves. And anyone who's spent any time online knows the Internet is full of pictures of cute dogs.

The *Times* faces its own challenges: much higher staffing costs, a print business that will eventually decline, and the difficulty of adapting to new technology as fast as its rival. But its print paper gives it an advantage on the Internet, and it recently started a neighborhood blog consortium to improve its reach online, where its Web site already draws three million readers a month, many of whom are probably local readers, and hence worth more to advertisers.[47]

"The basis of our Web site, which from a traffic standpoint is incredibly successful, is the content that's produced for print," Blethen says. "There's no way you could make enough money for this kind of newsroom online. There's a lot of hope that things will get better online, and I think we'll find some solutions, but a lot of it is wishful thinking."

CHAPTER 5

THE REVOLUTION
MAY NOT BE TELEVISED

HOW THE INTERNET
COULD KILL *MAD MEN*

I f the Israeli entrepreneur Avner Ronen has his way, the television business will be reinvented in a tenement turned office building in Chelsea,
a couple of miles and a world away from NBC's iconic headquarters at
30 Rockefeller Plaza. That's where Ronen runs Boxee, the start-up that
helps consumers watch on TV any video they can see on a computer
screen. The company's $200 Boxee Box brings the Internet into the liv-
ing room and takes all the video there along for the ride—whether it's
purchased or pirated.

A jet-black gadget the size of a Nintendo Wii, the Boxee Box lets
consumers use their TVs to navigate the Internet or stream video with
iPhone-style apps from YouTube, Netflix, and scores of other companies. For users, it's a miracle machine that can eliminate cable bills. But
television executives worry it will take away the $32 billion in annual
revenue those bills contribute to the cost of producing shows.[1] If devices
like the Boxee Box catch on—and several companies, including Google,
already make them—they could destroy television as we know it.

When I visit Boxee's office in February 2010, the company's two-
room headquarters isn't much to look at. Most of the company's thirty-
three employees work in Tel Aviv, where the Boxee software was written.
(It runs on computers as well as on the Boxee Box.) Here in New York, a
team of eleven works out of a small room filled with desks, each of which
has a shiny, new Mac on top of it. A kitchenette in the corner looks much

as it might have when the place was an apartment. There are no cubicles, perhaps because Boxee's ambitions are too large for the space.

Boxee has room to grow on the other side of a glass wall, where what passes for a conference room—two couches that face each other in front of a fireplace—gives Ronen room to demonstrate his product. Alongside the sitting area is a Ping-Pong table Ronen uses to sneak short breaks from the long days he spends running a start-up that has raised $10 million since it was founded in 2007.

When I walk in, Ronen—who always seems to have an exhausted entrepreneur's three-day stubble—gets off a conference call and decides it's time for one of those breaks. So we walk over to the table and hit the ball back and forth, first slow and high, then faster and lower. I'm decent, he's better, and he's playing to win.

Ronen plays public relations volleys the same way—aggressively, and with hard spin. The day before my visit, NBC Universal's chief executive at the time, Jeff Zucker, testified in front of Congress about the company's pending merger with Comcast. In response to a question about Hulu, the Web site that provides some of NBC's programming online, Zucker said it had blocked Boxee because Ronen's product was illegal.[2]

Within hours Ronen put up a post on Boxee's blog "to set the record straight." Since Boxee works much like any other Internet browser, he argued, it's perfectly legal. (He's right, but that doesn't mean Hulu can't block it.) "We believe the Internet represents a great opportunity for content owners," Ronen wrote, "and we hope that current artificial barriers put on distribution over the Internet will be taken down."[3] Within twenty-four hours, the post had received more than fifty comments, most of which took Zucker to task for failing to understand that television shows should be free online.

"It was an interesting day for us," Ronen says with a laugh that makes it clear he knows the dustup amounted to free promotion. "Our view is that consumers are gradually going to move towards entertainment consumption that is based mostly on the Internet, and they'll be able to access it from a variety of devices. Any artificial barrier you put up is not going to be understood."

That might sound promising for networks, since the young viewers advertisers want to reach are comfortable watching programs on laptops, tablets, and even smartphones. But most online advertising is worth a fraction of its off-line equivalent, just as it is in the newspaper business. And cable television isn't really a barrier—it's an admission gate.

Most viewers believe advertising funds television and cable bills cover the cost of delivering it. But that hasn't been true for more than a decade. About 40 percent of the revenue collected by cable companies gets divided among channels in the form of "carriage fees."[4] Most cable channels get about half their revenue from these payments.[5] Without them, smaller channels like FX and AMC wouldn't be able to fund smart shows like Sons of Anarchy and Mad Men, which don't reach a large enough audience to break even on advertising alone.

The business model those shows depend on is already in trouble. A report by the Yankee Group consultancy said one in eight consumers is planning to give up some of their cable services, presumably at least partly due to the availability of free online video.[6] The total number of cable and satellite video subscribers fell by 216,000 and 119,000 in the second and third quarters of 2010—a small decline, but the first one ever.[7] And Boxee is only one of many devices that could threaten cable. The Roku makes it convenient to watch movies from Netflix in streaming video, Apple TV lets users buy episodes directly from the iTunes Store, and Google TV makes it easy to search for any video online. Some new TVs even have Internet access built in.

More than anything else on the Internet, online access to video strikes at the beating heart of the entire entertainment business. Cable has become an increasingly important profit center for the six conglomerates that own major movie studios: NBC Universal, Sony, Time Warner, Viacom, the Walt Disney Company, and News Corporation (which owns the Fox Entertainment Group). All of them sell movies and television shows to cable, and all except for Sony own channels as well. Cable carriage fees make up 19 percent of revenue at Disney, and they usually account for a majority of operating profit at the five conglomerates that collect them. The cable business has become so important to Hollywood that five of the six executives who run the companies that own studios have backgrounds in cable, as does News Corp.'s chief operating officer, Chase Carey.

Most Americans have a far more favorable opinion of Hollywood than they do of the companies that provide cable service, which they associate with rising bills, interminable hold times for customer service, and technicians who never seem to show up on time. Boxee cultivates the opposite image—accessible and efficient, with open-source software consumers can download for free. The company even lets electronics manufacturers license its software for free, in order to build an audience.

The idea of using a TV to navigate the Internet goes back more than a decade to Microsoft's WebTV product, which never caught on. But Boxee's elegant interface quickly won it a following among gadget fans who spread the word on blogs. In December 2009, a couple of months before my visit, the company unveiled the beta version of its program at a packed New York nightclub.

A month later Boxee finally announced its business plan: using its platform to sell apps and taking a percentage of each transaction it processes payment for. (It doesn't make money on free apps like Netflix and YouTube, those that offer ad-supported content, or video that can be accessed on the Web itself.) "We're trying to push people toward legal consumption of content," Ronen says. He believes consumers with no legitimate options will turn to illegal file sharing—"and that's not good for anybody in the value chain."

Like many new-media entrepreneurs, Ronen wants to muscle his way into that value chain, whether companies that produce television programming want him there or not. Consumers who buy the Boxee Box will be that much more likely to cut their cable subscriptions and become potential customers for Boxee apps. As of the end of 2010, however, Boxee could not say what video providers would sell apps.

"We never actually spent much time on the business model," Ronen admits. In a business as large as television, he just assumed there would be plenty of opportunities for a start-up that helped users access online video from a TV—whether or not the companies that owned it wanted them to see it that way. "Maybe even now it's not completely clear how it's going to play out," he says, "but we know that if we're going to be in that position, we'll be able to make it work."

The television business has always been more complicated than it looks. Back before cable, the three networks had an easy time making money on advertising because they reached a mass audience without much competition. But even in the 1960s and 1970s, producers of more expensive shows would plan on losing money when they first aired and making a profit selling them for syndication later.

Over the course of the 1980s, the cable television business convinced Americans to pay for something they used to get for free—an accomplishment online media companies would do well to study. Cable's first real draws were movies, sports, and specialized programming like CNN and MTV, but most channels filled their schedules by airing old movies and repeats. (This is how Ted Turner made much of his fortune.) Original programming was less common and not nearly as ambitious as it is today.

The cable business exploded in the 1990s when the Clinton administration repealed the 1970 Financial Interest and Syndication Rules—"fin-syn" for short—that the Federal Communications Commission (FCC) designed to foster competition. These regulations limited how many self-produced programs networks could air, which required them to buy the rest from outside producers. Since the major movie studios produced so many television shows, this discouraged them from buying networks. Once the rules were eliminated, the studios started investing in television—to the point that they now dominate the business—and combining most of the larger cable channels into conglomerates.

At the time, cable relied mostly on advertising revenue. In 1996, when News Corp. introduced its Fox News channel, it *paid* cable companies to carry it.[8] As Americans grew accustomed, if not addicted, to cable, channels that had hit shows or sports rights found they could get higher fees from cable companies, even though they were also selling ads. Fox News now receives about seventy-five cents per subscriber, for example, from some of the same companies it used to pay.[9] Cable became, according to News Corp.'s former president Peter Chernin, "one of the all-time great business models."[10]

As consumers started watching more movies on DVD, cable channels, inspired by HBO's success with *The Sopranos* and *Sex and the City*, started investing more money in original programming. But they did it very differently from networks, and for good reason. Networks only made money on advertising, so they needed shows that reached as many viewers as possible, whether or not they felt strongly about them. This is the business model that brought us *Mister Ed*. Carriage fees gave cable channels a different incentive: to develop programs some viewers cared about so much that they could raise prices for them. This is the business model that brought us *Mad Men*.

"Hopefully, if you watch *Mad Men*, you didn't just sit down to watch TV, you sat down to watch that show," says Josh Sapan, chief executive of the company that owns AMC, which airs the show. "That's consumer allegiance. They would bug their cable operators if it wasn't on, and that enhances the value of AMC. If you perform and get a hit, you'll get rewarded." In the cable business, competition drives up quality and price—the opposite of what happens online, where free shows have to be produced as cheaply as possible.

Mad Men probably isn't popular enough to survive on advertising alone. At a reported cost of $2.3 million per episode, it isn't much cheaper to make than an average network drama.[11] But it draws a much smaller audience: the show's fourth season drew an average of 2.3 million viewers for the first broadcast of each episode—respectable for cable but less than a third of some network hits.[12] If AMC charged advertisers $20 to reach a thousand viewers, as is typical for a cable hit, it would bring in less than $1 million an episode. Alas, the Madison Avenue glory days the show celebrates are long gone.

As Sapan suggests, *Mad Men* makes money because it's good

enough to pay for. In 2007, when AMC started airing the show, it was an also-ran channel that charged cable companies an average of twenty-two cents a month per subscriber.[13] Since then, largely on the strength of that show and the critically acclaimed *Breaking Bad*, it has gained enough of a following to raise its rates. One analyst estimated that AMC increased its fees to twenty-four cents a subscriber in about ninety-five million homes in which the channel is available. That would generate almost $23 million more a year in fees. Others estimated the company actually gets significantly more per subscriber.

That money comes from viewers' cable bills, which have increased to an average of $68.[15] But much of that money goes to fund the most varied, ambitious programming in the history of television. Cable programs like *Battlestar Galactica* and *Burn Notice* wouldn't draw a large enough audience to work on networks; nor would HBO and Showtime programs like *The Wire* and *Dexter*, which have the moral complexity of independent films.

"The beauty of cable is that, because there are so many offerings, you don't have to be all things to all people," says Kevin Beggs, president of television programming and production for Lionsgate, which produces *Mad Men* for AMC and pays about a third of the show's production costs. (In exchange, the company gets rights to sell the show on DVD and in various overseas markets, including the U.K., where it has become a hit.) "It came out of that need to differentiate the channel and present something proprietary to cable operators and say, 'You have to pay us more.'"

The four networks have gone in the other direction. As they lose young viewers to cable and ad dollars to the Internet, they fund fewer scripted shows. That's the real reason why reality shows have become so popular: they're cheap. "Without a doubt, there's a trend on broadcast networks—and you see it in the number of reality shows that now populate prime time—to get as much audience as quickly and as inexpensively as you can, sell advertising, and move on to the next one," Sapan says. This is the business model that brought us *The Bachelor*.

These business models affect everything we see on TV. Consider the

2010 conflict over *The Tonight Show*. In the fall of 2009, when NBC moved Jay Leno's show to 10:00 p.m., it did so mostly to save money: the hour-long dramas that usually air at 10:00 p.m. typically cost more than $3 million an hour, while an episode of Leno's show costs around $400,000.[16] After Conan O'Brien's *Tonight Show* didn't draw as many viewers as NBC wanted, the late-night host got a contract with TBS, which wanted a show that appealed to a young audience and needed a marquee property to negotiate for higher carriage fees.

With the syndication market weakening and advertising prices down from the recession, the traditional networks are now asking cable companies for "retransmission fees" to carry their free over-the-air broadcasts on cable. (Network broadcasts can also still be seen with an antenna.) In late 2009, News Corp. asked Time Warner Cable for a payment to carry Fox's broadcast channels; a few months later Disney threatened to pull its ABC network from Cablevision right before the Academy Awards broadcast if the cable company didn't meet its price for programming.

"The cable companies are going to pay for retransmission because the stuff that's driving a huge amount of viewership is *American Idol* and [other broadcast shows]," says James Murdoch of News Corp. He's right, at least about the second part. In a fall 2010 survey conducted by the Needham & Company analyst Laura Martin, respondents who were asked what channels they'd need to get online in order to cut their cable subscription mentioned the four networks, then ESPN, as their top choices.[17]

But if television can be worth paying for, why have networks spent the last few years putting shows online for free?

In March 2007, NBC and Fox announced they were forming a joint venture to show some of their programming for free on a Web site they would later give the nonsensical new-media name of Hulu. In part, they worried that Google's then-recent purchase of YouTube would give the company a lock on the online video market before it really even got going. But they also worried that television shows were becoming popular on file-sharing services, and they figured that if someone was going to make their product available online for nothing, it might as well be them.

"We were very much aware of what was happening with YouTube, that it was a destination predominantly for pirated content, a lot of it ours," says Peter Levinsohn, the executive in charge of digital distribution at Fox. "We wanted to put a legitimate alternative in the marketplace."

As an old-media Internet venture, Hulu aroused the ire of technology business blogs like *TechCrunch* and *GigaOM*, which predict the decline of television networks with the shoe-banging subtlety of Nikita Khrushchev. The former gleefully reported that Google staffers had nicknamed the new venture "Clown Co." The latter ran a gag interview on the topic with the Pets.com sock puppet (which would seem to symbolize the hubris of technology start-ups rather than that of television networks).

When bloggers finally tried Hulu a year later, however, they liked what they saw. An intuitive interface lets users stream shows from NBC, Fox, and some of their related cable channels, and ABC joined in 2009. Hulu also offers an eclectic mix of programming from media companies that don't have a stake in it, including independent documentaries, Japanese anime, and videos from online sites like CollegeHumor. It has links to other legal sources of online television programming, such as the CBS and CW Web sites. Even the ads are easy on the eyes: Hulu only shows about six minutes of commercials per hour, and users can sometimes choose ones that interest them. By the end of 2008, when the Associated Press named Hulu its Web site of the year, Google staffers probably weren't laughing anymore.

Hulu started making a profit at the end of 2009, and it took in about a quarter-billion dollars of revenue in 2010.[18] It made money before YouTube, which takes in far more revenue, according to most estimates. (Google doesn't reveal earnings details.) Hulu uses far less bandwidth and storage, and it benefits from the fact that advertisers are more comfortable running commercials against *CSI* than against "Charlie Bit My Finger." The site gets about $40 per thousand viewer impressions—more than almost any other site online.

The former NBC Universal chief executive Jeff Zucker, who often said he didn't want to trade analog dollars for digital pennies, thinks the advertising economics of Hulu represent a step in the right direction. "I think we're making progress on the continuum of pennies to quarters," he says. (He spoke when he was running the company.) "Business models to support the digital revolution are still being developed—we're still very much in the beginning. But there's certainly more progress."

Unlike newspapers, which haven't been able to act together in a way that allows them to collect enough information about online readers to sell targeted advertising, Hulu tracks users and shows them relevant commercials. This gives it an advantage over television advertising. "You can't target ads any better in the living room than you could in 1955," says Hulu's chief executive, Jason Kilar. "It's astonishing to me that for fifty-five years the greatest innovation in terms of television advertising has been the movement from black and white to color."

Targeting helps Hulu charge a little more for commercials than prime-time network shows, and far more than daytime television or cable. That's important, since Hulu shows less than half as many ads; online viewers will only tolerate so many commercial interruptions, since many pirated shows have none at all. (Hulu still gets more ads to consumers than shows saved on digital video recorders, since about two-thirds of those viewers skip commercials entirely.) It doesn't generate carriage fees. Over the course of an hour, a Hulu viewer might be worth a third to two-thirds as much as someone who's watching traditional television.[19]

Does Hulu compete with traditional television? Network executives initially assumed they were offering online viewers a taste of shows they might enjoy on TV, as well as a convenient alternative to piracy. They never saw Hulu as a substitute for a cable subscription, since it was designed for a computer screen. Connecting a TV to a laptop requires a computer in the living room, a willingness to live without a remote control, and more patience than most people have when they're trying to relax.

That was the idea anyway. But the Internet can turn today's promotional push into tomorrow's replacement good. When Napster went online, technology executives argued that the file-sharing service offered music fans an easy way to sample recordings in low-quality audio so they could decide what CDs they might want to buy. At the time, that made sense. Within a few years, though, file-sharing services were filled with CD-quality songs that could serve as a replacement for the digital files sold at Apple's iTunes Store. For the same reason, network executives fear online video services will eventually threaten cable television.

And that's where Avner Ronen and Boxee came in.

To Ronen, the inconvenience of connecting a laptop to a TV was just another "artificial barrier" Internet users wouldn't like. So he turned that barrier into a business plan. The software Boxee introduced in 2009 makes watching online video on TV easy, with simple menus and the ability to use an iPhone as a remote control. For a few months at least, it made watching Hulu on TV as convenient as watching traditional television. And that made networks worry users would give up their cable subscriptions.

In February 2009, Hulu asked Boxee to cut access to video on Hulu, which it did. "Basically they told us, 'We don't want to have our content accessible or available on Boxee,'" Ronen says. For less than two-thirds of the revenue they would make on TV, why would they?

At first, Ronen wasn't content to leave that decision up to them. Hulu is the best source of television online, and it's easier to use than most of Boxee's apps. A month after Boxee first removed access to Hulu, it started using the site's RSS feeds to link directly to the videos, until Hulu blocked that as well. For the next year and a half, Boxee and Hulu played a game of cat and mouse, in which the start-up would find ways to access Hulu programming until the site blocked it again.

"We're very comfortable with Hulu staying on the PC," Levinsohn says, with considerable understatement. "To the extent that there were different business models that had different economic structures, would we be okay with it being on mobile devices or the television set? Yeah, probably. But in its current business model we're not comfortable with that."

Ronen is right when he says Boxee works like a Web browser—at least from a technical perspective. But that's not the whole story. On a computer, Hulu users see a frame around their video picture that offers controls and sometimes promotions for products or shows. Boxee eliminated this—a fact Ronen neglected to mention on his blog. "Boxee started out way over the line, to abuse access to Hulu in a way that boosted their economics and disadvantaged Hulu," says Rick Cotton, executive vice president and general counsel for NBC Universal. "They displaced advertising, and they disabled functionality."

Perhaps unsurprisingly, Ronen isn't sympathetic to this point of view. "I think that being upset with Boxee for making it easier for people to connect their computer to TV is naive," he says. "If they really don't want people to access their content for free online, they can fix it very easily—just don't put the content online. Then they risk piracy." That's exactly what some online music start-ups essentially said to labels: settle for less or get nothing at all.

Every time Hulu removes a show or blocks a service like Boxee, bloggers complain about the cluelessness of old media. So Jason Kilar tries to balance the expectations of an audience that got used to online media being free with those of Hulu's network shareholders who very much need it to make money. "Media companies invest billions of dollars every year to create shows like *30 Rock*, and it is absolutely their right to make decisions about how they make them available," Kilar says. "You can't ignore that. In the premium video business, you have at least two sets of customers—and by that I mean users and content owners—and we have to delight all of them."

Not all content owners are convinced. "Our view of Hulu is slightly contrary to the rest of the industry," says Josh Sapan, who doesn't show any AMC programs free online, except for promotional purposes. "We've taken what you could call a borderline fundamentalist approach as far as free video, because we want to protect our wholesale rate— what we ask cable operators to pay. In order to maintain that, we have restrained ourselves from putting these shows up for free on the Web. We have put them on iTunes because, if you have to pay a couple of bucks for an episode or more than that for a season, it reinforces the value of your cable subscription."

The words "value" and "cable subscription" are rarely found in such close proximity. Subscription prices have increased faster than inflation, and many consumers resent having to buy channels they never watch in order to get ones they do. But the average American watches 143 hours of television a month,[20] which makes cable a bargain at fifty cents an hour—much less than what Amazon and Apple charge for individual shows.

One threat to cable could come from Hulu itself, which introduced Hulu Plus in June 2010. For $7.99 per month, the service offers the entire current season of most network and some cable shows for streaming on computers, mobile devices like the iPhone and iPad, and Internet-connected TVs and video game consoles. Hulu Plus is even open to working with the makers of devices like the Boxee Box. For Hulu, it's a natural evolution: if someone is going to make your product available online for a small fee, it might as well be you.

The idea is to charge a modest premium for the convenient delivery of something that used to be free. "Years ago people wouldn't buy a bottle of water, and now bottled water is one of the most lucrative businesses beverage companies are in," Zucker says. "If we can make people understand that there's real value in paying for our content, I think it has a good chance of success."

For traditional broadcast networks, Hulu Plus could be even better than cable. "Hulu Plus allows us to actually exceed the carriage fees that you see in the living room," Kilar says. "If you take a look at the broadcast networks, how much are they getting for retransmission fees? I've heard anything from a quarter to maybe fifty cents at the high end. Hulu

Plus is $7.99, and we have worked very hard to make sure the economics that NBC gets in their portion of that subscription fee is well in excess of what they're getting from cable companies." That doesn't apply to cable channels, some of which may make more money from carriage fees.

As much as anything else, Hulu ensures the networks don't get stuck selling their products to the public through one dominant retailer, as record labels did with Apple. It gives them more negotiating power. "The notion that content businesses would simply cede to an Apple or a YouTube the aggregator role and let them become dominant is very unattractive," Cotton says. "So having Hulu out there as a competitor is a plus—and right now they are an important competitor."

As online video takes off, some of the most popular programming that isn't online consists of sports games. But NBC didn't win any medals for its coverage of the 2010 Winter Olympics in Vancouver. The network didn't present many events live online, and it delayed showing some of the biggest events until East Coast prime time, by which point some viewers who had checked the news on the Internet already knew who won. It also restricted access to some online video to viewers who could log in and prove they had a cable subscription.

From a public relations standpoint, this was a disaster: Twitter filled with indignant messages, while bloggers said NBC didn't understand the Internet. From a financial perspective, however, NBC's reasoning made perfect sense. The network presented events how and when they would bring in the most money and offered exclusive online video to cable viewers to reinforce the value of their subscriptions.

"To make record amounts of Olympic TV available to the U.S. public on both the broadcast and cable channels at a cost of around a billion dollars for sixteen days—$820 million in rights fees and around $200 million of production costs—requires a strategy designed to recoup that expense," NBC's Cotton says. "Some comes from advertising, some comes from cable exhibition and subscription fees, and there's advertising on the Internet site. And the online exhibition is managed with one eye on trying to generate revenue to support the overall enterprise." In other words, nothing personal, but we pay big money to show the Olympics, so you might have to spend something to watch them.

A more noteworthy question about the network's strategy came from Senator Herb Kohl (D-Wis.), chair of the Antitrust Subcommittee of the Senate Judiciary Committee, who wrote a letter to Jeff Zucker asking him to explain why viewers needed a cable subscription to see some online video. The context was NBC Universal's then-pending merger with Comcast. "I fear," Kohl wrote, "that this practice of locking up certain content only for pay-TV subscribers may be a preview of what is to come with respect to TV programming shown on the Internet."[21] He may be right. But some content has *always* been locked up for pay-TV subscribers. If it weren't, who would pay for it?

Now that television shows are so widely available online, both legally and not, sports provide even more of the value of cable subscriptions than they used to. Although athletic events account for a relatively small percentage of cable programming, the entire business revolves around them. ESPN gets higher carriage fees than any other channel, and sports in general makes up a large part of every cable bill, as well as most recent increases. No one wants to wait to watch a big game—or the Academy Awards, for that matter—until it's available from a file-sharing service.

In October 2010, the BTIG analyst Richard Greenfield conducted a survey of twelve hundred cable subscribers and found that 8 percent had some interest in cutting their cable subscriptions.[22] Many of the others cited sports as the reason they couldn't do so. Some of the answers were revealing: "Need my live sports!" "I cant live without fox sports [*sic*]," "If all sports were available online, we absolutely would get rid of satellite." An ESPN analysis of Nielsen data found zero cord cutting among heavy and medium viewers of sports.[23]

Unfortunately for the television business, live events can now be pirated as well. For the past few years, sites like Justin.tv and Ustream have been streaming sports games as they happen. Technology-savvy viewers run television signals into their computers, then upload them as live streams to sites that let anyone watch them. From a technical standpoint, these sites work like the live video-chat program Chatroulette, except the video is coming from a television broadcast instead of a Webcam.

Like YouTube, these sites don't make any video available themselves; they just let viewers upload footage of anything they want. (These sites are presumably covered by the Digital Millennium Copyright Act, which means content owners have to ask them to remove infringing material. But this doesn't do much good for live events, since the damage is done before sites can act.) Most of the live-streamed video features teenagers flirting with one another, much like Chatroulette, but there are also plenty of pirated shows. Visiting random channels on Justin.tv, I saw a teenage girl doing homework at her desk, a Harry Potter movie dubbed in Spanish, and several *South Park* episodes. (Although Comedy Central makes *South Park* available for free online, it remains a popular program for pirates.) These sites also allow U.S. West Coast residents to watch television shows earlier than they otherwise might.

Live-streaming sites emerged as a serious issue in the summer of 2008, when they offered real-time video of the Beijing Olympics. They've grown quickly since then. The English Premier League issued about fifteen hundred takedown notices to live-streaming sites that were hosting feeds of its soccer games in the 2008–2009 season, according to its top lawyer, Oliver Weingarten. In the 2009–2010 season, Weingarten says it issued ten times that many—mostly to Justin.tv and Ustream.

In December 2009, the House Judiciary Committee held a hearing on online sports piracy with testimony from executives from the Ultimate Fighting Championship and Major League Baseball, which has built a thriving business streaming games over the Internet itself. "Whatever features may have in the past distinguished live sports from other forms of content in terms of its susceptibility to online infringement are being rendered increasingly irrelevant by new technological means for misappropriating linear programming," said ESPN's executive vice president

Ed Durso. "And the quality of these sites is improving to the point that programming can be streamed in a form that is almost on par with that accessed through legitimate distribution channels."[24]

Live sports piracy isn't a big problem on computers, since it's not much fun to watch the big game on a small screen. But ESPN is already concerned. "This could become a bigger issue as technology advances and a better viewing environment emerges, which is what we're going to see with widgets on TV and more robust Internet connectivity to big screens," Durso says. "So we're working to confront it aggressively." Justin.tv has taken significant steps to cooperate with media companies, including creating a system that lets some antipiracy executives access the site to remove infringing content immediately. But other live-streaming sites use the Digital Millennium Copyright Act to justify not doing anything to discourage piracy; that means sports leagues need to monitor them in real time—an expensive prospect. Streams can also be found on scores of foreign sites that aren't subject to U.S. law. And they're getting easier to find all the time: one of Boxee's more popular apps is the one for Justin.tv.

When Boxee introduced the beta version of its software in December 2009, there wasn't much like it on the market. But by the time the Boxee Box came out, almost a year later, the start-up faced competition from much larger companies. Netflix and Hulu Plus stream television shows to video game consoles, Internet-connected TVs, and several other new devices. The $99 Apple TV offers ninety-nine-cent rentals for some shows as well as access to Netflix. And Google has deals to put its Google TV software into Sony TVs and Blu-ray players as well as stand-alone set-top boxes.

For all Ronen's bravado, his company doesn't have much of a sustainable advantage. And even if Boxee does take off, it's hard to imagine it will be able to sell much content. Its online store will need to compete with all the other video it can bring to a TV, and it will have a hard time competing with legitimate services like Netflix and services that make pirated shows available like Justin.tv. (Although Boxee no longer comes with the BitTorrent client included with the first version of the software, it still made the *TechCrunch* list of "9 Great Gifts for the Media Pirate in Your Life."[25]) It's amazing how easy the Internet makes it to destroy a business without creating another one in its place.

Whatever happens to Boxee, though, the future of television still lies online. So far, only early adopters have considered canceling their cable subscriptions. But that will change soon: about a fifth of TVs sold in 2010 can access the Internet directly,[26] and two-thirds of flat-screen models will be able to do so by 2013—many with their own app stores.[27] And some television executives worry that the modest decline in the number of cable subscribers so far actually understates the problem. College students who get used to watching shows online may never get cable. They're not cutting the cord; they never paid for one in the first place.

The $32 billion question is whether they'll ever get into the habit of paying for television at all. In a 2010 Nielsen survey, almost 80 percent of respondents said they wouldn't use a paid service like Netflix if they believed they could find the same content online for free.[28] And while some consumers will always pay for content and others will always take it without paying, the behavior of the vast majority of those in the middle depends on how the online television systems of the future will work.

Right now, cable television is an expensive, inefficient system that encourages competition for quality. In almost every way, it's the exact opposite of the more efficient Internet, where more content is pirated than purchased and the producers of shows are pressured into giving them away before another company can do it for them. Competition concerns cost and Google search ranking, and the winners are sites like the *Huffington Post*. If cable worked like the Internet, the result would be a race to the bottom: shows that are free to watch, cheap to make, and easy to forget.

The company that represents the greatest threat to television may be Google. In May 2010, the search giant announced Google TV, a platform that brings the Internet to a TV screen. As with Boxee, that means users can easily download video illegally as well as buy it. And as with Boxee, the conglomerates that own television channels are less than thrilled with that idea. When the first Google TV devices came out in October 2010, ABC, CBS, NBC, and Hulu blocked them from accessing their video; Fox and Viacom programs, initially available, soon disappeared as well.

One reason networks didn't make their shows available was that they didn't want to support a system that made piracy more convenient. Several companies asked Google to downgrade pirate sites in search results sent to Google TV devices, according to executives involved in the discussions.[29] Google did customize the search results for Google TV, a process that included downgrading pirate sites, according to studio executives. But networks think the company didn't go far enough. "You end up with the issue of whether Google is enabling easier access to stolen content," NBC Universal's Cotton says. "Google put it on the table in the sense of saying they've thought about it, but they said their judgments were not open to negotiation."

Networks also want Google to pay for their programming, just like cable companies do. If Google TV takes off, more consumers will cancel their cable subscriptions, and networks want to collect revenue without going directly to consumers. "No matter how they share it, they have to come to us for content," said CBS Corporation's chief executive, Les Moonves, in October 2010, speaking about online video services in general. "And we're going to get paid properly for it, or else we're not going to do it."[30]

Some technology pundits suggested the networks were being unreasonable, since—from a technology standpoint—Google TV worked much like any other browser. Since networks made video freely available for Firefox, shouldn't the same rules apply to Google TV? In October 2010, *TechCrunch* dismissed their "various timeworn concerns such as lack of a viable business model."[31] Oh, that again.

There's also an important difference between Firefox and Google TV: the latter will presumably sell advertising. So far, Google hasn't said much about how it plans to make money on Google TV. But the company gets most of its revenue from running ads against search queries, and there's no reason that wouldn't work on a screen that happens to sit in front of a couch instead of on top of a desk. Since Google TV would already have some control over how video is displayed, it could sell ads that would compete with those sold by networks. And Google would have an advantage, since it could have data on viewers' search habits or other aspects of their Internet use. Companies that spend millions of dollars to create content would have to compete for ads against one that had none of those costs, just as they do on the Internet now, and everyone online knows how that show ends.

In June 2009, Time Warner and Comcast announced a very different vision for the future of television. Called TV Everywhere, it would require Internet users to prove they have a cable subscription in order to watch some online video, in order to help the television business move into the digital age without sacrificing carriage fees. Confusingly, TV Everywhere is not always known by that name, and it's more of a general concept than a specific project: the networks involved can't cooperate with one another, for antitrust reasons. But it represents the most ambitious attempt in any media business to put the free-content genie back in its bottle.

At its most basic, TV Everywhere would just give cable subscribers another way to watch the shows they already pay for. This makes sense: if you're paying to watch *Mad Men*, it should be up to you whether you want to see it on a TV, a laptop, or another device. The implications are more complicated. Although channels that offer their programs to TV Everywhere would be free to make them available in other ways as well, one assumes that cable companies would pressure them to hold back their best shows. If *Mad Men* were available on Hulu as well as from cable companies—it's not—consumers would have one less reason to keep their subscriptions.

The idea behind TV Everywhere comes from Time Warner's chief executive, Jeff Bewkes, who agreed to make shows from his company's channels available to Comcast subscribers.[32] Compared with other chief executives of media companies, Bewkes has been more wary of businesses that make movies and shows available for a low price. He has also been vocal in his criticism of Netflix, which makes television programming available online through its streaming service. "For a year, [television companies] had some young digital-rights VP selling [programs] for an extra 10 percent and people said, 'You should give little Freddy a bonus because he made some extra money,'" he said in January 2011.[33] Bewkes worries that "extra" money could jeopardize more important revenue streams—mostly cable carriage fees, but also DVD sales and syndication rights.

Technology executives have trouble understanding why networks don't try to go around cable companies and sell shows directly to consumers. But this reflects their own industry's obsession with eliminating middlemen—going around travel agents to sell flights directly to consumers, for example. Networks like TV Everywhere because it's so similar to their current business model: they can keep dealing with a few distributors rather than millions of individual consumers.

More than anything, TV Everywhere would let media companies keep their bundling. When record labels started selling music by the song and newspapers ceded some control over presentation to aggregators and Google News, those industries were devastated. The cable subscription package could also become a relic; more viewers want to pick what shows they want to watch, as well as when they see them. But Bewkes wants to keep the economic structure that made cable so profitable for media companies and such an important source of smart shows for viewers. Although iTunes sales could potentially bring in good money for some shows, people tend to buy less when they make a series of individual purchasing decisions instead of one large one per month. Bewkes doesn't want consumers to pick and choose.

Bewkes's plan is the opposite of Google TV: controlled instead of open, packaged instead of atomized, run by companies devoted to maintaining the status quo instead of upending it. Naturally, TV Everywhere has enraged technology executives, as well as the groups allied with them. After Time Warner and Comcast announced TV Everywhere, Public Knowledge released a statement saying, "It is obvious that their 'TV Everywhere' is not 'TV for Everyone.'"[34] Obvious, indeed: nothing that costs money is ever for everyone.

In July 2010—two months after Google announced Google TV—Public Knowledge and the New America Foundation made a filing to the FCC that asked the agency "to protect consumer choice in home video."[35] The organizations put their support behind AllVid, a proposed open platform that would let any company make devices to help consumers access online video and essentially replace a cable operator's set-top box. The FCC wants more competition in the market for set-top boxes, both to encourage innovation and to drive down the monthly rental costs consumers have to pay with their subscription. But Google TV—which would be the most obvious beneficiary of the AllVid proposal—may not have been what they had in mind.

Most set-top boxes are fairly "dumb": they change channels and some can record shows with digital video recorder functionality, but that's about it. Google TV functions more like a computer that happens to connect to a TV, and it could let the search giant show its own ads against other companies' content. In its own FCC filing, Google asked the FCC to make the proposed AllVid standard open source, which Google TV, built on the company's Android platform, already is.[36] That would make it much easier to download video illegally. And since Google can afford to give away the Google TV software in order to build market share—as it already does with its Android mobile phone platform—it could end up dominating the market if AllVid becomes a reality. Although AllVid is supposed to encourage competition, who would pay for a Boxee Box when Google could subsidize a device with its own software?

It's hard to tell what actions the FCC will take on AllVid, as well as whether consumers will want it. (Google TV received a cool reception, in part because reviewers found it complicated.) But it's ironic that companies like Google are encouraging the FCC to take action on the restrictions imposed by cable companies at exactly the time they're start-ing to get looser anyway. A decade ago, anyone who wanted television shows had one way to buy them: from a cable company, in a package.

Now there are other options: Shows will be available from Netflix, Apple TV, Hulu Plus, and new television ventures coming from Amazon and Microsoft. Some programs might continue to be free online, as they are now. Others might be sold as individual episodes on iTunes. And if a few are held back on TV Everywhere to encourage consumers to subscribe to more expensive cable packages, what's wrong with that? The alternative is that video will get less and less expensive, until companies can't spend much money producing it. That's the business model that brought us "Charlie Bit My Finger."

CHAPTER 6

BOOKS OR KINDLE-ING?

HOW TECHNOLOGY COULD
TURN THE PAGE ON PUBLISHING

On January 28, 2010, John Sargent Jr. and Brian Napack, the chief executive and the president of Macmillan Publishers, flew to Seattle to give Amazon.com some news they knew the online retailer wouldn't like. A couple of days before, Macmillan had made a deal to sell its titles in Apple's iBookstore, just as Steve Jobs was set to introduce the company's new iPad. Rather than sell titles to Apple on a wholesale basis and let the company set a retail price, as it did with Amazon and other bookstores, Macmillan would set the price for its digital books itself and give Apple a 30 percent commission for selling them to consumers. Apple had also made similar deals with four of the other five major U.S. publishers.

But Amazon wanted to set book prices as well.

Since Amazon started selling downloadable e-books in the fall of 2007, it had priced best sellers at $9.99—usually $2.00 or $3.00 less than the wholesale price it paid publishers—in order to drive demand for its Kindle digital reading device. When Jobs introduced the iPad, Amazon controlled about 90 percent of the e-book market, and publishers worried that its ability to sell e-books at a loss would discourage other retailers from entering the business.[1]

Amazon seemed to be looking at Apple's iPod as a model for its Kindle: instead of giving away a razor to make money selling blades, the online retailer wanted to drive down the price of media and make money selling gadgets to consume it. The cheaper it became to buy e-books, the more value the Kindle would have to consumers. Because the e-books Amazon sells have digital copy protection, Kindle owners looking for a new reading device would find it easier to stick with the same brand. That's why Amazon didn't mind losing a few dollars on some sales.

Publishers didn't like this. Since Walmart also offers heavy discounts on some new books, they feared consumers would resent paying more than $20 for a new hardcover—and, more important, that stores selling them at that price wouldn't be able to compete. But until Apple introduced the iPad, no individual publisher believed it had enough negotiating power to change the nature of its deal with Amazon. Antitrust law prevented companies from acting together. In the end, what kept Amazon from becoming the next Apple was none other than Apple itself. By offering an alternative to the Kindle, the computer company gave publishers the leverage to change their deals with Amazon.

In Seattle, Sargent and Napack met with Russ Grandinetti, Amazon's vice president for Kindle content, and gave the company a choice: sell e-books under the same terms as Apple—using what came to be called the agency model—or Macmillan would hold back some forthcoming titles for several months.[2] Amazon, which controls about 20 percent of the mainstream U.S. bookselling business, is more accustomed to making demands than hearing them.[3] (The online retailer declined to comment on the negotiations.) Still, even the tense meeting didn't prepare Sargent and Napack for what happened next. By the time they got back to New York late the next day, a Friday, Amazon had removed the "buy" buttons from Macmillan's print books, as well as their digital versions, halting their sales.

In the fairly genteel publishing world, this amounted to a declaration of war. By all appearances, Amazon had Macmillan outgunned: The publisher depended on it more than the other way around. Amazon had the power to change the prices of e-books and their physical counterparts to make the former more appealing. And Macmillan couldn't predict the reactions of agents and authors, who might be more inclined to worry about losing sales in the short term than the economics of publishing in the future.

And yet, Amazon folded. On Sunday, January 31, Amazon

announced, "We will have to capitulate and accept Macmillan's terms because Macmillan has a monopoly over their own titles, and we will want to offer them to you even at prices we believe are needlessly high for e-books."[4] The line about Macmillan having a monopoly made little sense to most readers, but people in the technology world understood it to mean that Macmillan had too much control over its own products. By that logic, so does every other media company.

Four of the other five major publishers had also been planning to ask Amazon for more control over their pricing, according to the *New Yorker*, and within a week Simon & Schuster, HarperCollins, Penguin, and Hachette announced that they too would move to agency deals.[5] The exception was Random House, which continued to sell e-books to Amazon at a wholesale price until early 2011. (Random House owns my publisher in the U.S., Doubleday.[6]) Even then, negotiations didn't proceed without incident: in early April, Amazon temporarily removed the "buy" buttons from the e-book versions of a few titles from Penguin and the Hachette Book Group.[7]

Since Amazon's negotiations with Macmillan played out in public, bloggers followed along. Henry Blodget, the former equity analyst who now runs the Web site Business Insider, told Sargent to "take your $15 ebooks and shove them!" "The marginal cost of an incremental ebook is pretty much zero," Blodget wrote. "So why on earth should we pay $15 for it?"[8]

But books, like all media products, have *never* been priced according to their marginal cost: it doesn't cost anything close to $25.00 to print a single copy of a hardcover book. And although many bloggers implied that publishers were greedy, the new agency deals actually called for them to receive *less* money for each book they sold. Amazon had been paying publishers $12.00 or $13.00 for many new titles it sold for $9.99; under the new arrangement, publishers would get about $9.00 for a book priced at $13.00—and probably sell fewer of them at a higher price. The publishers were thinking about the long term, especially about how they could make sure other companies would be able to start selling e-books without having to do so at a loss in order to compete with Amazon.

"It was galvanizing," says Dennis Loy Johnson, co-publisher of the independent Melville House. "It was the first time anyone stood up to Amazon." A week after Amazon started selling the publisher's books again, a Macmillan representative at the American Booksellers Association Winter Institute program received a standing ovation from a crowd of independent store owners.[9]

Macmillan's skirmish with Amazon was only one battle in the ongoing war between authors and publishers and the technology companies that want to use their books to sell other products. A few months earlier, the *New York Times* had run an opinion piece by Sergey Brin in which the Google co-founder compared his company's plan to digitally scan all the world's books to the Library of Alexandria.[10] You can't fault his ambition: as of early 2011, the company had scanned more than fifteen million books. Google Books will be the most accessible repository of human knowledge ever assembled, and one of the most remarkable accomplishments of the digital age.

The Alexandrian parallel may be more apt than Brin would like, however. According to historical accounts, the ancient library had an unusual acquisition policy: it forced city visitors to give their books to scribes for duplication—the ancient antecedent of begging forgiveness rather than asking permission.[11] Nor does Google care much for niceties. Copyright law allowed it to scan books published before 1923, which are in the public domain, and it made deals with most U.S. publishers to scan newer works. But it was impractical to negotiate with—or, in some cases, even find—the millions of authors who got back their copyrights when their books went out of print, or the publishers who retained rights if they didn't. Many of the writers might have jumped at the chance to make their books available, since it was difficult to find new copies for sale (and they wouldn't get royalties on used editions). But the statutory damages for copyright infringement—up to $150,000 per work—had scared other organizations that tried to build digital libraries into limiting their efforts to books in the public domain and those they could get permission to scan.

In true Alexandrian fashion, Google saw copyright law as a Gordian knot and cut right through it. In December 2004, the company simply announced it would begin scanning the contents of the Harvard, Stanford, and Oxford libraries, among others. When the executive director of the Authors Guild, Paul Aiken, realized how extensive the project was, he says, "It sent me scrambling to figure out how this could be allowed under copyright law."

As with so many copyright questions, the answer wasn't entirely clear. Google argued that its scanning and indexing qualify as fair use, since the company initially planned to display only a limited amount of text.[12] But the project had a clear commercial purpose—giving Google's search engine an advantage competitors couldn't match, in addition to any direct benefits—and no one had ever used fair use to defend such an ambitious undertaking. Within a year, both the Authors Guild and the Association of American Publishers sued Google to stop the project.[13]

In the spring of 2006, in response to the lawsuits, Google started negotiating a settlement, which was submitted to the court in October 2008—and again, in an amended version, a year later.[14] The settlement would have allowed Google to display limited portions of millions of books for free, sell digital books to individuals for prices set by copyright holders, and offer licenses to schools and libraries that would have made the entire database available on computer terminals. In return, Google would have paid $125 million, $34.5 million of which would have funded a Book Rights Registry to disburse 63 percent of Google Books revenue to publishers and authors according to the use of their works.[15]

Most authors and publishers supported the deal. "It was so much better than either winning or losing, for both Google and the authors and the publishers," says Richard Sarnoff, who had served as chairman of the Association of American Publishers and as a senior executive at Bertelsmann, which owns Random House. If Google had prevailed in court, it would have had a library of scanned books but not permission to sell them. (The fair use defense it planned to use would have applied to scanning and indexing the books, but not selling digital copies.) Had the authors and publishers won, they would have received substantial damages but no way to sell out-of-print works. Perhaps most important, the settlement would have set an informal precedent that scanning books requires an agreement with publishers or authors. "The alternative was to take our chances on winning the lawsuit, and we probably would have," Aiken says. "But if we didn't, it would have been a catastrophe because [Google would have] millions of books scanned that authors and publishers would have no legal control over."

Like Amazon and Apple, Google sees books as a means to an end—in this case giving its search engine access to more information. "Probably the highest-quality knowledge is captured in books," Sergey Brin said.[16] Like record labels, publishers have become arms suppliers in a cold war between technology companies. By bringing Google into the business of selling books—and giving it enough of a selection to make it a legitimate competitor to Amazon and Apple—the proposed settlement could have given publishers more leverage.

In order to do this, however, the proposed settlement essentially turned copyright law on its head. In the vast majority of cases, copyright law is "opt in": creators or their representatives must give permission for their work to be sold, displayed, or performed in certain ways. The settlement would have essentially given Google permission to digitize and display books unless writers specifically objected. Marybeth Peters, who until the end of 2010 served as the United States register of copyrights, the country's top copyright official, testified before Congress that "the proposed settlement would give Google a license to infringe first and ask questions later."[17] Even some lawyers who supported the idea of an online library worried that Google and the Authors Guild were essentially using a private agreement to get around copyright law.

Opposition to the Google Books settlement made for some of the strangest bedfellows in legal history. In August 2009, the U.S. Department of Justice opened an antitrust investigation into the proposed settlement. A month later, Microsoft, Yahoo!, Amazon, and some writers groups came together to fight the settlement as the Open Book Alliance, under the leadership of Gary Reback, the attorney who pushed the antitrust case against Microsoft in the 1990s. A dislike for the deal also brought together strong believers in copyright with legal scholars like Pamela Samuelson, a professor at the University of California, Berkeley, who favors more exceptions to copyright and worries that the settlement will give Google a monopoly on out-of-print books. (Samuelson would have preferred that Google didn't settle and instead tried to set a precedent that scanning books qualifies as fair use.) And the Google Books settlement is certainly the only legal deal in history to draw objections from both DC Comics and the Federal Republic of Germany—the former due to concerns that it would cover material it might want to put back in print, and the latter because it would apply to works by German authors published in the United States.

In March 2011, after studying the amended settlement for more than a year, judge Denny Chin rejected it, partly on the grounds that it would "grant Google significant rights to exploit entire books, without permission of the copyright owners."[18] Although Google set out to display snippets of books, the settlement would have given it additional rights. As Chin pointed out, Google would have also gained a decisive advantage in the search business that Microsoft and other companies would never be able to match, since they wouldn't be able to scan copyrighted books without risking stratospheric damages. If information is the oil of online search, books contain the largest untapped reserve, and the Google Books settlement would have locked up the drilling rights. "The establishment of a mechanism for exploiting unclaimed books," Chin wrote, "is a matter more suited for Congress than this Court."[19]

Google and authors and publishers could submit another amended settlement to the court, but Chin objected to the opt-out provision at the heart of the arrangement, which is important to Google. The suit could also proceed, with considerable consequences for the losing side. More likely, Congress will again consider the issue of "orphan works"—those whose copyright holders can't be identified—in a way that would allow any company to digitize books as long as it conducted a search for their owners.

It's hard to know how Congress would act, and Google and other technology companies could easily take the opportunity to lobby for more sweeping changes to copyright. In the worst-case scenario, a law would allow technology companies to digitize books after a cursory search for rights holders. But legislation could also make the bookselling market more competitive. "A huge concern in the publishing industry is that there's going to be only one online portal that will have any significance for the sale of books," Aiken says. "A world in which Amazon controls all the growing parts of the industry is a dangerous one for authors."

The publishing world seldom conducts business with the shark-eat-shark aggressiveness common in Hollywood. But it may now have as much or more control over its online future, with two major technology companies selling digital versions of its products, plus Barnes & Noble getting into the e-book business and Sony selling digital reading devices. Unfortunately, publishers also get the most resistance to the prices of their products online.

Like Henry Blodget, most readers assume that books are priced according to the cost of printing, binding, and shipping them to stores. Since hardcovers almost always run between $25 and $30 and trade paperbacks usually sell for about $15, there's a tendency to think those prices have something to do with packaging. That's why a $15 e-book sounds so expensive; there is no packaging.

So what do we talk about when we talk about books? If you think about it, $25.00 is a lot of money for a sheaf of paper held together by cardboard. But that's not what most people pay for, of course; they buy the text itself. And that's the largest source of cost as well as value. Publishers only spend about $3.50 to print and distribute a hardcover.[20] (Hardcovers are sold on a returnable basis, so the costs of retailer returns of unsold stock adds about another dollar or so to the price of each book, depending on how they're accounted for.) In many cases, the biggest expense in traditional book publishing is royalty payments to the writer, who can make more than the publisher (especially when sales don't make up for a large, nonreturnable advance against royalties). But those expenses don't change much in the digital world—Macmillan actually raised author royalties on e-books—nor does the need for editing or marketing.

As for the difference in price between hardcovers and paperbacks, a better binding doesn't cost another $10 any more than the larger seats and better food in first class cost airlines an extra $1,000 per passenger. Like first-class travel, hardcovers represent a way to maximize revenue in order to meet a high fixed cost—in this case, the money required to acquire, edit, and market a book. In many cases, publishers wouldn't be able to sell enough $15 paperbacks to make back their investment. Hardcovers let them do that. A book's price doesn't come from its packaging—its packaging comes from the price.

Publishers were "windowing" new releases before Hollywood. Most readers buy hardcovers because they're available earlier, not because of the binding, and publishers want to keep that strategy as they move online.[21] They could make titles available initially for $15, lower the price to $8 or $10 over the course of a year, then bring them down further when they wish. Airlines use a more complicated version of the same strategy: they try to get passengers to pay as much as they can without losing potential customers. Planes fill up, while books don't, but the idea is the same: defray a high fixed cost by pricing in order to maximize revenue.

Traditionally, this strategy also served the interests of retailers. But like Walmart, which sometimes sells certain titles below cost to draw shoppers into stores, Amazon doesn't really need to make money on book sales. Until June 2010, when Amazon reduced the price of the Kindle in the face of competition from Apple, the company was making between $80 and $100 on each $259 device, according to analysts.[22] So it made financial sense to sell popular e-books at a loss in order to drive demand for the reader, much as Apple forgoes significant profit on music sales to push the iPod and iPhone.

Therein lay a problem for publishers. If Amazon had kept using its Kindle profits to compensate for lower margins on e-books, booksellers without an outside source of profit might not be able to compete. That would limit the number of e-book retailers in a way that would ultimately hurt publishers, just as iTunes dominated the digital music market because it was too hard to make money selling music at ninety-nine cents a track without also having a device to promote. "That $9.99 price may have been reinforcing one player's business model, so it wasn't a spur to competition in the market," Sarnoff says. "Other players that wanted to be good sellers didn't want to have the loss-leader approach, and this was the genesis of the so-called agency model." The Authors Guild has said that, by changing the dynamic of the e-book market, Apple made it possible for Barnes & Noble to compete.

Some technology executives say publishers need to cut e-book prices to discourage illegal downloading, which has become a problem in the book business now that digital reading devices have become more popular. But the experience of record labels suggests that some consumers will pirate books no matter what their price, others will always buy them, and the behavior of the rest depends more on convenience than anything else.

Amazon tells publishers that by cutting prices, they'll sell more books, and it promotes the fact that Kindle owners buy three times as many books as they did before purchasing the device. But although several publishing executives do believe Kindle owners buy more books overall and Amazon says it drives sales of older books from popular authors, this statistic is deceptive, since it only compares digital and physical sales from Amazon itself. Imagine that a regular reader of physical books does about a third of his shopping from Amazon.com and the rest at local stores. If he buys a Kindle, he'll probably change his habits, since e-books are cheaper and more convenient to buy—and he can only buy them from Amazon. So the online retailer might sell three times as many books to that reader, but that doesn't mean more titles are being sold—just that Amazon gets a larger share of them.

Taking a larger share of book sales is a key part of Amazon's Kindle strategy. In the physical book business, Amazon has to compete for every sale. In the digital world, once Amazon sells a Kindle, it knows customers will buy almost all their books from its site. So it wants to speed the move to e-books as fast as it can. Publishing executives would prefer the transition to proceed more slowly. Bookstore displays are an important part of their promotion strategies, as are retailer recommendations, especially for new fiction. And as sales of physical books decline, the production expenses for each physical book will rise, since costs for warehousing and shipping will be divided among fewer units. The adjustment will be far easier if it happens more slowly.

"If people keep moving to e-books because of extremely low prices, then physical bookstores will be in trouble," Napack says. "Throughout history publishers have counted on retailers wanting to keep prices up in order to make money. If the reading public is willing to pay $28 for what's between the covers of a book, it troubles me that someone came into the market and, for their own strategic reasons, consistently undervalued it."

Amazon seems to see publishers the way technology executives see record labels: as companies that manufacture and distribute physical goods no one needs anymore. Naturally, it wants to deal directly with writers and cut out what it sees as the middleman. So, starting in June 2010, the company began offering 70 percent royalties to authors and publishers who agreed to sell their books on Amazon's Kindle platform for between $2.99 and $9.99, and at least 20 percent below the print version. In December 2009, the business advice writer Stephen R. Covey signed a deal to make two of his books available as digital editions exclusively on Amazon.com for a year.[23] (Print versions of the same titles will still come out through Simon & Schuster.) And in December

2010 the marketing author Seth Godin announced that he would write and package a series of "Idea Manifestos" using Amazon's distribution for both digital and traditional print editions.

Like Radiohead and Nine Inch Nails, Covey and Godin are stars of a sort, so they don't need the promotion and marketing that publishers provide. They can get higher royalties by dealing directly with Amazon. And since business advice authors generally make good money performing live, they can cut the price of their books to reach more potential speaking clients.

But what does Amazon offer less established writers? Just as Napster didn't really replace labels, an online retailer can't replace publishers—just their printing and distribution infrastructure. (Technology companies never say they want to disrupt the shipping and warehousing business; it's not nearly as cool.) Like record labels, publishers do much more than manufacture and distribute; they advance money to creators, shape projects, and help them find an audience. Doing those things well is far more complicated than getting a book to a store on time.

Amazon does an efficient job fulfilling demand for books, which small publishers sometimes have trouble with. But a more important function of publishers, like labels, is *generating* demand, which Amazon doesn't have much experience with. While the Internet makes it less expensive to reach prospective readers, by using tools like Twitter and Facebook, so many authors are taking advantage of this that breaking through the clutter still requires expertise, money, or some combination of the two. Independent writers can hire independent editors or marketers, of course, but that means Amazon's higher royalties get offset by expenses that publishers once covered.

It's hard to write a book about the book business without referring to my own experience, so I'll say up front that there's no way I could have written this without a publisher. Even if I had the money to hire an editor and a marketing expert, it would have meant gambling a substantial amount of time and money on a single project, without having any idea how much, if anything, I'd make on it. Publishers spread out their risk among scores of books in a way that writers can't.

Although technology has revolutionized the process of distributing books, it hasn't fundamentally changed the process of writing one. The Internet makes it easier to find information quickly, and computers have transformed the editing process. But reporting and writing are still painstaking work, and they can get expensive as well. Work on this book took me to Los Angeles, Washington, D.C., London, Brussels, Copenhagen, and Düsseldorf. I hired reporters who each gave me a few days of help with interviews and translations in German, French, and Swedish; paid a fact-checker and a lawyer to make sure the book was accurate; and worked with a part-time researcher to help me make my deadline (or at least miss it by less than I might have otherwise). All of this costs money, which authors need while they write, rather than later. That's basically what Ken Auletta explained to Sergey Brin: it's not that easy to give a book away, since it's harder than most people realize to write one.

Just like in the music business, most of the ideas to change publishing run into some version of this problem. Writers could give away books and earn money on the speaking circuit, but that works best for authors like Godin, whose books are practically written in PowerPoint form already. Even if that works, what would authors live on for one or two years—or, in some cases, more—while they write? It's far more practical to borrow money against the delivery of a copyrighted work than against the vague prospect of speaking fees.

Unlike Hollywood, book publishing hasn't exactly been swimming in money for some time: annual sales grew 1.6 percent between 2002 and 2008,[24] independent bookstores are closing, and Borders filed for bankruptcy in February 2011. But physical books may decline more slowly than other forms of traditional media. Unlike CDs and DVDs, books aren't tied to a particular platform; they work just fine on their own. It's hard to find anyone who misses the cheap, plastic packaging of CDs or DVDs, but books are appealing objects to own and display. (It could take years for people to figure out what else to put on bookshelves.) Priced right and marketed well, books could have a slow, steady decline instead of a steep, sudden drop. That would be a huge help to publishers, who need more time to prepare for a digital market.

One question is what kinds of books will sell in that market. In October 2010, Amazon announced it would launch Kindle Singles— written works that are longer than a magazine article but shorter than most books.[25] The company suggested they would range from ten thousand to thirty thousand words, "the perfect, natural length to lay out a single killer idea, well researched, well argued and well illustrated— whether it's a business lesson, a political point of view, a scientific argument, or a beautifully crafted essay on a current event."[26] Amazon sells Singles from publishers as well as direct from writers, but the business model seems better suited for the latter, and Amazon's descriptions of Singles—"lesson, . . . argument, . . . essay"—don't exactly make it sound like a format for reported work that would require significant time and money. In most cases, it seems unlikely that editing would be part of the package.

"Their interest is fundamentally different from yours as a publisher—they're interested in driving traffic," Napack says. While publishers commit to particular authors and books, Amazon doesn't care what it sells, as long as it can be read on a Kindle. That's a significant difference. "There was a time when the advantage of being a big publisher over little publishers or an individual is that we had the infrastructure to get a book printed, ship it to a warehouse, ship it to a bookstore, and take returns," Napack says. "In the digital world, that becomes less important. We have to rely again on what we did well—what should have been a core advantage all along—which is editing and marketing books."

CHAPTER 7

MOVING PICTURES

CAN HOLLYWOOD CONQUER THE CLOUD?

As befits a business devoted to the art of illusion, Hollywood likes to accentuate the positive. Each Monday brings news of the weekend's box office grosses, which together accounted for a record $10.6 billion for 2009 in the United States and Canada.[1] New 3-D technology kept ticket sales close to that level in 2010.[2] Foreign revenue has grown as new theaters in China and other developing countries expand the market for American movies.[3] With numbers like that, few observers realize just how much the Internet is hurting filmmakers of all sizes.

Although studios like to talk about box office revenue, it only accounts for between a fifth and a quarter of the money most movies take in. Per capita movie theater attendance has fallen steadily since the introduction of television, and films make most of their money from various television rights, Blu-ray discs, and especially DVDs. Hollywood relies on the business of selling plastic discs almost as much as the music industry. But U.S. revenue from sales and rentals of DVDs and Blu-ray discs has fallen by a quarter since its 2004 peak, and the decline accelerated in 2009 and 2010.[4] And while there are several reasons for this decline—including the convenience of Netflix and consumer fatigue with the idea of film ownership—much of it is almost certainly due to piracy.

Since the 1980s, movie studios haven't been in the business of selling tickets to see films so much as selling an array of different rights to show them. "Windowing" allows them to offer the same film at different times to pay-per-view television, premium cable, pay cable, and network television, as well as a similar array of foreign outlets. But the Internet is disrupting this business, and it could eventually destroy it entirely. Foreign audiences can now download movies that haven't yet opened locally—sometimes even in their own language, since pirates often record audio tracks intended for hearing-impaired cinemagoers, then sync them with video to create dubbed versions—and television stations don't pay as much now that films are so easy to download.

In the long run, this matters far more than ticket sales. "The business model that formed the underpinning of the modern-day motion picture business is changing right before our eyes, in profound ways," said Disney's chief executive, Bob Iger, in an October 2009 speech at a University of Southern California business conference. "That means you're going to have to change your business in profound ways, or you will no longer have a business."[5]

Although the major studios operate as divisions of media conglomerates that can be cagey about the performance of their film divisions, analysts believe their earnings are down, an assumption reinforced by layoffs and division closings. When MGM's assets went on sale in early 2010, the company drew bids for less than half of its 2004 price.[6] In 2008 both Warner Independent and Paramount Vantage were folded into their respective parent companies; Disney sold Miramax two years later. Worried about the prospects for smaller films, studios are focusing more on blockbusters.

Studios are negotiating to build new businesses online, even as they try to limit piracy by suing commercial infringers. But the nature of the conflict is changing as online media consumption evolves beyond downloading tracks from iTunes to using services like Spotify, which lets consumers listen to music wherever they have an Internet connection. In technology terms, such services store media in the "cloud"—online servers that interact with PCs and other devices—and charge consumers a subscription fee to access it online. They're selling *access*, not products—a business model that many believe represents the future, not just for music, but for all media. But there's no reason the same services can't be offered illegally—and Hollywood is already facing off against pirate sites that are free, popular, and growing fast.

RapidShare is one of the biggest companies in the cloud, but it keeps a low profile in the physical world. The company has its headquarters in picturesque Cham, Switzerland, a mountain village about a half-hour drive from Zurich. On the door of one of the offices is a cartoonish sketch of a seated figure and a logo that says, "RapidChair"—a way for the sixty or so mostly young employees to make fun of the idea that hardly anyone who delivers their mail has heard of the company.[7] Not many people over forty have.

In 2009, RapidShare generated about 1 percent of the world's Internet traffic from this modest setting—about as much as Facebook.[8] It was the seventeenth most popular site in the world, with seventy-seven million users a month, mostly from outside the United States.[9] The company stored about fifteen petabytes' worth of data; that's fifteen million gigabytes, or enough to fill the hard drives on sixty thousand average new computers.

RapidShare is an online locker service, the best known of a dozen or so large sites—there are also scores of small ones—that offer Internet users cheap digital storage as well as the ability to share anything they've uploaded with anyone they want. (They're also called file-hosting services, or one-click hosting services.) It offers limited access for free and sells RapidPro accounts that provide faster service and more storage space for €4.95 (about $7) a month. When users upload a file, they receive a Web address that allows anyone to download it, which they can keep to themselves, share with friends over e-mail, or link to from blogs or other sites. Every day the company takes in 400,000 files of all types—text, music, videos, software—from users who are either short on hard drive space or looking for a way to distribute files that are too big for e-mail. Many of those files, probably most of them, are pirated. Which is why RapidShare and other online locker services—

Hotfile, Megaupload, and MediaFire, among others—are starting to do to Hollywood what file sharing did to the music business.

For a company that generates so much data traffic, not much is known about RapidShare. The company was founded in 2005 by Christian Schmid, a teenager in Freiburg, Germany, who later moved near Cham to live with his girlfriend. Schmid is so private that it's difficult to find a photograph of him online, and he has never given an interview. The only thing anyone knows about him for sure is that he's very, very rich: a movie business estimate places RapidShare's annual profit at a minimum of $45 million.[10]

Online locker services are growing at the expense of file sharing, which has fallen as a percentage of global Internet traffic since 2007, as lawsuits drove away companies and scared users.[11] "Peer-to-peer [file sharing] is declining, and when you look at RapidShare and Megaupload, that's where the traffic is going," says Craig Labovitz, chief scientist at Arbor Networks which makes software used by internet service providers. "We believe that online lockers are growing faster than the Internet, which is growing at 45 percent a year." According to one study, online locker services account for about 7 percent of all online traffic, and more than 90 percent of the non-pornographic material stored on them is copyrighted.[12]

Online locker services don't index their own files—you can't go to Hotfile.com and search the site—but a Google search will return links posted on other sites. Functionally, these services are the online equivalent of a self-storage business, except that anyone with the right Web address can download the file there with a single click. Given the site's location, a better analogy might be a Swiss bank. Like Swiss accounts, online locker services have plenty of legitimate uses—backing up files, making content available to multiple divisions of a company—but they make it a point not to ask questions and, intentionally or not, attract unsavory activity on a massive scale. Do a Google search for "Rapid-Share" or "Hotfile" and any popular movie—even one that's still in cinemas—and you'll find pages of links to illegal downloads.

Online locker services have essentially crowdsourced copyright infringement: they store files but leave the linking to others. Some sites, like the ones Ellen Seidler found her independent film on, consist of nothing *but* links to movies, plus ads to bring in money. Although these "link farms" don't have formal ties with online locker services, they depend on each other. Lockers pay for storage and bandwidth, so link farms don't have to. And link farms bring users to online locker services, where downloading large files may convince them to buy memberships so they can do so faster.

Any piracy on RapidShare is the result of consumers finding an illegal use for a legitimate service, says Daniel Raimer, RapidShare's main outside lawyer and de facto spokesman. Although several major German publications have covered the company, our January 2010 conversation at his Düsseldorf law office marked the first substantial interview the company has done with the English-language media. "It's not RapidShare's business to violate copyrights," Raimer says. "RapidShare's business is to offer Web space. That's pretty much it." Raimer says RapidShare is covered in Germany by the 2007 Telemediengesetz, or Telemedia Act, which offers online intermediaries the same kind of safe harbor as the Digital Millennium Copyright Act. When studio or label executives point out a pirated version of a movie or album, the company takes it down. "If you do illegal things, that's a serious problem," Raimer says, "but it's not our main business to deal with that."

Some online locker services, such as Dropbox and Microsoft's Windows Live SkyDrive, seem designed to help users who want to back up the contents of their own computers. But Schmid seems to have realized early on that the most effective way to market RapidPro accounts was to make sure his service was filled with files people wanted to download. So until the spring of 2010, RapidShare encouraged users to upload files they thought would be popular by awarding them RapidPoints based on how many times these files were downloaded. The strategy seems to have worked: a study by the networking company Sandvine says the site has more download than upload traffic;[13] Raimer says the average file is downloaded five to ten times, although he cautions the range is so wide that this doesn't mean much.

With some justification, media companies think online locker services depend on piracy, and several have sued RapidShare in Germany. Lower courts have granted preliminary injunctions to several book publishers, three German film companies, and the music collection society GEMA; two of those decisions were later overturned by the appellate court in Düsseldorf. The injunctions only require RapidShare to block specific works, which the company says it can't do. It uses a very basic filter to screen out copyrighted material, but it has refused to use a stronger content-identification system, as YouTube now does. It has also declined to block uploads based on file names, since that might flag legitimate content that uses the same words, such as home movies named "Avatar" or "Inception."

The legality of online locker services is now being tested in the United States, in a case that could set an important precedent. In February 2011, the MPAA sued Hotfile.com for copyright infringement.[14] Although the technology behind the site is almost certainly legal—it operates under the same principles as SkyDrive or Google Docs—the way Hotfile runs its business could make it liable for infringement under the "inducement" doctrine outlined by the Supreme Court in its Grokster decision. Hotfile pays individuals who upload files between $2 and $15 for every thousand downloads of their material. Although one could upload anything, the fact that potential downloaders can't preview files makes it a tough way to distribute works they're not familiar with. The easiest way to generate enough downloads to make money is to put up popular movies or albums.

The other big online locker service is Megaupload, owned by a Hong Kong-based company that also runs the streaming service Megavideo and the self-explanatory Megaporn. Megaupload is even more secretive than RapidShare, but both Raimer and several Hollywood antipiracy executives say it's owned by Kim Schmitz, an obese German hacker who is both literally and figuratively larger than life. (Megaupload, which has never said anything about its ownership structure, did not respond to requests for comment.) Schmitz served twenty months in jail for insider trading starting in 2002, and his habit of appearing in photographs with expensive cars and beautiful women made him a tabloid figure in his home country. One antipiracy executive, who says Schmitz lives in a top-floor suite in the Hong Kong Hyatt, compared his colorful life to a figure in a James Bond movie. In early 2010, according to the *New Zealand Herald*, Schmitz purchased the most expensive private house in New Zealand for $NZ30 million ($22 million).[15] Apparently, the movie distribution business can be quite lucrative if you don't have to cover the expense of making films in the first place.

Online locker services have worried labels and studios for years. But over the course of 2010, as gadgets like Boxee and Google TV made it easier to connect TVs to the Internet, the problem threatened to become a crisis. Until recently, most movie piracy has taken place on computer screens, which don't offer the same viewing experience as big-screen TVs. As consumers connect their TVs to the Internet, however, they could be able to download movies from Hotfile or stream them from Megavideo as easily as they can buy or rent them from legitimate outlets like iTunes and Netflix. And that means Hollywood might never develop an online movie business to replace the DVD sales it's losing.

To understand why movie piracy seems harmless, as well as why it's not, consider *X-Men Origins: Wolverine*, the kind of comic-book action flick studios depend on. In the spring of 2009, a month before the 20th Century Fox film opened, a work print of the film leaked online. It was downloaded more than four million times,[16] an issue the studio took so seriously that the FoxNews.com gossip writer Roger Friedman reportedly parted company with Fox News for reviewing the unfinished version and describing how easy it was to get. The movie still grossed $85 million on its opening weekend—less than the last X-Men movie, but certainly respectable—and made $179.9 million over the course of its run in U.S. theaters.[17] It took in a total of $373 million worldwide.[18] How much damage could the online leak have possibly done?

Enough to matter. *Wolverine* had a $140 million budget.[19] Studios don't reveal what they spend on marketing, but they usually allot an amount equal to half the production budget. So Fox probably spent about $210 million before *Wolverine* even popped out his claws. As for the $373 million, a box office gross is just that—a *gross*. Studios usually end up with about 50 percent of U.S. theatrical revenue, in this case $90 million. For a variety of reasons, including taxes and local distribution expenses, studios usually end up with only around 30 percent of foreign box office receipts—another $46 million. (Fox declined to comment on the movie's financial performance, so all of these figures are based on industry rules of thumb.) In other words, out of that $373 million in box office income, Fox probably took in about $136 million—for a movie on which it had spent $210 million.

Now let's look at the effect of piracy. It's foolish to argue that each of the four million people who downloaded the movie illegally represented a lost ticket sale, as some industry-funded studies of piracy do.[20] But it seems even more absurd to suggest that none of them did. Let's say one in twenty downloaders represents a lost ticket sale—a fairly conservative estimate.[21] That's 200,000 unsold tickets—around $2 million in lost box office revenue. That's real money.

But that's just the beginning of the damage. To understand how illegal downloading really hurts Hollywood, let's look at what happens once *Wolverine* claws its way to the home video market. To make up the $60 million gap between the movie's cost and its revenue, Fox counted on DVD sales, especially important for a movie that appeals to teenagers and young men. *Wolverine* sold 4.4 million DVDs in the United States, with a gross of $73.5 million.[22] (No reliable figures on international DVD sales are available.) Studios have much higher margins on DVDs—about two-thirds, even allowing for additional marketing expenses—so those sales probably brought Fox another $50 million.

Those DVD sales also suffered from piracy, however. Since its theatrical release *Wolverine* has been downloaded more than four million times from file-sharing services alone[23]—let's assume five million, counting other sources of piracy. Assuming that one in ten of those downloaders decides not to buy a $15 DVD—a moderate estimate—that adds up to another $7.5 million in losses.[24] That means Fox lost almost $10 million to piracy, and that's not counting lost DVD rentals or the lowered price of pay-per-view or television deals. In the end, *Wolverine* almost certainly made a profit. But Fox needs some of that money to run its business and offset losses on other films.

The United States also needs the resulting economic activity. Hollywood is more American than the rest of the entertainment business. Five of the six major studios are owned by U.S. corporations, and film business jobs are still mostly located in the United States. (Even when movies are shot elsewhere, they tend to be conceived, financed, and marketed in California.) Perhaps most important, at a time when the U.S. trade deficit is becoming a bigger problem, Hollywood still generates a significant trade surplus. The demand for U.S. movies isn't likely to change soon; countries with homegrown film businesses rarely produce effects-driven popcorn fare like *Wolverine*. But exporting them relies on international recognition of copyright, which the Internet is eroding.

Movies also shape the world's idea of what the United States stands for, as a cable written by an American diplomat in Saudi Arabia released on WikiLeaks showed. "It's still all about the War of Ideas here, and the American programming on [the television channels] MBC and Rotana is winning over ordinary Saudis in a way that [the U.S.-funded satellite channel] 'Al Hurra' and other U.S. propaganda never could," read the May 2009 message.[25] Titled "David Letterman: Agent of Influence," it mentioned *Friends* and *Desperate Housewives* as being particularly popular. "We should say that copyright theft and copyright abuse is more than just an economic disaster," says Simon Renshaw, who manages the Dixie Chicks. "You could argue that it's a national security issue since content exports—American culture in the form of films, television, and music—is American soft power at its finest."

International trade has always shaped copyright policy, since countries that produce music and film need them protected while those that don't would prefer to use them for free. For much of the nineteenth century, the United States did not recognize British copyrights, which left American publishers free to print unauthorized editions of books by Charles Dickens and other authors. (This also hurt American authors, since it had the effect of making homegrown works expensive by comparison.) More recently, the United States has campaigned for stronger copyright protection in Asia.

Most academics tend to see copyright as yet another set of regulations that let the West take advantage of developing countries, while others point out that the Indian and Nigerian film businesses thrive without much enforcement of copyright laws. But few filmmakers in those countries have the budget to make movies with production values that are up to international standards, and that means they're rarely exported in a way that generates money for the countries that make them. A detailed 2010 study by the Organization for Economic Cooperation and Development found that improved protection of intellectual property rights generally helps developing economies.[26]

From an international perspective, it's hard to make a case that copyright laws don't play an important role in developing a strong culture business. The vast majority of the popular culture we consume comes from countries with strong copyright laws: the United States, the U.K., France, northern Europe, and Japan. Nations without them, like Russia and China, don't export much music and film, considering their size and influence. Countries with copyright may be more developed for other reasons. But consider East and West Germany, which were fairly similar when they were divided after World War II. Over the next four decades, West Germany exported movies by Wim Wenders, Werner Herzog, and Rainer Werner Fassbinder, plus music by influential recording artists like Kraftwerk and Neu! East Germany, where artists essentially worked for the state, didn't produce a single figure of comparable influence. Whatever the future of the film business looks like, it will be shaped by law as well as technology.

Mitch Singer, chief technology officer of Sony Pictures Entertainment, has the kind of office that Silicon Valley executives probably imagine when they make fun of Hollywood: larger than some New York apartments, with tasteful art and modern furniture. This is where

Singer planned Hollywood's strategy to introduce its own cloud-based movie format, with more features and flexibility than illegal downloads. Although it's being marketed to consumers as UltraViolet, its official name is considerably geekier: the Digital Entertainment Content Ecosystem, or DECE.

Notice how there's no reference to a physical object? What sets DECE apart from videocassettes and DVDs is that it's a purely digital format, much like iTunes files. Unlike iTunes files, though, UltraViolet content is stored in the cloud, on Internet servers; it can be streamed and downloaded as needed. Consumers establish an account that tracks what films they have rights to, and they can watch them from any connected UltraViolet device, including computers, video game consoles, and Blu-ray players with Internet connections. If it succeeds, it will give the studios an online product that could replace the DVD—and perhaps much of the revenue it represents.

Singer, who is also president of DECE, is a Hollywood executive with a law degree, but he sees the conflict between technology and the content business with a coolly logical worldview more common among Silicon Valley engineers. He has longish hair and glasses and speaks quickly, in complete paragraphs that might include references to economics, encryption algorithms, or network design. And he started worrying about how downloading would hit Hollywood as soon as he saw what happened to record labels.

"I'd say, 'There, but for the grace of bandwidth, go us," he says with a smile.

As Singer points out, there have always been two schools of thought on how movie and music companies should respond to online piracy. Most entertainment companies believe they need to litigate to prevent illegal downloading, which risks alienating fans. Technology executives say that media companies need to "compete with free" by drastically lowering prices, but that makes it hard to make money, and this didn't work so well for the newspaper business. The answer may lie somewhere in the middle: lawsuits don't work if content isn't available from legal outlets, while lowering prices won't help if a free alternative is just as convenient. "I think RapidShare is a major concern for the content industry," Singer says.

Assuming consumers act rationally, entertainment companies need to compete with pirates on both price and convenience. Since pirates almost always offer content for free and studios and labels can only cut costs so much, the competition really comes down to convenience. That means coming up with a product that can be played on different devices with minimal hassle, just like downloads from Hotfile or streams from Megavideo. But it also means issuing takedown notices and pressuring Google to remove search results that link to illegal sites, in order to make piracy as much of a hassle as possible. "We believe in speed bumps," Singer says. "You don't want to get caught up in focusing solely on protecting content."

Singer believes movie studios need to focus their antipiracy efforts on films that are still in theaters, then accept the fact that illegal downloading can't be stopped and concentrate on making UltraViolet as appealing as possible. Although UltraViolet movies are copy protected and limited to compatible devices, users don't have to worry about moving them between devices, because they're stored remotely and accessible from anywhere. (All UltraViolet movies come with at least three downloads and unlimited streaming for a year, and buyers can play movies on up to twelve devices at once.) In addition to using copy protection to limit access, Singer wants to use it to let consumers watch their movies wherever they are.

Singer had the idea that evolved into UltraViolet in 2002, when he was messing around with his multimedia system, trying to transfer some movies to his PC so he could watch them on other screens in his house. This was hard to do with DVDs, which are encrypted to foil copying. So Singer started thinking about a format that would make it easy. "I said, 'Okay, technology exists to enable some really cool functionality here,'" he remembers. "We're going to take what's limited today and give you more expansive rights."

The idea behind UltraViolet is "Buy once, play anywhere." Although UltraViolet movies can be downloaded to watch away from an Internet connection, the idea is to give consumers the right to enjoy the movies they bought with more flexibility. (The system could also be used for books, music, or other digital media.) Consumers will be able to buy UltraViolet movies in physical stores—where they'll be included with DVDs or Blu-ray discs, and potentially other physical products as well—and from online retailers and cable companies. Once they own those movies, they'll be able to watch them from services run by any of the partners, which will check what movies they have and offer to stream them, in some cases for a fee. Comcast's cable service will stream UltraViolet movies on your TV from the same system Microsoft's Xbox Live does.

This compatibility is important, since it could make UltraViolet more convenient than piracy. The main challenge for most media formats is support: Few people purchased movies on Sony's Universal Media Disc format, since they couldn't watch them at a friend's house. DVDs can be watched on any player—with a few geographic restrictions—but you have to carry them around. With UltraViolet, you could start watching a film with your Comcast cable service, then go to a friend's house and, after signing in to your account, finish watching the same movie on his Xbox Live connection. (The relevant standards were set by the DECE organization.) Both companies, as well as many others, will draw information from the UltraViolet database.

If this sounds complicated, Singer says, think of it as an ATM system for movies. Much like ATMs, UltraViolet companies check in with a central database that tracks who can "withdraw" what content. Much as ATMs dispense their own cash, UltraViolet providers handle the resulting streams or downloads and charge their own access fees. "I was on a panel and some guy says, 'Are you telling me I have to pay for my content again after I bought it?'" Singer says. "And my response to him was 'You pay for money that you already have.' It's convenience."

The trick will be making UltraViolet as easy to use as the ATM system. So far, efforts to come up with copy-protected files compatible with a variety of devices have failed—often embarrassingly. Intel's Viiv platform never took off, and Microsoft's PlaysForSure music format proved so unworthy of its name that the company itself abandoned it. And free culture activists have become so hostile to the idea of digital rights management that bloggers started insulting UltraViolet before it had even been introduced.

UltraViolet can count on widespread support within Hollywood; the venture includes five of the six major studios, as well as some independents, plus Best Buy, Comcast, Microsoft, Motorola, and Netflix. Essentially, it has the support of most companies that make and sell movies, as well as the makers and sellers of the equipment on which they play. But the four companies missing are big ones: Disney, Apple, Google, and Walmart. The last of those is more important than most consumers realize, because the retailer controls more than a third of DVD sales; in 2010 it bought the company Vudu to get into the online movie business itself. Apple isn't expected to sell UltraViolet movies in its iTunes Store, but the iPad and the Apple TV could play UltraViolet movies in apps, the way they do Netflix films. Disney has introduced Keychest, a system similar to UltraViolet, but other studios kept their distance, and in November 2010 Disney's chief executive, Bob Iger, said movies in that format could be compatible with UltraViolet.[27]

"People have wanted it to feel like a format war, and I don't think it really is," says Mark Teitell, DECE's executive director. If anything, studios will promote UltraViolet by packaging it with DVDs and Blu-ray discs, in order to offer consumers the picture quality of a disc as well as the flexibility of a cloud-based format. "UltraViolet should really help us build value for people who buy Blu-ray discs," Teitell says.

UltraViolet will still have to compete against online stores committed to other formats. In order to maximize sales, studios will continue to make movies available through Netflix, iTunes, and new high-definition pay-per-view services that offer films that are still in cinemas. "UltraViolet certainly is a priority for our company, and we'd like it to have some success in the marketplace, because we genuinely believe that a digital locker is critical to the success of digital consumption," says Peter Levinsohn, the executive in charge of digital distribution at Fox. "But UltraViolet will not be the only solution to this."

It may be the best solution for Hollywood, however. Over the past decade, studios have grown accustomed to selling DVDs in stores for $10 to $15, and rental models like Netflix don't generate nearly as much money. No one knows whether consumers will buy movies they can't put on a shelf, but UltraViolet may offer enough convenience to convince them. "What consumers want is flexibility with the content they've purchased," Levinsohn says. "The more valuable we make the products and services we offer the consumer, the more people will consume them."

Over the course of 2010, as DECE finalized its technical specifications and prepared to introduce UltraViolet, RapidShare began cleaning up its act. During the spring, the company gradually dismantled its RapidPoints program and started having more productive conversations with music labels and movie studios. (Several movie business sources say the company was threatened with a lawsuit, but Raimer says negotiations improved when studios stopped insisting on content filtering.) "We listen to their concerns and try to find a solution," Raimer says. "But we have very strong feelings about privacy. We don't screen files."

For advice, RapidShare turned to the lawyer Andrew Bridges, a partner at Winston & Strawn, who successfully represented Diamond Multimedia against the RIAA in the case that established that MP3 players don't face the levy intended for digital recording media. Two months after RapidShare landed on the congressional International Piracy Watch List, it also hired the lobbyist firm Dutko Worldwide to convince politicians it had been lumped in with pirates unfairly. "We were really not happy about that," Raimer says in December 2010, almost a year after we first spoke. "We're trying to convince politicians and the guys from [the Congressional International] Anti-Piracy Caucus that Rapid-Share is a legitimate company."

Judging by RapidShare's traffic, its decision to focus on the legitimate market has been an expensive one. According to Quantcast, the service had 3.7 million U.S. users a month in January 2011, down from 5.3 million the year before.[28] "It's been a significant decrease in uploads, and honestly we're not really sad about that, because a lot of the guys who were doing illegal things have left RapidShare and gone to other companies like Megaupload or Hotfile," Raimer says. "Windows Live Sky-Drive, Google Docs, these are the companies we want to compete with. If that means Megaupload is bigger than we are, that's okay with us."

Entertainment companies are still pressing RapidShare to do more, perhaps with a more sophisticated filter. Since dedicated pirates would get around it, perhaps by encrypting their files, Raimer says there's no point. Unsurprisingly, studio executives disagree. "That's silly and wrong," says NBC's general counsel, Rick Cotton. "There's no reason why they can't employ a similar kind of filtering technology to that used by YouTube, as an example."

Until the MPAA sued Hotfile, online locker services had only faced one U.S. lawsuit, a case brought in November 2009 by Perfect 10, a soft-core pornography Web site that specializes in photographs of natural-looking women and has sued a number of Internet companies.[29] The court denied Perfect 10 a preliminary injunction, RapidShare counter-sued, and the two sides settled in July 2010.[30] RapidShare can make a solid argument that it's covered under the safe harbor provision of the Digital Millennium Copyright Act, since it can reasonably say it doesn't know what's stored on its servers; unlike YouTube, it has no search function or "most popular" list. But several movie studio lawyers suggest that RapidShare may have "induced" copyright infringement by offering RapidPoints to users whose files proved to be popular downloads.

Raimer disputes this; he says RapidPoints could only be turned in for small prizes. "We had T-shirts and [key-chain] lanyards," he says. Some users got so interested in accumulating points that they'd send RapidShare takedown notices for popular movies, then put the films back online themselves so they could collect points when they were downloaded. Partly for that reason, RapidShare cut the program.

Raimer believes that changing RapidShare's policies leaves the service in the clear. "The technology Hotfile has is the same as what we have—it's also the same as what Microsoft's SkyDrive and Apple's MobileMe have—so the issue might be what companies do with it," Raimer says.

"I think people will agree that the basic technology of file hosting is the kind of thing the [Digital Millennium Copyright Act] covers."

Hotfile offered studios a better target for a lawsuit, since it pays uploaders cash. (The studios also may have been reluctant to face Bridges, who has a reputation as an effective litigator.) Hollywood wants to shut down Hotfile, but it also wants to set a precedent that would make other online locker services do more to filter content. This will be controversial, since any regulations could also affect Microsoft, Apple, and Google. But setting up some basic rules wouldn't just help Hollywood in the present; it would protect its future. The harder it is to access and store pirated content, the more consumers will want to do so legally—perhaps with UltraViolet.

Mitch Singer has studied what happened to the music business in order to avoid making the same mistakes. In the late 1990s, when he did some work for Sony Music, he attended a few meetings of the Secure Digital Music Initiative, which the major labels set up to develop a copy-protected album format. Historically, electronics makers and entertainment companies had always cooperated to introduce new formats. But once MP3 files became common, electronics manufacturers realized their devices would sell better if they could play pirated music, so they had no financial incentive to incorporate copy protection. "The iPod developed around getting content from ripping CDs or getting MP3 files from Napster," Singer says. "It wasn't until eighteen months later that iTunes launched." When it finally did, the major labels were under so much pressure that they agreed to sell music under Apple's conditions.

Singer likes to contrast the development of iTunes with the introduction of the DVD. When the movie studios and electronics companies established the DVD Consortium, neither side could go ahead without the other: movies weren't on the market in a compatible format the way MP3 files were available on the Internet before Apple started selling the iPod. So electronics companies had to give the studios the copy protection they wanted. The actual protection they came up with wasn't all that strong: it was broken a few years later by a teenager.[31] But by that time the studios had some legal protection in the form of the Digital Millennium Copyright Act.

Technology executives like to mock the law's anti-circumvention provision, since any digital rights management system eventually gets cracked. But that's not really the point. The law also made it illegal to sell a DVD copying device at Walmart, and it gives some consumers pause. "Every time people want to use [the DVD copying program] DeCSS, they have to download it, they have to worry about viruses, and perhaps a twinge of guilt goes through their brain," says Fox's senior vice president of content protection, Ron Wheeler. "None of that has ever been true for CDs. That's the difference, and it's all because of the DMCA."

Unlike Apple's copy-protection system for the iPod, the DVD Consortium created technology that could be licensed by any electronics company willing to pay the necessary fee. The DVD player became a commodity, which encouraged price competition. "The manufacturers were completely independent, and that put downward pressure on prices," Singer said. Within a decade after the format's 1996 introduction, the price of a DVD player went from more than $1,000 to less than $50. This created a giant market for movies and gave studios the power to set their price. "DVDs are now thirteen years old, and we're still selling them for roughly the same price we sold them for at launch," Singer says. In some cases, there's more profit in selling a single DVD than the machine that plays it.

"Maybe," Singer says, "the heading of this white paper would be 'Who's Commoditizing Whom?'" Just as cheap digital music helped Apple market its iPod, so inexpensive DVD players helped Hollywood sell more DVDs. The advantage can go either way, but piracy tends to cost entertainment companies their negotiating leverage.

Singer knew he needed to offer technology companies an incentive to respect copyright rather than turn a blind eye to infringement, and two things changed in the last half decade that made this easier. First, many technology companies have become more interested in selling services than gadgets; Microsoft makes money selling Xbox Live subscriptions and games, not the video game console itself. Second, the Internet service providers that benefited from the widespread availability of pirated content had started to worry that the use of file-sharing services was clogging their networks. UltraViolet gives both groups of companies a service to sell.

For Internet service providers, selling UltraViolet movies will be much easier if potential buyers aren't illegally downloading the same films from file-sharing networks. So it could also give Internet providers an incentive to cut piracy on their networks. It's hard to know how effective they could be, especially without a government mandate. But giving them a reason to try would be a significant step in the direction of legitimate commerce.

Theoretically, at least, UltraViolet should also encourage competition among retailers, much as the DVD player did. While DECE sets technical specifications, it doesn't mandate how retailers sell movies. That means Best Buy could package UltraViolet movies with physical DVDs, Comcast could use them to buttress its video-on-demand options, and Netflix could use them to "upsell" subscribers into buying films instead of just renting them. It also means that all of those companies will compete to offer hit movies for the cheapest price. Since studios set wholesale prices, the resulting competition should benefit them.

This assumes that UltraViolet works. Although DECE hoped to introduce UltraViolet products in time for the 2010 Christmas season, it took too long to agree on all the necessary standards. "People have been really skeptical that a group of sixty companies—many of which are large, powerful companies with different business models—could get anything done," Teitell says. "But they were partly right: it's challenging."

DECE also faces a more complex world than the Blu-ray or DVD format. "Home entertainment is moving from something that involved two companies—the content company that owned something and the retailer that sold it—into something that involves multiple parties," Teitell says. "UltraViolet will be a combination of something you buy now and an ongoing service that comes with it."

At least for now, pirate sites won't be able to offer a similar service. "What we hope will happen with DECE is that consumers will want the extra functionality we can offer them," Singer says. "And if we create an environment that's better than free, I think we can bring back digital sell-through."

CHAPTER 8

DISQUIET ON
THE EUROPEAN FRONT

WHY FRANCE FAVORS ART
OVER THE INTERNET

A specter is haunting Europe—the specter of piracy. And on a typi-cally gray day in Brussels, seventy-five executives from media trade associations all over the Continent have gathered in the headquarters of the Motion Picture Association (MPA) for a series of presentations on how to fight back. The MPA is the international affiliate of the American MPAA—it lobbies the European Union in Brussels, much as the MPAA works in Washington, D.C.—but this event is aimed at the operators in the trenches who try to prevent pirates from acquiring, distributing, and making money from their films. In modern Europe, where files and funds flow easily across borders, this work can be as painstakingly com-plicated as unraveling financial fraud.

The executives are listening to Pascal Hetzscholdt, a laid-back, tech-savvy Dutch guy with a mop of dark hair who runs the MPA's online antipiracy efforts for Europe. Gesturing at a PowerPoint slide, Hetz-scholdt reads a quotation from a science book about how predators and prey need to evolve along with each other in order to survive. For now, piracy still depends largely on file-sharing services, which can be moni-tored. But it's increasingly moving to streaming sites like Megavideo, online locker services like Hotfile, and link farms that direct users to both. As piracy becomes more decentralized, the movie business has to adapt accordingly.

Unglamorous as it sounds, the executives in this beige conference room will help determine the future of the film business. No one expects them to stop piracy or reverse the slide in DVD sales that's hitting various European countries at different rates. What they want to do is keep pirate Web sites less convenient than legal movie services so ventures like iTunes and UltraViolet can build an audience. They've declined to file mass lawsuits against ordinary individual uploaders in order to focus on taking down some of the larger commercial operations and keeping the rest too busy switching names and online addresses to build up a mass audience.

Hetzscholdt and the MPA have stronger laws on their side than their U.S. counterparts. In October 2009, the Constitutional Council of France approved the Creation and Internet Law—also known as the HADOPI law after the organization that will administer it—which could deny Internet access to repeat copyright infringers.[1] In April 2010, the U.K. approved the Digital Economy Act, a more complicated piece of legislation that calls for repeat infringers to suffer consequences that would most likely consist of having their access slowed or suspended. (Both of these are called graduated-response laws, since users who infringe copyrights will receive a letter, then a warning, and eventually a limitation of service.) And in December 2010, the European Commission released a report that said online piracy in the European Union was "alarming" and stronger laws—perhaps requiring the cooperation of Internet service providers—might be needed to enforce intellectual property rights.[2]

It's hard to tell how much of a difference the British and French laws will make, since they both call for monitoring file-sharing networks, but not online locker services or streaming sites. But they show that Europe is getting more serious about piracy and that it won't hesitate to make Internet service providers play a role in limiting it. That could help more legal online services get the momentum they need to grow into sustainable businesses.

This is more important than it might seem, since Europe's decisions on these matters affect the world. The first French copyright law states, "The most sacred, the most unassailable, and the most personal of all properties is the composition, the fruit of the writer's thought."[3] This attitude, so different from that of the United States, has played a role in shaping international copyright treaties since the 1886 Berne Convention for the Protection of Literary and Artistic Works. Even now, when intellectual property is regulated by an alphabet soup of agencies and agreements—including the World Intellectual Property Organization (WIPO) and the Agreement on Trade-Related Aspects of Intellectual Property Rights (TRIPS)—Europe still wields considerable influence.

Just as important, the European Union hasn't been afraid to regulate U.S. technology companies in ways that have forced them to adjust their business worldwide: it penalized Microsoft and Intel for anticompetitive behavior, and it opened an antitrust inquiry into Google in November 2010. Perhaps because they aren't homegrown, Europeans don't see Google, Apple, and Amazon in the same soft light Americans do, especially when it comes to their power over culture. Germany prohibits the discounting of books in ways that have made it difficult for Amazon to launch its Kindle there.[4] The French parliament considered, but rejected, a bill to mandate that iPods play music purchased from online stores other than iTunes.[5] And the proposed Google Books settlement inspired the European Commission to create its own online culture archive and recommend that libraries limit Google's exclusivity regarding the materials it scans.[6] The Internet may be international, but Europeans tend to see Google as *très américain*—dynamic, but disinclined to bother about matters of international law.

"The Google Books compromise in America, which was agreed upon with publishers because they had to give in, overlooks the fact that copyright is an international law," says Michael Naumann, a German publishing executive who ran Henry Holt in the United States and subsequently served as his country's culture minister from 1998 to 2001. "Google can lobby their butt off. We won't bow to their commercial interest."

The Internet is an irresistible force, but Europe is full of immovable governments. And anyone who believes countries there can't regulate the online world should consider what happened when Yahoo! told a court in France it couldn't follow laws there. In February 2000, after Nazi memorabilia was offered for sale on a Yahoo! auction site, the company was sued in France, where it is effectively illegal to sell such items. Yahoo! warned that limiting what it characterized as free speech would set a dangerous precedent for the online world. And like many technology companies before and since, it argued that it couldn't exert any control over the Internet, in this case to block French users from its site.

At the time, according to Jack Goldsmith and Tim Wu's *Who Controls the Internet? Illusions of a Borderless World*, it seemed entirely possible that France would give in. Internet utopians claimed such censorship was impossible anyway. "It's not that laws aren't relevant," the MIT Media Lab's co-founder Nicholas Negroponte said at the time, "it's that the nation-state is not relevant."[7] France, this line of thinking implied, would just have to accept the new reality of a borderless world.

But France does not even fully accept the reality of Sunday shop openings. "It became clear," Goldsmith and Wu write, "that the irrelevance of the nation-state would not go uncontested."[8] When Yahoo! claimed France could not impose its laws on a U.S. company, the advocacy groups that sued it argued back that the United States should not push its free speech laws on France. "Should we have to accept this *barbarism*?" asked Marc Knobel, one of the activists who organized the lawsuits. "In America they have the First Amendment, which makes legal action against such sites difficult. But in France, as in other countries, we have laws, and these laws must be respected."[9]

The court agreed: in May 2000, Judge Jean-Jacques Gomez gave Yahoo! three months to figure out how to block its site from Internet users in France. Yahoo! said it would be impossible. But when Judge Gomez consulted a group of technology experts, they said it could be done—not perfectly, but pretty well—employing the same technology Yahoo! used to make sure French users saw ads in their own language. Judge Gomez ordered Yahoo! to do so. The company apparently got over its philosophical attachment to free speech: two years later, as Goldsmith and Wu pointed out, Yahoo! agreed to restrict its search results in order to do business in China.

For a variety of reasons and in a variety of ways, the culture of the Internet has come to resemble the United States in both its enthusiasm for capitalism and its resistance to regulation. Like U.S. law, online culture and the companies that dominate it value privacy less than an anything-goes approach to free speech. (Very few people in France would say their country lacks freedom of expression; they just define it differently.) The U.S. approach to copyright also dominates the Web: many online companies outside the United States respond to Digital Millennium Copyright Act takedown notices, and technology companies have adopted the U.S. view of copyright as a way to give creators an economic incentive, but not control over their work.

Since the Internet has global reach, technology executives worry their companies could be subject to the most onerous regulations of any country in which they operate—"a world of Singaporean free speech, American tort law, Russian commercial regulation, and Chinese civil rights," as Goldsmith and Wu describe it.[10] When Judge Gomez issued his Yahoo! decision, online activists worried it set a precedent that would allow any country to impose its laws on the online world. "We now risk a race to the bottom," said Alan Davidson, an attorney with the Center for Democracy and Technology who has since become the top lobbyist at Google. "The most restrictive rules about Internet content—influenced by any country—could have an impact on people around the world."[11]

This is certainly worth worrying about, but it could be seen as a very American view. In Western Europe, voters tend to see regulations on commerce as a way to protect their rights rather than limit them; generally speaking, they tend to want freedom *from* the market, rather than for it. So they worry about another kind of race to the bottom, where the *least* restrictive rules in the world undermine their laws—on hate speech, consumer protection, and especially privacy. And many European countries already support their culture businesses using the French idea of *l'exception culturelle*—the cultural exception—which protects culture from the free market by requiring companies to invest in new works and imposing quotas on the airing and distribution of French music and film.[12] France has subsidized newspapers and considered a tax on search engines that would mainly affect Google.

Any country that regulates DVD release dates in order to protect movie theaters, as France does, won't hesitate to protect its film business from the Internet.[13] So as soon as Nicolas Sarkozy became president of France in May 2007, he set out to do just that. He asked Denis Olivennes, then chief executive of the entertainment retailer Fnac, to prepare a report on the problem of piracy. Olivennes's report recommended a "three strikes" policy of cutting off Internet access to repeat copyright infringers—an idea no other country had yet seriously contemplated—and French lawmakers put it into the HADOPI law.[14]

When the bill that would become the HADOPI law was first presented to the French Senate in June 2008, the reaction of online activists could be summarized as *Quelle horreur!* Several groups protested on the grounds that using the Internet was a fundamental right. There's not much in French law to support this: it's difficult to function without online access, but the same could be said of a car, and few would argue that the government can't suspend one's right to drive.

The possibility of false accusations raised more serious concerns. In June 2009, the French Constitutional Council declared this first version of the HADOPI law unconstitutional because it did not provide for proper due process. Around the same time, members of the European Parliament in Brussels tried to insert a passage in Europe-wide telecom legislation that would forbid countries to cut off Internet access for copyright infringement without allowing users to request an official hearing on the matter. (Companies would not, of course, need a proceeding to cut off users who did not pay their bills.) Although some members of the Parliament became uncomfortable with the idea of disconnections in general, the court approved a version of HADOPI that provided for judicial review.

In the U.K., momentum for similar regulation started building in October 2008, when the country launched its Digital Britain project, aimed at helping the country improve its online infrastructure. Among other recommendations, the resulting report suggested forcing Internet service providers to follow a code to deal with copyright infringement.[15] But it also emphasized how important it was for copyright holders to make it easier for consumers to buy music and movies online.

The Digital Economy Act, which takes the graduated-response idea from HADOPI, was presented in March 2010 and voted on the next month—a rushed process that left members of Parliament on both sides of the issue complaining that they didn't have enough time for debate. (The law doesn't mandate a specific number of offenses or penalty; repeat infringers are subject to "technical measures," which could include a limit on broadband speed.) The influence of lobbyists was obvious: the *Guardian* reported that an amendment that could block sites that repeatedly infringed copyright was taken nearly verbatim from a document from the British Phonographic Industry (BPI), the U.K. recording business trade group.[16] As with HADOPI, the difficulty of matching the Internet protocol addresses used by computers that download pirated music with individual users raises the likelihood of false accusations— someone could use a neighbor's open WiFi system to download illegal material—but the bill provides for an appeals process.

The music industry was conflicted, with some artists and their representatives protesting that the law's penalties were too harsh. "I think a bunch of us were a bit anti the Digital Economy Act because it was more stick than carrot," says Radiohead's manager, Brian Message. Although Radiohead famously let fans name their own price for one of its albums, Message manages other acts on major labels, and he wants to make sure artists don't get taken advantage of by them *or* technology companies. "I quite like the attention it put on the issues, and I'm definitely interested to see how it actually works," he says. "But I do worry that we spend so much time on a negative slant where we're not spending enough time necessarily working out how we can use this to our best advantage."

Although online activists criticized these laws for strengthening copyright, they didn't actually give creators any additional rights. As in the United States, it was already illegal in the U.K. and France to make copyrighted work available online without permission, and British and French copyright laws are generally more restrictive than those in the United States. (The U.K. has a "fair dealing" doctrine that's similar but a bit stricter than fair use; French law contains specific "statutory exceptions" to copyright.) The problem was that these laws were difficult to enforce, since Internet service providers had little responsibility for copyright infringement, due to laws modeled on the Digital Millennium Copyright Act.

"You have a lot of perfectly good copyright legislation in a lot of areas, and what you need is new ways of managing copyright that go with the grain of technology rather than a last-ditch attempt to manage the status quo," says James Murdoch, chief executive of News Corporation in Europe and Asia. "But you also need an enforcement agenda that works and doesn't turn a blind eye to theft."

Although scores of bloggers lambasted the bill, their feelings don't seem typical of the British public. In June 2010, a survey by the research company Ipsos MORI found that 52 percent of respondents agreed that it was acceptable to limit the online access of repeat copyright infringers, while only 18 percent disagreed.[17] Those results nearly matched a spring 2010 survey by the law firm Wiggin LLP (which works for media companies).[18] And the law isn't designed so much to get infringers off the Internet as to scare them straight.

"For us, what's always been more important about the technical measures is not the imposition of them but the threat of them," says Richard Mollet, the BPI's former director of public affairs. (He became chief executive of the U.K. Publishers Association in October 2010.) It's not in the interests of copyright holders to actually cut off people's Internet access, if only for selfish reasons: it limits their access to online stores. Mollet thinks most consumers will stop downloading illegally once they receive a letter that says they've been caught, while others will have a stern talk with their kids.

The debate about piracy in Europe has a depressing familiarity. Just as they do in the United States, media companies cite studies that exaggerate the effects of file sharing, while online activists point to the flawed Oberholzer-Gee and Strumpf study that said it's harmless, even though the authors themselves have since concluded otherwise. Copyright holders talk about theft, while technology companies hide behind the public interest. The only difference is that everyone has more rights—artists to their work and individuals to their privacy—in a way that makes it difficult to enforce laws online.

In France, this conflict set the Socialists, the country's major left-wing party, against themselves. During the debate over HADOPI, *Le Monde* published a letter from four prominent French artists defending the traditional French view of copyright as a human right, one the Left had often defended.[19] But the French Socialist deputy Christian Paul instead spoke out to praise the ideas of Jean Zay, the late-1930s leftist French minister of national education and fine arts, who promoted the idea of artists as *travailleurs intellectuels*—"intellectual workers"—who would entrust some of their rights to the government.[20] "Then, there was a great debate on the future of creative production and the future of the artist in a society in the midst of transformation," Paul said at a National Assembly hearing. "But that debate, you won't have it after HADOPI, which opens the way to a society of repression, whereas we wish for a society of freedom for artists and the public." Of course, the public's freedom to access a work can interfere with an artist's freedom to sell it.

"Zay supported the access of people to culture," says Catherine Trautmann, the former French culture minister who now serves as a Socialist member of the European Parliament. "I think we are in a new period of rights—cultural rights. First there were individual rights, then social rights, now cultural rights."

A more cynical view would be that the Socialists got caught in a classic left-wing dilemma: Defend the rights of a few or offer their stuff to the many? "There is a tradition of the Socialists defending the 'cultural exception'—the right for the cultural product to escape the usual market law," says Denis Olivennes, now chief executive of Europe 1 Radio. "But now they are siding with young people against what they call 'the artist lobbies.' They think they are defending consumers, but they are the advocates of international corporations with huge profit, like the telecom operators and Google. How can the Socialists, who are in favor of regulation for everything—for finance, for the workforce—want to totally deregulate culture?"

Meanwhile, as file sharing grows more popular in Spain and Scandinavia, music and movie sales in those countries have suffered more than elsewhere in Europe. Courts rarely hold anyone liable for file sharing in Spain, which is quickly becoming the worst-case scenario for the future of the entertainment business.[21] The country's recorded music business is only a third the size it was a decade ago, and no new Spanish artist had a Top 50 album during 2010.[22] DVD sales have fallen so much that the chairman of Sony Pictures Entertainment, Michael Lynton, has said Spain is "on the brink of no longer being a viable home entertainment market for us."[23]

Scandinavia, especially Sweden, has seen a backlash against creators' rights that stems from a May 2006 police raid on the offices of the Pirate Bay, a major file-sharing service based in Stockholm. In Sweden, where fast Internet connections made illegal downloading popular before it took off elsewhere, many people had a hard time believing copyright infringement justified such a severe response. When the Pirate Bay's four founders faced criminal charges for contributory copyright infringement, the trial that followed drew hundreds of new members to the Pirate Party, a previously obscure Swedish political party that wants to severely limit copyright and patent protections and to expand privacy rights.[24]

The four Pirate Bay founders charged in the case—Peter Sunde, Gottfrid Svartholm, Fredrik Neij, and Carl Lundström—saw the controversy as a growth opportunity. Instead of acting on takedown notices from music and movie companies, they posted them on the site and mocked them. Unlike other file-sharing services, they didn't bother to talk about their respect for copyright; they just said it had run its course as a useful policy. Asked about his ideas on copying in November 2007, Sunde, who acted as spokesman for the group, told a BBC reporter, "If I want it, I take it, 'cause I can. It might be [im]moral to some people but I think it's up to me to decide."[25]

Much like European Internet regulations, what happens to the Pirate Bay could have a profound effect on the U.S. media business. Although the Pirate Bay operates in Sweden, it attracts users and illegally distributes work from every country with Internet access. Allowing such a service to operate legally in Sweden wouldn't only undermine copyright there; it would do so all over the world. This, too, is a race to the bottom.

By the fall of 2008, the Pirate Bay had twenty-five million users and represented a tenth of all Internet traffic.[26] As the Swedish prosecutor prepared its case against them, Sunde, Svartholm, and Neij continued to present themselves as forward-thinking champions of free speech. (Lundström, who had provided funding for the venture, was older and acted it.) A 2008 article in *Condé Nast Portfolio* presented Sunde, the group's spokesman, as "a bit of a philosopher when it comes to what his site does." "We're not even a company," Sunde told the magazine.[27] Elsewhere, he said the service had made just $80,000 in profit in three years because "there's no good way to monetize something which is political."[28]

Sunde, Svartholm, and Neij deliberately turned their February 2009 trial into a media circus—a "spectrial," in their words. In a pretrial press conference at the Swedish National Museum of Science and Technology (from which publications that had been critical of the Pirate Bay were barred), Sunde claimed that the BitTorrent file-sharing protocol accounted for 80 percent of all Internet traffic and 40 percent of that came from the Pirate Bay—figures that were probably exaggerated. Sunde, who did most of the speaking for the group, compared the Pirate Bay to Google, since it merely helped users search for files to download.

In April 2009, the four founders each received a year in jail and a collective fine of about $3.5 million. They requested a retrial after Swedish Radio reported that a judge in the case, Tomas Norström, belonged to the Swedish Copyright Association, but the Swedish Court of Appeals took the case instead. The Pirate Bay remained online, and interest in its cause only grew.

Fueled by controversy surrounding the Pirate Bay, the Swedish Pirate Party gradually grew into an international movement. In June 2009, it won two seats in the European Parliament in Brussels. (It has no seats in the Swedish parliament.) The German Pirate Party won enough of a following to make the Green Party address the issue of copyright, and Pirate Parties International was founded in April 2010 to coordinate the activities of more than thirty national organizations. But the movement never got much traction outside northern Europe.

The Pirate Party's main argument is that governments face a choice between protecting copyright or privacy, an important right in most of Europe. Since people wouldn't tolerate the government opening their mail, why would they allow it to examine what they download? But there are ways to compensate copyright holders that don't involve looking at every work acquired: cable television companies don't need to monitor what customers watch, since a single fee covers all the programming they want. And the fact that governments don't open letters sent from within the country doesn't mean they have no authority over large packages sent from outside it.

Perhaps most important, the technology companies that lobby against enforcing copyright laws are the same ones that collect information about users themselves. "With the Internet community, whatever you do to protect the interests of artists, they argue that intellectual property protection leads to a surveillance culture," says Helga Trüpel, a member of the German Green Party who serves as the vice-chair of the Committee on Culture and Education in the European Parliament. "But when Google is watching them, it's okay."

According to the Pirate Bay e-mails found on computers seized as evidence by the Swedish police in 2006, none of the founders were nearly as interested in any of these issues as they were in building a profitable business that happened to be illegal.[29] Initial funding came from Lundström, the heir to a crisp-bread fortune, who financed several right-wing nationalist organizations, according to the Swedish newsweekly *Veckans Affärer*.[30] (There is no evidence that the other three founders share his political ideas or that the Pirate Bay ever promoted them.) "We'll make some sort of offshore company of it," Lundström wrote in a March 2005 e-mail that Neij was copied on. He said the Pirate Bay was already making money, with much less traffic than it eventually attracted.[31] A few days later, he copied Neij and Svartholm on an e-mail in which he said, "We're attacking the international market now, which means even more ad revenue."[32]

The Pirate Bay gradually built up a serious ad sales operation. It hired Random Media, a consulting company based in Israel and run by a man named Daniel Oded, to sell most of its advertising. In May 2006, Oded e-mailed Lundström and Svartholm to say that he and Sunde had met with a company that wanted to buy $100,000 worth of advertising.[33] According to a 2006 article in the Swedish daily *Svenska Dagbladet*, another company that worked with the Pirate Bay, Eastpoint Media, brought in SKR600,000 ($94,000) a month just selling advertising in Scandinavia.[34]

No one knows how much money the Pirate Bay made on advertising: Swedish prosecutors haven't been able to find the money, and the founders either say they don't remember or give a number close to $80,000. "Pirate Bay maintain that all the revenue went back into the site, but that's highly unlikely," says Anders Rydell, author of *Piraterna* (The Pirates).

Judging from their e-mail, one cause the Pirate Bay founders did feel very strongly about was avoiding taxes. According to *Svenska Dagbladet*, the Pirate Bay had advertisers send money to a company in Switzerland that shared an address with a firm that offered advice on how to avoid taxes.[35] A February 2006 e-mail from Neij to Svartholm referenced a company Lundström set up to launder money,[36] while another asked if it was smart to wire money into a Swedish account since "the taxman has big eyes and a long crooked nose."[37] Although these e-mails are openly available, and those sent to and by Oded are in English, the Pirate Bay's tax planning hasn't received nearly as much media attention as its professed politics.

The Pirate Bay has proved very difficult to shut down. Sunde has said the founders no longer own it, but a series of shell companies makes it difficult to find out who does. In 2009 and 2010, injunctions prevented two hosting services from keeping the site on their servers. But the Swedish Pirate Party started hosting it in May 2010, and Sunde suggested that shutting it down now would be seen as political censorship.[38]

More than a year after the first Pirate Bay trial, in November 2010, the Swedish Court of Appeals upheld the district court's guilty verdict. Neij, Sunde, and Lundström all got jail time—ten, eight, and four months, respectively—and were ordered to pay about $7 million in damages. (Svartholm did not appear in court, due to illness, and will have a separate trial in appeals court.) Neij, Sunde, and Lundström immediately filed an appeal to the Swedish Supreme Court, as did the music and movie business groups suing them, which are seeking a higher penalty.

According to the Swedish Court of Appeals verdict in the Pirate Bay case, Sunde had a previous conviction. In February 2009, according to Swedish court records, he was convicted for accounting fraud in connection with not declaring income of a business he controlled, High Availability Intelligence Quality Sweden.[39] Sunde said in court that he had given the company's payment records to its accountant, who did not file them. (Sunde did not respond to interview requests.) In February 2010, Sunde, who had left the Pirate Bay in August 2009, announced that he was founding Flattr, an online payment system that would let users make "micropayments" to artists they wanted to support by clicking on their Web pages.

In the United States, as piracy lowers the value of media, technology companies have essentially managed to set the price of music and video, and tried to do the same for books. No matter what something costs to make, Amazon and iTunes try to sell it for as little as possible, since they make money in other ways. This can be beneficial for consumers—but in the same way Walmart is, and with the same kind of long-term cost. In this digital version of Walmart capitalism, retailers set prices and conditions, and suppliers meet them by cutting costs however they can.

That's exactly the kind of outcome European countries try to avoid. Consider the book business in Germany, which sees publishing the way France views film: as a business it invented, developed, and needs to protect. Gutenberg invented modern printing in what is now Germany, and the first incarnation of the Frankfurt Book Fair started nearby soon after. For more than a century, the Buchpreisbindung—Book Pricing Law—has forced retailers to sell books for list prices to prevent chains from dominating the business through aggressive discounting.[40] "You don't have this [situation in the United States] where bookstores like Barnes & Noble and Borders sell $25.00 books for $9.99," says Michael Naumann, the publishing executive.

As Naumann sees it, the law keeps the country's book business healthy. The lack of price competition means books cost more than they otherwise would, but many Germans credit it with preserving independent bookstores, small publishers, and the diversity of German-language writing; Germany has more bookstores and releases more books per capita than the United States.[41] (France, Italy, and Spain all have similar regulations, albeit with less tradition attached.) When Naumann was culture minister, he prevented the European Commission from overruling the pricing law. "It was a long and hard fight," he says. "The German book business is a sacred cow."

Whether this amounts to savvy protection or silly protectionism, it certainly conflicts with Amazon's strategy of distributing books in ways that are more efficient for readers but less profitable for authors and publishers. Amazon does not discount German-language books in Germany, and as of early 2011 it hadn't announced plans to market the Kindle there. The trade organization Börsenverein des Deutschen Buchhandels—the German Publishers and Booksellers Association—has declared the book price law would apply to digital books, and so far no one has challenged it.

To fend off Amazon and Google, the Börsenverein has also created its own online publishing platform. Launched in 2007, the online platform libreka! lets publishers and retailers sell digital books for publishers' prices, either in shops or through online storefronts they run.

It represents a plan to maintain the traditional structure of the publishing business, including physical stores, in a new world that seems to have little use for them. By all available evidence, it is failing. Lower prices are one of the main advantages of e-books, and Germans have shown little interest in the service, which only sells 31,000 titles, compared with the 810,000 available for the Kindle.[42] The weekly newsmagazine *Der Spiegel* called it a "platform to prevent e-book sales."[43] It certainly seems to be stalling them.

"I'm not sure we have the power to speed it up or slow it down," says Ronald Schild, who runs libreka! "The power of libreka! is to maintain the position of publishers in the value chain. Apple and Amazon can make [the spread of e-books] faster, but publishers don't want to have to accept Amazon's terms." Like Hulu, libreka! is essentially run by the business whose products it sells, which gives the participating companies control over pricing. "We go all over the world to talk about it," Schild says, "and publishers in other countries are jealous."

If Germany is wary of Amazon, imagine what a country so conscious of its literary heritage thinks of Google's plan to archive all the world's books. An amicus brief the country submitted about the proposed Google Books settlement called it "a privately-negotiated document that is shrouded in secrecy, formulated behind closed doors by three interested parties, the Authors Guild, the Association of American Publishers and Google, Inc., resulting in a commercially driven document that is contrary to established international treaties and laws."[44] Although the settlement could help U.S. publishers, it certainly goes against several copyright treaties, and German law does not have the concept of fair use on which Google's legal argument would rest. The Börsenverein des Deutschen Buchhandels has already said it does not want its out-of-print books to be covered by the settlement. In 2011 the German National Library plans to launch a Web site with books and artifacts from thirty thousand institutions, which it will then integrate with the European Commission's project Europeana.

Germany has also debated defending its print culture by passing an "ancillary copyright" law to protect newspapers and magazines. According to a draft leaked to the free culture Web site iRights.info, the publishing giants Hubert Burda Media and Axel Springer AG are lobbying for a law that would essentially require online aggregators and search engines to pay a licensing fee in order to excerpt their news articles. This could be easier than it sounds, since the concept of fair use that Google News relies on to index content in the United States has no basis in German law. (Germany, like other countries in Continental Europe, has specific exceptions to copyright law.) And if Google is selling ads against this information, why shouldn't it pay?

Whatever happens to the law, it shows how Germany, like France, may be more willing to defend its culture businesses than the United States. "The German government has a clear position," said Chancellor Angela Merkel in an address before the 2009 Frankfurt Book Fair. "Copyrights have to be protected on the Internet."

By sheer force of its market size and willingness to regulate the Internet, Europe's decisions about technology and culture will exert a pull on the rest of the world, however they play out. But this might not help media companies as much as they'd like. As of early 2011, the Pirate Bay was still operating, the HADOPI law hadn't had an impact, and the Digital Economy Act was stuck in a process of reviews.

In France, a University of Rennes survey conducted just after the HADOPI law came into effect found that file sharing had actually grown.[45] As of early 2011, HADOPI had yet to issue a single penalty; it wasn't even allowed to start sending second notices until January 2011. "These policies are destined to fail," says Jérémie Zimmermann, a spokesman for La Quadrature du Net, a French online activist group. "The fact that they stuck a judge in there [when the Constitutional Council forced a change in the law] killed HADOPI. There will never be a conviction." If the law does cut file sharing, it might just push users toward online locker services like RapidShare.

This might make it easier for Pascal Hetzscholdt and the antipiracy executives he works with, however, since link farms and online lockers are easier to shut down than file-sharing services. As Hetzscholdt points out, pirate sites depend on hosting companies, domain registrars, and either ad networks or firms that process credit card payments, and this web of relationships makes them vulnerable. Legitimate businesses all respond to pressure, and they're easy to find. "You can go to the registrar, the hosting providers, the ad broker, or the payment processor," Hetzscholdt says. "In most cases that's sufficient." The idea isn't to eliminate piracy—just keep it inconvenient enough that most people will buy or rent from legitimate retailers.

In the U.K., the Digital Economy Act handles online lockers by calling for the government to order Internet service providers to block sites that persist in infringing copyrights. This saves U.K. copyright holders the considerable expense of suing online services located in other countries and allows the U.K. to enforce the law within its borders, which, after all, is the whole point of having a country. "Site blocking is far better for us because we are able to go after the commercial infringers," says Oliver Weingarten, commercial solicitor for the English Premier League. "We'd be able to have an effective remedy against the problem with live sites."

Like the HADOPI law, however, the Digital Economy Act isn't exactly moving at Internet speed. Some of this is due to the nature of the law itself: so much is left to the discretion of the U.K. Office of Communications—popularly known as Ofcom—that it almost seems as though Parliament passed a bill before it decided what it would do. The law defines obligations and limits, then leaves it to Ofcom to produce a regulatory code, as well as progress reports.

That should provide controversy for years to come. After Ofcom released the first draft of its enforcement guidelines in May 2010, the U.K. Internet service provider TalkTalk said that "copyright owners are the only ones that will benefit from this system, so unless the government decides that these companies should fully reimburse ISPs' costs, broadband customers will in effect be forced to subsidize the profits of large music and film companies."[46] TalkTalk didn't seem so bothered by the fact that music and film had been subsidizing its profits for years. In July 2010, TalkTalk and the Internet service provider BT successfully requested a judicial review of the law, on the grounds that it wasn't consistent with privacy law or European Union telecom regulations. In February 2011, the U.K.'s culture secretary, Jeremy Hunt, asked Ofcom to look into the feasibility of actually blocking sites that were almost entirely devoted to providing pirated material.

All of this is taking place at a time when Prime Minister David Cameron seems even more entranced by Google than President Obama is. In February 2009, Cameron appointed Eric Schmidt as an adviser on the Conservative Party's economic policy. In November 2010, Schmidt co-wrote a *Daily Telegraph* opinion piece with George Osborne, the chancellor of the Exchequer, which concluded that the Internet would fuel an increasing amount of economic growth—according to a report by Google.[47] (The Internet is obviously a crucial source of growth, but surely there's another study that says so.) And Cameron's director of strategy, Steve Hilton, is married to Rachel Whetstone, a vice president for public policy and communications at Google.

Cameron seems especially interested in Google's opinions on U.K. copyright law. In November 2010, when Cameron announced a "tech city" for start-ups in London, he mentioned that the U.K. would also review its intellectual property laws, "to see if we can make them fit for the internet age."[48] Cameron was frank about his motivations: he mentioned that the founders of Google "feel our copyright system is not as friendly to this sort of innovation as it is in the United States." The science and universities minister, David Willetts, also spoke, stating that he would look into making it easier to patent software—an issue that represents a potentially serious block to innovation in a way copyright hardly ever does.

In late 2010, the government announced that an independent review of intellectual property would be led by the former *Financial Times* editor Ian Hargreaves. More upsetting for copyright holders, the panel will include James Boyle, a law professor at Duke who is a former chairman of Creative Commons. To convey his views on intellectual property,

Boyle wrote a comic book on the subject that portrays Lawrence Lessig as the Statue of Liberty.[49]

Whatever happens with U.K. copyright law—and Hargreaves's panel will only deliver recommendations—changing the poisoned relationship between media companies and Internet service providers will require new ideas. One of the most promising is the concept of a blanket license, which would add a fee to Internet connections, allow file sharing or other forms of downloading, and divide up the money to compensate copyright holders for the use of their work. And it will be difficult to make progress on that idea until technology companies face more pressure to negotiate.

This would help European economies more than any ideas that come out of Hargreaves's panel. Copyright-based businesses generate a significant number of jobs in Europe, just as they do in the United States. Ultimately, says Tim Renner, former chief executive of Universal Music Germany, "for Europe and the United States, it's in our mutual interest that there is some value behind ideas."

CHAPTER 9

BLANKET PROTECTION

TURNING COPYRIGHT INTO COPY*RISK*

About ten years ago, Jim Griffin was reading a book about the history of risk when he had an idea about how to save the music industry—by making it more like the insurance business.

Griffin, a bespectacled, slightly hyperactive consultant who has advised both music and technology companies, holds the distinction of having put the first major-label song online back in 1994, when he worked as technology director for Geffen Records. It was an Aerosmith track—"Head First," appropriately enough—that the label offered for free to promote the band's *Get a Grip* album. Back then, it took more than twenty minutes to download from the online service CompuServe.

Since leaving Geffen a few years later, Griffin has built a reputation for thinking presciently about how the music business might actually work in a digital world. In 2000, during congressional hearings held as the Napster case unfolded, Griffin testified that "music can and should be made to feel free, even when it is not free"—much like on radio.[1] He knew enough about technology to understand even then how hard it would be for entertainment companies to control the way their products were traded online. But he was realistic enough to realize that artists still needed to be compensated for their work.

Instead of selling music by the album or song, Griffin suggested in his testimony, why couldn't labels sell access to all of their recordings, the way cable companies carry television channels? In exchange for a monthly payment, consumers could listen to everything they wanted—

either on a streaming service or as downloads—and then leave it to labels to divide up the money. Consumers would get music, artists would get paid, and no one would get sued.

This idea is not unique to Griffin, as he himself says, although he has become its most visible proponent. It would require a blanket license—also called a collective license—under which an organization designated by the labels would grant rights to distribute recordings to Internet service providers, collect money from them, and distribute the funds to copyright holders. It sounds like a complicated arrangement, but it has been working for decades with musical compositions. (Remember: each piece of music involves two copyrights—one for the recording and another for the composition—that may or may not be owned by the same entity.) In the United States, radio stations, restaurants, and other businesses that play music in public pay the collecting societies ASCAP, BMI, and SESAC, which figure out what songs are most popular and disburse royalties accordingly to songwriters and the music publishers that represent them.

Under a blanket license, composers and the publishers that work with them essentially forfeit their ability to determine where their work is heard in exchange for the knowledge that they will get paid for it. Since the Internet makes it harder to control media of any kind, this idea—"compensation without control," some call it—is being pushed by a few entertainment and technology executives, as well as some European politicians. And while the plan represents a rational compromise, some technology bloggers have already started maligning it by inaccurately calling it a "music tax."

So what does all of this have to do with the insurance business?

As Griffin read *Against the Gods: The Remarkable Story of Risk* by the economist Peter Bernstein, he saw how the need to allocate risk on the voyages of English merchant ships in the eighteenth century led to the advent of "actuarial economics."[2] As opposed to "transactional economics," which involves the purchase of individual items, actuarial businesses gather pools of money and divide them according to the outcome of subsequent events. Such pools can be used to defray the risk to anything, from an eighteenth-century trade vessel to a teenager's Toyota. Griffin points out that Ooma, the voice-over-Internet system he uses for long-distance service instead of Skype, works on an actuarial model, since customers buy the machine from the company, which then covers the cost of all their calls out of that price. And he consulted on Nokia's Comes with Music service—it didn't catch on—which made music free with the price of a cell phone.

"I increasingly think of copyright as copy*risk*," Griffin says. "I say that you're undergoing a risk as an author or a creative person and we should address your *risk*, not your *right*. To the extent that you think it's your right to stop someone from making a copy—and it may be a legal right or a moral right—good luck enforcing it."

Griffin, who in his spare time runs an online mailing list dedicated to the future of music, doesn't mean to sound insensitive. He's just acknowledging an obvious truth: it's difficult to stop people from spreading information using technology designed for that very purpose. "Copyright is what we wish were true, but the technologist in me knows it's a check we can't cash," he says. "I can't stop someone from making a copy of someone else's work, and I'll be increasingly unable to do so in the future."

Griffin points out that we usually don't address risk by trying to eliminate it: we do so by insuring against it. "We run a risk when we let someone take a Corvette off an auto dealer's lot," he says, "but the way we address risk as a society is more through monetization than through actual rules." In other words, all the seat belts and speed limits in the world won't make a sports car perfectly safe, so we've come to accept the fact that it can't be done, at least not beyond a certain point. Instead, we require drivers to buy insurance to compensate themselves and others for potential losses. Griffin is in no way suggesting that illegal downloading is as serious as a car wreck. He just believes that collecting and distributing a pool of money to compensate creators would be more practical than regulating the Internet with laws that can be difficult to enforce.

"Technology is like that Corvette: it runs into your rights," Griffin says. "Every year it gets more and more powerful, even more so than a car. You and I, we both have multiple music copying machines in our pockets right now. And they make photocopy machines look trivial!" As Griffin points out, we *already* treat photocopy machines the way he wants to deal with online music. Starting in 1978, the nonprofit Copyright Clearance Center has licensed some owners of copiers in much the same way ASCAP and BMI license restaurants. In exchange for a flat fee, owners get the right to duplicate certain scholarly journals and reference materials. The center then divides the money according to its assessment of the popularity of different works. No one would argue that this is a perfect system. But it's certainly more practical than either forbidding researchers to make copies or trying to monitor them as they do.

There are several ways this could be applied to online music, and none of them is simple. Ideally, Griffin wants to license Internet service providers for music downloads. They essentially already use music to attract customers, and this would give them a way to compensate copyright holders that could be easier and cheaper than setting up a system to deal with infringing users, as they now have to do in the U.K. and France. In a less elaborate version, Internet service providers could set up their own music streaming services. They would determine what users listen to, by either counting every song or monitoring a sample and extrapolating, in order to divide royalties appropriately. (Services could store the information without listeners' names attached, as Google does with search data, so no one knows who's listening to Air Supply.)

Implemented correctly, a blanket license system could preserve the best aspects of both the recorded music business and the Internet as it exists now. Labels would have an incentive to invest in and market artists in order to make as much money as possible, while technology companies wouldn't have to worry about barriers to the use of online music. Both Lawrence Lessig and the Electronic Frontier Foundation favor versions of the idea.

So far, though, the concept of blanket licensing doesn't have much traction in the United States. In 2008, Griffin founded Choruss, a venture backed by Warner Music Group, and offered blanket license deals to a few U.S. universities for about $5 per student per month as an experiment. In exchange, students would have been able to use Choruss's custom file-sharing system, based on the Audiogalaxy program, to download as much music as they wanted. Choruss would have legalized—and monetized—the way many college students get music anyway. But although Griffin secured cooperation from six colleges, as well as limited support from the other major labels and publishers, disagreements among labels delayed the project, and the fact that Warner owned Choruss presented potential antitrust problems that prevented it from launching. Griffin left Warner in March 2010 but kept running Choruss as an independent company.

"I thought, and think, it's something that ought to be done," says Warner Music Group's chief executive, Edgar Bronfman Jr. "But I think maybe we were early or under-resourced or both, because to make something like Choruss work, you need a whole bunch of foot soldiers, and we couldn't afford to do that on our own without knowing we had the support of the other majors and the publishers."

The biggest problem with blanket licensing is that it would be difficult to do without help from the government. Right now, U.S. law provides little incentive for Internet service providers to negotiate deals with content owners; since their subscribers already download content for free, albeit illegally, they have little to gain. Any proposed licensing organization could run into antitrust issues; the U.S. collecting societies ASCAP and BMI both operate under consent decrees from the U.S. Department of Justice.[3] And both labels and technology companies would fight a government-imposed solution that didn't favor their side's interests.

At the same time, the idea is gaining traction in Europe. The French and British three-strikes laws have put pressure on Internet service providers to negotiate licensing deals. The Internet service providers TDC and Eircom already run all-you-can-eat streaming music services in Denmark and Ireland, respectively. And the French National Assembly has discussed the idea. It would be an appropriate homecoming for an idea that has its origins in nineteenth-century Paris.

A French composer walks into a bar, orders a sugar water, and hears the band playing his song. This sounds like the beginning of a surrealist joke. But the 1847 incident—involving the songwriter Ernest Bourget, the stylish café Les Ambassadeurs, and a fashionable drink of the time—marked the beginning of blanket licensing for musical compositions. When the waiter presented the bill, Bourget declined to pay, on the grounds that the café didn't pay him to use his music to attract patrons.

Like so many businesses today, Les Ambassadeurs believed that music should be free. But when Bourget sued to settle the matter, the Tribunal de Commerce de la Seine found the café liable for damages. Composers had the right to be compensated for public performances of their music. Two years later, that decision was upheld by the Cour d'Appel de Paris.[4]

This created a new problem: How could composers possibly license their songs to every bar and café in France? Fortunately, they had an innovative business model to look at: a new kind of organization called a collecting society. So along with two colleagues, both of whom were with him at the café, Bourget formed the organization that became the French collecting society SACEM (Société des Auteurs, Compositeurs, et Éditeurs de Musique).

The idea of a collecting society originated in 1777 with Pierre-Augustin Caron de Beaumarchais, a prominent French intellectual who started his career as a watchmaker, served as a royal adviser, and later became a spy for Louis XV. He is best remembered for writing plays, including *The Barber of Seville* and *The Marriage of Figaro*, which were hits at the time. (The operas of the same names are based on his work.) At the time, most theatrical companies pressured authors to sell all rights to their work, but Beaumarchais gathered twenty of his fellow playwrights and founded an agency that allowed them to bargain collectively and collect a fee for each performance. When France formally recognized copyright in 1791, Beaumarchais's society got a legal foundation.

Playwrights could strike deals with individual theaters, of which there were a limited number. But music presented a greater challenge, since it was played in every restaurant and café that could afford a band—and, later, a phonograph. Composers couldn't deal with all of these venues, but SACEM could offer a simple contract that allowed them to play all the works it controlled. Essentially, French songwriters gave up control in order to protect their compensation.

The concept came to the United States in 1914, when the operetta composer Victor Herbert founded ASCAP (American Society of Composers, Authors, and Publishers), which quickly attracted Irving Berlin, John Philip Sousa, and others. The organization had its sugar-water moment when Herbert sued Shanley's Restaurant for playing his music without compensation in a case that went all the way to the Supreme Court. In the decision, Justice Oliver Wendell Holmes stated that venues had to pay composers for public performances of their work, since "the purpose of employing it is profit."[5]

Could a system like this work for recordings heard or downloaded online?

Intuitively, the idea makes sense. Internet service providers and file-sharing services benefit from recorded music, just as restaurants do from compositions, and it's so difficult to exercise any control that labels and artists might be smart to settle for compensation. Until recently, they could have both, since recordings were attached to a physical object. At this point, it would be easier to let the Internet spread them around and then collect money for their use. But this would require a historic shift in thinking on the part of the recorded music business.

Until recently, the music business has always thought about recordings in terms of *sales*. To labels, radio just served to promote sales. But even if consumers prefer to buy access to streaming music or unlimited downloads over a period of time, labels need to find a way to sell it. And decades' worth of laws and artist contracts are set up in ways that would make this difficult.

Although it didn't get much attention at the time, the idea of a blanket license for the online use of recorded music was first proposed by Bennett Lincoff, the former director of legal affairs for new media at ASCAP, who wrote a *Billboard* op-ed on the subject in 1995.[6] He realized that thorny legal problems would arise from the tangle of separate rights needed to use recordings online, so he suggested Congress replace them with a single right for the digital transmission of recorded music.

A new collecting society could then be set up to license online services, distribute fees among rights holders, and pursue legal action against sites that offered music without permission. But while this could solve any number of legal problems, it would also require changes to copyright law that would be unlikely to pass Congress anytime soon.

The concept also got attention during the 1997 congressional hearings on the law that became the Digital Millennium Copyright Act. Since ASCAP and BMI already collected money for songwriters from radio and television stations, said Allee Willis, who wrote the theme song for *Friends* and testified for BMI, why not treat Internet service providers the same way? (This would have compensated songwriters but not recording artists or their labels.) "I think you would have to ask the on-line providers why they find the idea of blanket license so onerous," said John Bettis, an ASCAP songwriter and board member. "I haven't got a clue."[7] The testimony was essentially ignored.

Blanket licensing won attention in the technology world in 2004 when the Harvard Law School professor William "Terry" W. Fisher III published *Promises to Keep: Technology, Law, and the Future of Entertainment*. The book proposed a government-controlled plan to fund music and other art with tax revenue. Culture would be "free" to consumers, with tax revenue distributed to content creators according to the popularity of their work. Fisher pointed out that this could legalize and advance "semiotic democracy," the phenomenon of amateur artists making mashups, music remixes, and other work from copyrighted content.

Like Griffin, Fisher started a company to put his ideas into practice, but neither creators nor technology companies expressed much interest. Labels were disinclined to allow a government agency to set the value of their recordings. Technology companies benefit from the status quo, which allows them to profit from media first and face legal consequences later, if ever. And in the United States at least, it's hard to imagine Congress would pass a law to fund culture. (If you think Fox News hosts hate rap music now, wait until it's supported by tax dollars!) "Americans distrust government," Fisher says, "and these systems indicate government control over what are perceived as private property rights."

Fisher's idea for government funding captured more imaginations in Europe, where he still speaks about it. Lincoff, who has worked on his single-right idea as a hobby for more than a decade, recently found an enthusiastic audience in Sweden and Finland. "In 1998, after I left ASCAP to go out on my own, people weren't responding to this idea—they were laughing," he remembers. "Now I'm hearing things like, 'If we could snap our fingers and have this implemented in a moment without going through the transition, we would do it.' That's progress! And as the crisis deepens, the difficulty may seem not as great."

So far, the idea of blanket licensing seems to appeal more to countries with strong traditions of thinking collectively.

Since April 2008, customers of the Danish telecom company TDC have downloaded more than 200 million tracks for free. The Internet service provider has paid copyright owners for every single one of them. In fact, as TDC's music manager, Tejs Bautrup, explains in a movie theater café that oozes low-key Scandinavian charm, doing so is key to his company's business strategy.

Like other Internet service providers, TDC spends an enormous amount of money to build and maintain a network, so it wants to attract as many customers as possible. That usually means spending money on advertising and marketing. But Bautrup, who frankly admits he's more of a business guy than a music fan, realized that it would be more effective to reduce TDC's expenses by finding a way to keep the users it already had.

Most European Internet service providers compete only on price: they offer a certain amount of speed, measured in megabytes per second, for a fixed monthly fee. In a competitive market like Denmark, where much of the population can choose among several providers, this can quickly become a bruising battle that drives down profit margins. So TDC, which also sells cable television and mobile packages, started offering additional services to keep customers happy. Right now the one that works best is TDC Play, a music system it includes free with online access that allows users to stream songs to their computers and download songs to their mobile devices for as long as they subscribe. In Denmark—a country ahead of most in the popularity and speed of broadband access—Internet service providers see record labels as partners, not opponents.

"The churn is 10 percent to 20 percent less for customers who use the service," Bautrup says—which means TDC saves so much on marketing that Play pays for itself. TDC pays a fee for each consumer who uses the service; no one will say how much, but it's probably about $5 a month, based on the structure of similar deals. Some of that money goes to the Danish collecting society KODA, which represents songwriters, much as ASCAP does in the United States, while the rest is divided by labels according to the popularity of their recordings.

So far, the labels like what they see. In April 2010 they accepted a guaranteed payment of 25 percent less than their first two-year deal, partly because TDC Play seems to be hurting radio ratings more than music sales. "It's not yet a clear picture, but so far we are happy with the money we get," says Sony Music Denmark's managing director, Henrik Daldorph. "We're trying to understand the demographic that uses it and if this use takes away from other music sales or if it is the opposite—the more they sample, the more they get into music, the more likely they are to make a purchase."

To everyone involved, TDC Play offers a look at a possible future of the media business—one in which Internet service providers have an incentive to cut piracy. (TDC sends warning notices to customers who share songs downloaded from its music service.) Bautrup says telecom executives from around the world call to ask about the project. And to labels, Denmark is a small enough market in which to experiment. As with Griffin's plan to set up Choruss at universities, the potential losses are limited.

"We love the business model, and the fact that they went through a term and then renewed because it helped them retain subscribers is good," says Michael Nash, Warner Music Group's executive vice president for digital strategy and business development. CD sales in Denmark have continued to decline as record stores close and other retailers cut the space they devote to music. "But iTunes sales have continued to grow, which is the chief barometer we're concerned about. The perspective in that market is that it has had no cannibalistic impact."

Some technology executives say the major labels resist innovation for fear of losing their share of the music market: they don't want to compete with independent companies on a more even playing field. But so far, Bautrup says, their market share isn't all that different from the physical CD market. He says a few Danish labels have thrived at the majors' expense, mostly because they have devoted more attention to packaging, or its virtual equivalent. At the same time, however, TDC Play's popularity among men in their thirties and forties guarantees a steady demand for the kind of classic rock that's almost entirely on major labels.

The only dissent comes from KODA, the collecting society that represents Danish songwriters, which is literally located right around the corner from Sony in a neighborhood of charming old buildings. Like most European collecting societies, KODA is a legal monopoly that wields far more power than its U.S. counterparts. After KODA's first two-year contract with TDC ran out in April 2010, the two sides could not agree on a new deal, although they proceeded under a temporary agreement. TDC asked for a ruling from the Danish Copyright Tribunal, which has the power to set license rates if companies cannot come to terms.[8]

"TDC wanted to renew at a lower rate and we offered a reduction, but they wanted more of a reduction than we offered," says Jakob Hüttel, KODA's head of international legal affairs. Both sides agreed to abide by the tribunal's decision. In stereotypical Scandinavian fashion, both KODA and TDC were refreshingly polite about the dispute, especially compared with their counterparts in other countries. "This is strictly business," Bautrup says. "I like KODA. We pay them a lot of money, but that's how it is, and they take care of the administrative costs of paying songwriters."

KODA's dispute with TDC points to one of the biggest problems with blanket licensing: labels and publishers don't always agree on how to split the money. So far, they've treated iTunes downloads as sales, although not without some objections. But what about services that offer unlimited downloads or streaming? If labels don't have to bear the costs of manufacturing and distributing CDs, publishers argue, shouldn't publishers get a larger share of royalties? In turn, labels point out that they still bear more of an act's expenses, including production, promotion, and marketing. Sony's Daldorph and the Danish labels favor TDC's side in the dispute—yet another example of how the music business isn't as monolithic as some technology executives imagine.[9]

Hüttel says KODA needs to protect its members, since it runs as a songwriters' collective. It has a reputation as a hard bargainer, and as of early 2011 it had declined to make deals with YouTube or Spotify. Although KODA says it's eager to strike deals with online services, start-ups often ask for low rates to get their businesses off the ground, and it doesn't want to license them music so cheaply that it gives them an advantage over existing businesses. "Why should we help some businesses give music away without earning any money on it when there are successful models with which they're competing?" Hüttel asks.

Although this sounds harsh, KODA has to look after the interests of its members. TDC Play seems to take listening hours away from radio, a major source of KODA's income. At the same time, companies like Spotify and TDC resent that collecting societies in some countries charge more than those in others. "Payments have come to the level where Spotify cannot launch, where they're higher than Holland or Sweden," Daldorph says.

TDC Play continued to operate during the dispute, and the two sides reached an agreement in April 2011. "TDC is clearly an evolution along this path, and actuarial thinking is very common in Scandinavian countries," says Griffin, who spent most of 2007 in Finland consulting for Nokia on Comes with Music. "It's the foundation of their society in the sense that they've socialized any number of expenses that others would view as private."

As anyone involved in health care can tell you, what works smoothly in Scandinavia can start fights in the United States. And as Griffin tried to strike a balance between the culture business and the culture of the Internet, he ran straight into the latter. Even before Warner Music's incarnation of Choruss finalized any deals, bloggers started calling the plan a "music tax." In a fit of objectivist outrage, an engineer from Akamai, the online company, even suggested that "failure to pay their tax will ultimately result in people with guns coming to your door."[10] At one point, Griffin says, he was e-mailed a death threat, through two anonymous mail servers, that Warner took seriously enough to hire a private detective to investigate.[11]

The "tax" talking point scored well online, even though it is legally and logically inaccurate. Choruss would be more accurately described as a "levy," since it would organize an easy way for rights holders to collect money they're entitled to by law. It's *already* illegal to download copyrighted music without paying under most circumstances—that's why people get sued for it—and Choruss would eliminate those lawsuits and make sure artists got compensated. Like ASCAP and BMI, it would monitor and monetize a right that already exists. Some people objected to the idea that colleges would charge students for music, but many schools already assess activity fees that cover cable television, campus concerts, and other cultural activities. And since a 2008 law gives universities a legal obligation to reduce illicit file sharing, taking a license from Choruss might be easier than policing student use of computer networks.[12]

Over the course of 2008, Griffin signed up six schools: the University of Colorado, Boulder; the University of Washington; Seton Hall University; California State University, San Bernardino; Murray State University; and the Berklee College of Music. But as Choruss came under fire, Warner Music grew reluctant to talk about it, partly because of antitrust concerns. The air of mystery led some students to expect stringent limitations on service.

"They didn't understand it, and they hate anything that has the stench of major labels on it," Griffin says. This is ironic because Griffin has also criticized labels, albeit in fairly measured ways. He even sits on the advisory board of the Electronic Frontier Foundation, which is hardly a friend to the entertainment industry.

Like most Internet idealists, Griffin wants to use technology to distribute creative works as widely as possible; he just wants to make sure their creators get paid. "A civilized society could not long tolerate purely voluntary payments for culture and art," Griffin says. "If you turn it into a tip jar, society starts to crumble. But the same thing happens if you condition access to those materials on one's ability to pay—or, worse, the size of their parents' wallet. A child should be able to hear any age-appropriate song, watch any movie, read any book." It's a remarkably utopian vision for a man the *TechCrunch* blog accused of planning a "protection racket."[13]

Warner Music's involvement didn't guarantee Griffin smooth sailing within the industry, either. Like TDC Play, Choruss needed to convince publishers they would come out ahead overall by lowering their usual fee for downloads. Some labels were also wary: Universal Music, the major label with the largest market share, approaches some blanket license deals by asking for a guaranteed share of revenue, according to executives familiar with the negotiations. For some rights holders, participating in Choruss means sacrificing a short-term advantage for the good of the overall music business. You could call the lack of industry support for Choruss shortsighted, but an economist would call it a market failure.

In the United States, the government has traditionally stepped in to resolve such situations. In 1909, Congress created a "statutory license" that allows performers to cover any song that has already been released as long as they pay a "mechanical royalty" set by a rate court.[14] Other such government arrangements were made for the retransmission of broadcast television on cable systems and for online radio services like Pandora, which don't allow users to choose which songs they hear.[15] (Services like Spotify, which do allow users to choose specific songs, aren't covered by that arrangement, which is why they need to make deals directly with labels.) So far, U.S. labels and Internet service providers have not expressed interest in such an arrangement—the former because it could further erode music prices and the latter because it would raise their costs. Labels have grown more interested in cutting private deals, but in the United States at least the Internet service providers have little incentive to negotiate with them. Why pay to give users what they're already taking for free?

Ultimately, there's no reason why a blanket license couldn't also apply to other media, although the way the film business uses release windows to maximize revenue makes it impractical for Hollywood. Television carriage fees are already split up by cable companies, albeit in a very different way. So far, though, the only other business looking into blanket licensing is journalism. Like music, it spreads easily online in ways that don't benefit its creators, and the companies involved are faring so badly that they need to experiment with new business models.

As in music, publications already have the right to receive compensation for many uses of their stories. In most cases, this right wouldn't apply to one- or two-paragraph excerpts, which would fall under fair use, but it would certainly apply to blogs with advertising that republish articles in their entirety. As with Choruss, collecting money in these cases wouldn't require any adjustment to copyright law, since those who reprint entire articles already have to pay for them—they're just not doing so. An organization like ASCAP could collect money and divide up the resulting revenue. And one of the hot news cases being litigated by news organizations could set a precedent like the one in Victor Herbert's case against Shanley's Restaurant.

Any blanket licensing plan will almost certainly begin in the music business, which is more comfortable than most with actuarial economics. Music publishers have fared better than labels did during the last decade, and they have a record of being more fair to songwriters than labels are with artists. But any such arrangement would fundamentally change the nature of the recorded music business. Instead of focusing on raw sales volume, labels would need to focus on raising their average revenue per user, or ARPU, a metric used by telecom companies, among others.

Could this work? As of October 2009, about seventy-five million U.S. homes had broadband connections[16]—just less than 65 percent of all U.S. households.[17] For the sake of argument, let's assume broadband usage climbs to a hundred million households over the next decade. And let's assume that about two-thirds of those households would want an unlimited music service for $10 a month—a good value compared with cable television. (Perhaps half of the remaining third don't like music, while the other half of that third simply refuse to pay for it.) Of the $120 that each subscriber brings in annually, perhaps $30 might go to the Internet service provider. That would still leave sixty-six million households paying $90 a year into a pool of money that would be worth $5.9 billion a year.[18]

To make comparisons easier, let's assume the money record labels would save on manufacturing and distribution would now go to collecting, managing, and disbursing this pool of money. So we can directly compare this $5.9 billion with the $6.3 billion that labels made in 2009 on music sales and licensing. But publishers would almost certainly demand more of that money than the dollar or so per CD they get now—perhaps another eighth in addition to what they get now, which is about an eighth of wholesale revenue. (These estimates are rough but realistic.) That would leave about $5.2 billion for the labels.

Labels could also charge money for access to music over mobile phones. This could be a more lucrative business, since there are many more mobile phone users than there are households with online connections. But this idea, like many other mobile business models, requires drawing a distinction between broadband and wireless Internet connections that seems increasingly artificial. It might make sense for labels to charge $5 for a broadband connection and another $5 or $10 for a mobile phone, but that's only possible if there's a discernible difference between the two.

Artists or labels could also make money selling other products—vinyl records to collectors, CDs to listeners of a certain age—and artists who wanted greater investment from labels could license their rights to concert tickets or merchandise. Right now, one of the most valuable rights artists have is the ability to license songs for use in commercials, films, and television shows, which has grown more important as music sales have fallen. Under the model William Fisher proposes in *Promises to Keep*, artists who allow others to remix their material would get a higher level of compensation. In principle, this is an elegant idea. In practice, who would decide what constitutes a remix? Using a pop song in a home video might not affect its potential licensing value, but putting it in a commercial online video certainly could. (And since so many YouTube clips run with advertising, aren't many home movies now commercial in nature anyway?) Songs from artists who rarely license their work command a premium, so those who granted remix permission could lose significant revenue. Putting Fisher's ideas into practice would require significantly more money in the pool.

Under such a broad-based plan, "I don't see how you'd get the consumer to agree to pay a sum that would match what we have at present," says Frances Moore, chief executive of the International Federation of the Phonographic Industry (IFPI), the international equivalent of the RIAA. "What's great about TDC is that it's one of many models that the consumer has available. The problem with [a government-run plan] is it takes away all other models." Labels would receive guaranteed income, but they'd have a hard time entering new businesses.

Under any blanket license plan, labels could immediately face a severe drop in revenue, although it would eventually rise again. Consider a streaming music service that charges $5 per month. Its first customers would be dedicated fans, the consumers who might now spend $100 or so a month on music. Once they buy a subscription, they might spend less. In the long run, this might not matter, because other subscribers—the consumers who now buy one or two CDs a year—will spend much more than they did before. The problem is that they might not buy a subscription for some time.

Any blanket licensing system will also have to be transparent enough to satisfy labels, performers, and songwriters that they'll get the money owed to them. Some worried that Choruss would not collect enough money for everyone. "This idea appeals to people who haven't done their homework because they all say, 'All we have to do is license this and then make money from it,'" says the president of the Songwriters Guild of America, Rick Carnes. "They don't look at the details, and the devil is in the details." Among them are how labels and publishers will split revenue, what organization will monitor the popularity of various works, and even contractual issues between artists and their record companies. Seemingly minor legalities—like whether blanket licensing deals legally count as sales or licensing—would make a huge difference in the money that goes to labels, artists, and songwriters.

Ironically, the same copyright laws that protect labels also make it difficult to launch a project like Choruss without government support. As Griffin planned it, Choruss would work like existing file-sharing programs, meaning users could trade any music they wished. But if someone uploaded a recording to which Choruss did not have rights, its copyright holder could still sue him. That would eliminate one of Choruss's main advantages and leave students wondering why the legitimate service they were paying for offered less music than the illegal one they had been using for free. It also means that smaller rights holders can serve as spoilers, essentially forcing organizations to pay them a premium to keep them from litigating. To prevent this, some Nordic countries use an "extended blanket license," which covers all rights holders once a certain percentage of them agree to terms. The majority rules, then takes everyone else along.

Mostly for this reason, Griffin put Choruss on hold in October 2010 to start working on a better way to track who owns what rights. The leading venture to do this is the Global Repertoire Database Working Group, a Europe Union venture of eight companies to make music licensing easier across international borders.[19] Griffin is working on a similar project for the World Intellectual Property Organization.

"I love Choruss, but I know it's not a good idea until we have a database," Griffin says. "Everyone had come to understand that it's a predicate to progress. We should not be creating pools of money if we cannot allocate them fairly."

The biggest problem with blanket licenses will be getting technology companies to collect a reasonable fee, or else convincing individuals to pay one. Consumers obviously value professional content: more U.S. households have cable television than broadband Internet connections, even though the former is more expensive. But the widespread availability of pirated content has changed consumers' attitudes, as have public interest groups aligned with the technology business.

"I like the idea of a voluntary license fee, but it's got to be for all content," says Gigi Sohn, president of Public Knowledge, which is partly funded by technology companies. "I think you have maybe one small fee—maybe $5—and it gets split up among various and sundry copyright holders."

That's laughably low; it would fund a smaller music business than the United States has now and leave nothing for movies, television, or any form of journalism. Charging more would be unfair, Sohn says, since it would raise Internet access bills. But many consumers are taking this content *already*—they're just not paying for it—and this content is what gives Internet access most of its value. Blanket licenses would better align the value of broadband Internet with its price, and eliminate unproductive lawsuits along the way.

Whatever Choruss's faults, some of its critics keep comparing it with an ideal system, rather than the considerably messier state of affairs we have now. As music sales continue to decline, difficult solutions could become more appealing. Ultimately, Griffin thinks the government might have to step in. "In relation to my experience, I now believe we may need a statutory approach," he says. "And I do think it's coming."

Like Formula 1 racing and Robbie Williams, the idea of a government-mandated blanket license seems appealing to Europeans in a way Americans may never understand. French politicians discussed a "global license" for all media before debating the HADOPI law, and the German Green and Social Democratic parties have proposed a similar idea called the "culture flat rate." As three-strikes laws become unpopular with young people, the idea of a blanket license becomes more difficult for politicians to dismiss.

"When in politics one is confronted with two options that both don't work one should look for a third one," said the German Green Party's Helga Trüpel. Speaking at a Berlin press conference in April 2009, the day after the French National Assembly approved an early version of the HADOPI law, Trüpel rejected both that approach and the idea that content should be free online and put her support behind a German blanket license for all media. She said an Institute of European Media Law study concluded that an online blanket license could conform to German and European copyright laws.[20]

Germany's Green Party added the culture flat rate to its official platform in 2007, partly to compete with the Pirate Party for the votes and attention of left-leaning young people. The idea came to them from Volker Grassmuck, a German sociologist active in the free culture movement, who took it in turn from Fisher's book, *Promises to Keep*. Grassmuck points out that Germany has solved problems with collective licensing before. In the 1960s, the German collecting society GEMA sued a company that made tape recorders—not cassettes, the old reel-to-reel models—for the right to license users to make copies of compositions. Since Germany's strict privacy laws would not allow companies to reveal who bought their products, legislators created a "private copying exception" that covered a limited number of duplicates for friends and family. Unlike fair use, which is left up to judicial interpretation, this is defined in law.

"Lawmakers addressed this by controlling what can be controlled and remunerating by a levy what can't be controlled," Grassmuck says. Because it couldn't determine how recorders were used, the German government added to the price of each machine a levy that is divided among rights holders. As technology developed, most Continental European countries eventually applied the same principle to a variety of devices with an alphabet soup of collecting agencies.

Like any European leftist, Grassmuck is skeptical of private solutions to what he sees as a public problem. He calls the Electronic Frontier Foundation's proposal for a voluntary license an "extreme neoliberal antistatist manifesto," since it leaves too much up to the market. He doesn't care for TDC Play either: what the company sees as an extra service, he sees as a way to tie in users. Like many online activists, he believes Internet service providers should compete only on price and steer away from providing additional services. The companies that invested most in the Internet infrastructure would essentially become utilities, while Google and other technology companies would be left almost unregulated.

The Green Party plan has problems as well, however. Left of Germany's Social Democratic Party, which itself leans left of America's Democrats, it does not inspire the confidence of executives in the technology or entertainment business. It has already discussed how to provide tax-subsidized media for the poor, even before it has come up with a workable formula to divide funds among the industries in question. "The artists are against it," admits Oliver Passek, spokesperson for the Green Party Working Group on Media Policy. "But the 'net citizens'"—German online activists—"are more important to the party."

In the past year, Trüpel has had a change of heart about whether any kind of blanket license will work after all. "According to my interpretation, this culture flat rate must be very expensive for everything that would be distributed—they said it would be more than €100 per month—and the Greens were only talking about €5 or €10," says Trüpel, who now favors a "digital rights fair trade" policy that would encourage private companies to make deals that don't involve litigation against consumers. "Consumers will never accept a compulsory flat rate where they will have to pay €100, and I don't want a state-run culture market in the EU and especially not in Germany."

A more realistic idea that has gained traction in the Social

Democratic Party is the "culture flat rate *mit Kontrahierungszwang*" —with compulsory licensing. Under this plan, the labels and the Internet service providers would negotiate a license fee for recorded music, with the government stepping in if they can't come to terms on a price. Like radio stations, Internet service providers would then be free to pursue any kind of business model they wanted, as long as they paid for the music on their networks. Some could offer music free to users, while others could charge for access, or even for specific track downloads.

"What we have here is a market failure, and by German legal logic the state is supposed to intervene," says Tim Renner, the former head of Universal Music Germany, who supports this idea. Under this plan, since Internet service providers would have to pay for the music on their networks, they would have a strong incentive to limit illegal file sharing. "The market would start working again," Renner says. "Then they would compete for customers, so you have two advantages for the consumer—good prices and better convenience." Renner's license plan would repair the market—not replace it—in a way that would open up opportunities for all kinds of businesses.

It's hard to negotiate a private blanket license deal until Internet service providers have an incentive to come to the table. For TDC, this came in the form of competition. But the broadband market in Denmark is more advanced than it is in most countries. The most obvious way to motivate companies in other markets is to make them take at least some responsibility for what users are doing on their networks.

"Legislators in Europe are moving in that direction anyway," says Paul Hitchman, co-founder and chief executive of Media Service Provider, a British company set up to run unlimited music streaming services for Internet service providers. "Three strikes is many things to many people, but it's absolutely doomed to fail unless it goes hand in hand with the delivery of new services. It's the alignment of interests that's important: The threat of imposing graduated response tends to bring the [Internet service providers] to the table and then the government brings the labels to the table."

Media Service Provider's first major project involves running the MusicHub service for the Irish Internet service provider Eircom. It's part of a deal that offers something to both sides. Eircom agreed to enforce antipiracy rules with a graduated response program, while the labels signed a deal that has Eircom pay them in order to offer free music streaming to its customers and sell downloads for less than Apple's iTunes store—€5.99 ($8.50) for 15 tracks a month.[21] Labels and artists get paid, and Eircom gets a service for its customers. But the path to this deal ran straight through a courtroom.

In January 2009, the Irish Recorded Music Association (IRMA), an organization that represents the major labels and Irish independents, sought an Irish High Court injunction to hold Eircom responsible for the copyright infringement that took place on its network. After three days, the two sides arrived at an out-of-court settlement that required Eircom to introduce a graduated-response program to notify infringers that it knew about their activities and, eventually, restrict their access in some way. (This could involve a reduction in speed or an interruption of service rather than a disconnection.) The agreement also required IRMA to negotiate with other Internet service providers to pursue the same policy, so Eircom wouldn't have a disadvantage.

"This was a stand-alone decision in Ireland, since our sales had gone through the floor," says IRMA's director general, Dick Doyle. Since widespread broadband access came to Ireland later than other European countries, its falloff in music sales was more sudden: label revenue fell 26 percent in 2009 alone. Doyle says that suing copyright infringers didn't help the situation.

Once the labels started talking to Eircom, they realized that a penalty for illegal behavior wouldn't change consumer habits unless it was paired with a reasonable legal alternative. "We said, rather than have a stick and no carrot, let's think about a deal we could do," says EMI Ireland's managing director, Willie Kavanagh. "The nice thing about the way we structured the deal is that the streaming is free to Eircom customers and they pay us, so it becomes part of their bundle for consumers."

In October 2010, when IRMA filed a case against UPC, one of Eircom's competitors, Justice Peter Charleton ruled that the company could not be held liable for secondary copyright infringement, since Ireland had not correctly adapted European Union copyright laws. For UPC, this was a technical victory at best: Charleton wrote that piracy "ruins the ability of a generation of creative people in Ireland, and elsewhere, to establish a viable living."[22]

Eircom initially worried it would be the only Internet service provider to enforce limits on piracy, but the company's head of content and services strategy, Mark Taylor, doesn't think the combination of enforcement with a legal alternative will drive customers away. "You would think that if Eircom implemented graduated response unilaterally, it would be suicide, but most of our customers are families and many of them are aligned with this policy," he says. "It's the teens and twentysomethings who have a philosophical objection to restrictions on the Internet. We want to change consumer behavior to using legal alternatives."

Hitchman hopes to provide services for more of these deals, and he hopes they'll get easier to set up as time goes on. So far, he's looking at small markets, in which labels might be willing to experiment, or ones where piracy has already become a devastating problem. But he thinks both labels and Internet service providers will study the Eircom deal to see if it cannibalizes traditional music sales. "Our big opportunity is if the terms of these deals become standard, or if we see a licensed wholesale market, where platforms like ours can just slot into Internet service providers," Hitchman says. But he also says the Eircom deal would have been difficult to negotiate without the legal case that preceded it.

By removing all responsibility for copyright infringement from Internet service providers, laws like the Digital Millennium Copyright Act allowed the Internet to flourish. But they also gave Internet service providers a perverse incentive to ignore the problems of the entertainment industry. If online companies have nothing to lose, they have no reason to negotiate. Any solution has to start with giving Internet service providers an incentive to reduce piracy without strengthening copyright so much that music labels and movie studios lose their incentive to come to terms. Both sides have to realize they can't get everything they want: Internet service providers can't blithely dismiss piracy, while labels have to start selling services as well as products.

"My dad, the union negotiator, told me that if both sides are unhappy, you made a good deal," Griffin says. "Until you give up your fantasy, you can't achieve your dreams."

CHAPTER 10

THE FUTURE OF THE FUTURE

CHOOSING COMMERCE OR CHAOS?

In big, bold letters—black, against a red background—the cover of the September 2010 issue of *Wired* declared, "The Web Is Dead." The accompanying article, written by the magazine's editor in chief, Chris Anderson, argued that "one of the most important shifts in the digital world has been the move from the wide-open Web to semiclosed platforms."[1] He was referring to the fact that online networks like Microsoft's Xbox Live and Apple's iPhone App Store are generating more data traffic at the expense of the Web.[2] If this trend continues, it could fundamentally change the balance of power between media and technology companies.

The Web we have known so far is an almost perfectly open platform, ungoverned by a central authority: anyone can put up a page, and any browser can access one. That has proved to be both its strength and its weakness. The same lack of barriers that makes it easy to disseminate media also makes it difficult to sell it, and, as Anderson also pointed out, the ease of generating Web pages has driven down the price of online advertising. This is leading many media companies to experiment with paywalls and more closed systems, such as iPhone apps, many of which are available only to those who pay to download them. Anderson wasn't the only one to notice this shift. The idea that the Internet would split into "walled gardens" goes back to *The Future of the Internet and How to Stop It*, a 2008 book by the Berkman Center professor Jonathan Zittrain, and it began to receive mainstream attention after a January 2010 Forrester Research report predicted the coming of the "Splinternet."[3]

Over the next decade, we will choose between two competing visions for the online world: media companies want the Internet to work more like cable television, while technology companies want cable to run more like the Internet. Just as the Web is open, cable is closed: broadcasting requires permission, and watching requires payment. Apple's iPhone operates much the same way, since apps must be approved for sale and, generally, purchased by users. (The iPhone can also access the Web, so it's not restricted to a closed system; it just favors one.) These kinds of partly controlled systems tend to make it much easier and more appealing to buy music or movies than to take them without paying. Piracy isn't impossible, but it is inconvenient—just like in the real world.

Google and the "Web 2.0" companies that have evolved to thrive on the wide-open Web are pushing to open cable television systems and mobile phone networks to the Internet as it exists today. Google has pushed the FCC to enact an AllVid proposal that would favor its Google TV platform,[4] and it supports groups that want to require companies like Apple to open the iPhone to its products.[5] These open systems give consumers more freedom and flexibility, but they also give Google more power, since it can cut through the clutter. Much like media conglomerates, technology companies want the government to keep communications networks just as they were when they were on top.

The Internet has been so open for so long that many people just assume its structure is the inevitable result of the technological advances that created it. That's not really the case. Technology makes certain things inevitable: broadband speeds will get faster, computers will get more powerful, and almost everything related to either one will get cheaper. But it doesn't dictate how engineers set up the resulting networks, much less how politicians regulate them. Those are our choices. And fully closed *or* fully open networks would be the worst two choices we could make.

Washington helped create the Internet as it exists today, by passing the Digital Millennium Copyright Act, letting the Internet operate freely across borders, and encouraging the growth of online commerce in a variety of ways. In next few years, a series of regulatory decisions coming to a head there and in other capitals will either lock in the status quo or open the possibility of change. Among the most important decisions are on "net neutrality": proposals that would forbid Internet service providers from favoring some services and sites or slowing down others. Other decisions involve how much control companies like Apple can exercise over how their devices interact with the Internet and whether the United States can block Web sites that violate its laws. Although online companies play up the idea of keeping the Internet "unregulated," establishing this openness would actually require regulating Internet service providers, device makers, and other companies. For all their talk of innovation, Google and other technology giants have the same agenda as the media companies and Internet service providers they lobby against: *regulation for thee but not for me.*

Online activists present the choice about our online future as one between control and creativity, but it's really about commerce or chaos. A completely closed system would indeed defeat the purpose of the Internet; it would limit both commerce and creativity. But so would an absolutely open one, where selling digital media—or anything that can be reduced to zeros and ones—would be almost impossible in the long run. We'd have a twenty-first-century communications infrastructure supporting a seventeenth-century economy, where artists need patrons and only physical items have value. That doesn't sound like progress.

In fact—although reports of its death have been greatly exaggerated—one reason for the Web's decline relative to the app world is the fact that it's hard to sell media there and even harder to make money giving it away. Condé Nast, which owns *Wired*, seems to agree. An iPad app of the magazine's June 2010 issue sold more than 100,000 copies—more than its print counterpart, for the same $4.99 price.[6] The magazine gets 70 percent of that, plus advertising revenue. And although apps based on subsequent issues sold fewer copies, publishers are still learning how to build appealing apps, and the iPad is still growing as a platform. Condé Nast saw so much potential in Apple's device that it made the *Wired* app designer, Scott Dadich, its executive director of digital magazine development. Suddenly, it seems, the future involves paying for stuff.

But that future can only come about if there's an effective way to make sure more stuff is paid for than taken. That means revisiting or interpreting the Digital Millennium Copyright Act to give Internet service providers, online locker services, and ad networks at least some responsibility for how their products are used. As Congress recognized at the time, it would be impractical for Internet service providers to have legal responsibility for everything they carry on their networks. But it seems increasingly irresponsible for them to do nothing. The way some Web sites and online locker services maintain willful ignorance about copyright infringement—arguing that it's someone else's problem—is no way to run a legitimate business. Giving safe harbor if they use a basic level of filtering, as YouTube does now, would be a reasonable compromise. This wouldn't slow innovation; it would encourage it. As pirate sites lost their unfair advantage, legitimate services would attract more investment and prosper. Online companies could try to make things better, not just cheaper.

Questions about the future of the online world are becoming more urgent as consumers connect televisions and other devices to the Internet. For now, film and television companies still count on a steady stream of revenue from cable, a closed system that makes piracy impractical. But devices like Google TV will increasingly bring the Internet into the living room—online locker services, Russian pirate movie sites, and all. In order to preserve the free-for-all that helps them thrive, technology companies are promoting regulations that would nearly forbid Internet service providers to stop them.[7] "We need to be conservative in this debate and preserve what has worked in driving this economy," Lawrence Lessig said at an April 2008 FCC hearing, "and what has worked is a neutral network."[8]

But this status quo works far better for technology companies than for creators. If a country had a market where about a quarter of all commerce was illegal and the rest was dominated by a few large companies, no one would call that economy a success. You can't have a functioning economy without a market, you can't have a market without some form of property rights, and those rights don't mean anything if they can't be enforced. Do we really want to risk destroying a centuries-old market for cultural products to ensure that the Internet can continue to work the way it did in 1995?

Google and the public advocacy organizations allied with it promote the idea of an "open Internet," which refers to several loosely intertwined ideas, including net neutrality and an absence of barriers to the exchange of data. The goal of an open Internet is promoted as a progressive idea, and the phrase is filled with positive associations: After all, who doesn't want to be *open*? Public advocacy groups say this openness is the key to preserving free expression online, but it allows corporations as well as people to act as they wish, which isn't progressive at all. On an Internet of sites that exchange data without restrictions, the information that wants to be free could include a record of everything you've ever done online.

These notions of open and closed aren't absolutes, of course; it makes more sense to think of them as points on a continuum. Both have their advantages. Linux, the open-source operating system, has both flexibility and power. *Wikipedia*, the ultimate open media product, is a fantastic tool for accessing information. And crowdsourcing journalism that involves combing through massive amounts of data has been very effective.[9]

Closed systems seem better suited to commerce, though. It's one reason DVDs became such a moneymaker for Hollywood studios. It's why video game publishers have cut investment in PC titles to focus on closed consoles like Microsoft's Xbox 360 and Nintendo's Wii. (The most successful PC game of recent years, *World of Warcraft*, is a closed system of its own; it charges a subscription fee.) And it's why apps sell much better for Apple's iPhone platform than for Google's Android operating system.[10] The online world needs to support both.

To some in the technology business, this sort of thinking is nothing short of sacrilege. In the December 2010 issue of *Scientific American*, Tim Berners-Lee, the computer scientist credited with developing the World Wide Web, wrote "a call for continued open standards."[11] He suggested that Facebook shouldn't keep its data behind walls and said that "the tendency for magazines, for example, to produce smartphone 'apps' rather than Web apps is disturbing, because that material is off the Web. You can't bookmark it or e-mail a link to a page within it. You can't tweet it." But if the Web was *entirely* open—to the point that any site could present the text or video from any other site—you also couldn't *sell* it. In the long run, that means you couldn't continue to produce it either.

In the short term, the move toward partly closed platforms will be bad news for consumers, who naturally want to pay as little as possible for the media they consume. But if media gets more expensive, much of the resulting revenue will be invested in making better products. That goes for digital media as well. News Corporation spent a reported $30 million to develop the *Daily*, its multimedia newspaper for the iPad, because it believed a product it could sell would justify the investment. Compare that with AOL's free Patch community journalism sites, which depend on overworked reporters churning out short articles filled with keywords to place high in Google's search results. The first needs to deliver a product readers will pay for—the second just has to draw the attention of as many people as possible.

To understand how technology executives see issues involving open platforms, remember that their perspective is informed by Apple's 1980s struggle with Microsoft for the personal computer business. Then, as now, Steve Jobs wanted to control his products, so he declined to license the Macintosh operating system software to other computer makers. Since Microsoft didn't make machines, it made deals to supply its operating system software to every PC clone company it could. As more companies began making computers that used Intel chips and Microsoft's Windows operating system, competition drove down prices, "Wintel" machines dominated the industry, and Apple became an also-ran in the business it invented. Open beat closed. Then, after the Internet's open standards drew audiences away from walled gardens like America Online, it became an article of faith in the technology world that open systems always win.

But the open systems that offer freedom in the short term can also stifle innovation in the long run. Just look at the PC market. As Wintel computers grew increasingly alike, the companies that made them waged brutal price wars, to the point that many went out of business, the rest have thin profit margins, and few spend much money on research and development. All the profit in the PC market went to Intel and Microsoft, which created standards, set prices, and watched money roll in. Both companies were penalized by the European Commission for anticompetitive practices.

Google wants to be to the online world what Microsoft was to the PC: the company that dominates an open ecosystem by providing most of the value and uses that power as leverage to get an advantage in other businesses. The "Quadroid" platform—Qualcomm chips and Android software—is already becoming a standard for mobile phones.[12] Google's strength in search gives it such an economic advantage in new businesses that it's hard for other companies to compete; no other mobile company can sell ads with so much knowledge about users, for example. Although Google "may represent open systems," as Michael Wolff wrote in an article than ran with Anderson's in *Wired*, "it came to almost completely control that openness. It's difficult to imagine another industry so thoroughly subservient to one player. In the Google model, there is one distributor of movies, which also owns all the theaters."[13]

Many academics believe otherwise. In April 2010, when Apple introduced the iPad, the New America Foundation fellow Tim Wu—who coined the term "net neutrality"—wrote in *Slate* that Steve Jobs's hostility to the hacker ethic made Apple "a self-professed revolutionary that is closely allied with establishment forces like the entertainment conglomerates and the telecommunications industry."[14] (The real rebels work for Google!) Around the same time, Wu participated in the New America Foundation panel called "Why Your Cell Phone Is So Terrible," and the explanation had a lot to do with closed systems.[15] In his 2010 book, *The Master Switch: The Rise and Fall of Information Empires*, Wu shows how AT&T used its monopoly over the U.S. telephone system to prevent innovation until a 1968 FCC decision held that consumers could connect devices made by other companies, including modems and fax machines. Wu believes the Internet succeeded at least partly because it didn't have such restrictions, and to some extent he's right. But does that mean every communications network needs to work the same way?

Many consumers have come to prefer Apple products, and the company's walled-garden strategy has made it the most valuable technology company in the world.[16] When the iPad came out, some online activists slammed it as a high-priced toy because it couldn't be used in ways Apple didn't intend.[17] But the simplicity that technology true believers tend to regard as a bug, many consumers see as a feature. It's easy to dismiss Apple's walled garden as a kind of sanitized online Disney World. But it's worth remembering that many people really *like* Disney World, and they might *want* a high-priced toy.

Media companies also feel more comfortable with platforms that have a built-in bias toward legitimate commerce. Apple's control over the iPhone and iPad app stores means a program that makes copying movies quick and easy would have a hard time getting distribution. (On Google's Android platform—which powers Google TV as well as mobile phones—it would be much easier.) But helping to create a functioning online market for entertainment is the kind of behavior that gets Apple branded as part of the "establishment."

In the United States, Republican victories in the 2010 election make it unlikely that the FCC will enact very strict net neutrality rules in the near future,[18] although the agency voted for a limited version of these regulations in December 2010.[19] (The fight isn't over: Senator Maria Cantwell [D-Wash.] introduced a bill to broaden the rules in January 2011,[20] and Verizon filed a legal challenge.[21]) At this point, though, so many consumers have become accustomed to the Internet being open that at least some degree of net neutrality will probably remain the de facto standard, whether or not it becomes law.

The larger questions involve how to enforce any kind of law on the Internet, as well as whether the same ones will apply to mobile and television devices. Companies like Spotify—which have trouble selling online music subscriptions at least partly because the same material is available for free—have an easier time doing business on mobile platforms that impose some limits or favor legitimate software. The same is true of other devices. On a PC, Netflix has to compete with illegal movie streaming sites; on an Apple TV, it's so much easier to use Netflix that the choice is obvious. (As in the real world, piracy is possible—just enough of a hassle that fewer people bother.) Forcing smartphones and Internet TV devices to access the open Internet without preferring certain apps, as Google would like to see them do, wouldn't just hurt the entertainment business; it would undermine technology companies like Netflix and Spotify.

Even the "open" Web will be regulated to some extent. "I actually don't believe that responsible government officials mean that open access means the right to break the law or to do anything people want to do on the Internet," says NBC Universal's Rick Cotton. "Particularly when the Internet is the platform on which policy makers want to see most communications in the U.S. take place. It has to follow that the rule of law needs to exist. So there's a broad policy discussion that needs to take place and hasn't yet."

The longer the current online chaos lasts, the more bitter the fight between creators and copyright infringers gets. In December 2008, the RIAA announced it would stop suing individual uploaders in favor of finding a way to cut piracy by cooperating with Internet service providers.[22] But a few small film studios and porn producers have retained lawyers to file copyright infringement lawsuits against individuals, seemingly as a moneymaking venture. From early 2010 to January 2011, a law firm called the U.S. Copyright Group filed almost 100,000 lawsuits against U.S. residents who had uploaded films such as *The Hurt Locker* and *Far Cry*, and then sent letters offering to settle for $1,500.[23] While creators have the right to seek redress for infringement, these mass suits are turning the justice system into a reverse lottery that addresses widespread losses by trying to collect absurd amounts of money from an unlucky few. Several organizations, including the Electronic Frontier Foundation (EFF), have lined up to help fight the suits, most of which will probably end up being dismissed for jurisdictional or technical reasons.

Copyright laws do need to be revised to bring some order to the Internet; we need shorter terms of protection, a way to take quicker action against commercial-scale pirates, and less draconian damages for individual infringers. Specifically, a small-claims court for copyright infringement would allow independent artists to assert their rights without burdening the court system and distinguish casual downloaders from moneymaking operations. To deal with the former, it's much fairer to sue 100,000 illegal downloaders for $50 each than it is to sue 50 users for $100,000 each, and the law should make that possible. Making such suits an unpleasant but routine event—like getting a speeding ticket—would cut down on infringement as well.

Passing new laws will be difficult: copyright holders know the current level of potential damages gives them negotiating leverage with technology companies, and online activists still hope to legalize file sharing. For the near future at least, the fight will be over how—or even *if*—the copyright laws we already have will be enforced. And for all the Obama administration's admiration for Google, Hollywood has enormous influence with the Democrats, and Vice President Joe Biden has always championed the protection of intellectual property.

In June 2010, Biden threw down the gauntlet at a press conference and said "piracy is theft."[24] He appeared with Victoria Espinel, a former negotiator in the Office of the U.S. Trade Representative, whom Obama had appointed the first "copyright czar."[25] In a report released that day, Espinel introduced a strategy to fight online piracy and trafficking in counterfeit goods that focuses on interagency cooperation and an insistence on seeing infringement—along with patent and trademark violations—as an issue that negatively affects several sectors of the U.S. economy.[26] (Formally, Espinel holds the title of U.S. intellectual property enforcement coordinator, with a purview that extends to patents, trademarks, and counterfeit goods off-line as well as on the Internet.) Espinel's report also recommended cooperating more extensively with foreign governments and, in a significant nod to fair use, asserted that "strong intellectual property enforcement efforts should be focused on stopping those stealing the work of others, not those who are appropriately building upon it."[27]

Espinel, who has won respect in both Hollywood and Silicon Valley—no small feat—doesn't think we have to choose between the media business and the Internet. "One of the things that I'm trying to avoid is having people view policies—net neutrality is a good example—as creating a conflict with intellectual property enforcement," she says. "There's this view that the administration has two policy goals—one is to keep the Internet open and accessible, and the other is to enforce intellectual property laws—and one of those needs to be sacrificed for the benefit of the other. That's not my view, and I think we should be able to move forward and accomplish both of those goals, and I think that's true in a number of areas."

But some technology executives seem to resent the idea that copyright laws will be enforced at all. Many mocked Espinel's report, which said movie and video piracy cost the U.S. economy $20.5 billion a year. (The number is probably exaggerated, but even a quarter of that would be way too much.) Michael Arrington, the founder of the *TechCrunch* blog, wrote about an off-the-record meeting he attended between Espinel and several top technology executives and complained that "Espinel has a single agenda when it comes to copyright issues."[28] But that agenda is *enforcing the law*.[29] According to his post, Espinel reminded him, "My job title *is* Intellectual Property *Enforcement* after all."

That enforcement became much more visible at the end of June, when U.S. Immigration and Customs Enforcement seized the domain names of nine Web sites offering pirated copies of films still playing in cinemas.[30] (The National Intellectual Property Rights Coordination Center works closely with Customs and oversees enforcement against counterfeit products, as well as large-scale copyright infringement.) Although some of the sites were hosted in other countries, the government went to their domain name registrars and had their addresses redirect to an intimidating-looking image that read, "This domain name has been seized by ICE—Homeland Security Investigations, pursuant to a seizure warrant issued by a United States District Court." Immigration and Customs Enforcement also seized assets from several PayPal accounts. The idea of Operation in Our Sites—get it?—was to disrupt criminal operations in foreign countries by working with legitimate companies based in the United States. And although it's hard to know how much of an effect this had—some of the operations went up again at new addresses—it was done without suing any individuals.

There have been more seizures since then, as well as a sense—hopeful on one side, despondent on the other—that this could provide a blueprint for a way to target commercial-scale piracy. In September 2010, Senator Patrick Leahy (D-Vt.) introduced the Combating Online Infringement and Counterfeits Act (COICA), which would authorize the U.S. attorney general to seize the domain names of sites that are "dedicated to infringing activities." (The sites could still be reached by typing in an IP address directly or through a virtual private network that first connects to a computer outside the United States, but most people probably wouldn't bother.) It would also require U.S. banks and ad companies to stop doing business with them. While the law wouldn't stop dedicated pirates—who are lost to the entertainment industry as consumers anyway—it could reduce traffic to the worst offenders, like the Pirate Bay.

To the Electronic Frontier Foundation, "COICA looks like another misguided gift to a shortsighted industry whose first instinct with respect to the Internet is to try to break it."[31] (One could also say that the current state of affairs is a misguided gift to a few giant technology companies whose first instinct with respect to culture is to try to take it.) The organization said the bill would crush online freedom of speech, but it's hard to imagine the First Amendment value of a Russian pirate site like ZML.com, which sold subscription access to movies still in cinemas. (Users complained it overcharged their credit cards, which just goes to show there's no honor among thieves.[32]) If anything, under the principle that copyright is "the engine of free expression," widespread piracy *endangers* free speech by reducing the incentive of artists to create new work.[33]

Several groups, including the Electronic Frontier Foundation and Public Knowledge, also suggested the bill would signal to other countries that the United States approves of censorship. But there's a significant difference between selling pirated copies of *Iron Man 2* and questioning China's policies in Tibet. And if China hasn't been convinced to change its online censorship policy by a decade of diplomatic entreaties and an Olympics the whole world was watching, does anyone *really* believe it would do so just because the United States allows pirates to sell movies illegally?

The Senate Judiciary Committee approved the bill in November, but Senator Ron Wyden (D-Ore.) blocked it. "The collateral damage of this statute could be American innovation, American jobs, and a secure Internet," Wyden said, referring to fears that interfering with the domain name system would destabilize the online world.

"We were a little bit surprised," says NBC Universal's Cotton, who pushed for the bill, about the amount of opposition it met with. "But when you look at the objections and you look at the conduct [of the sites], there's a big difference." When Cotton talks about the bill, he starts by showing some of the sites that might be affected, which consist *entirely* of illegal copies of music and movies. "Free speech is a complete red herring," he says. "This is about sites that are simply stealing. When you start discussions that way, you don't get to a discussion about free speech."

Whether that's entirely true could depend on how the law is written and interpreted. COICA definitely needs to define more narrowly the circumstances under which a site can be blocked, and there are valid concerns that it will interfere with the domain name referral system used on the Internet. But it would set an important precedent that countries can enforce their own laws within their own borders, and it would do so by penalizing commercial offenders, not teenagers looking for a free movie. What really endangers American innovation and jobs is the status quo, which is why several unions supported COICA.

If the lawmaking process stalls, a private agreement could accomplish some of the same goals. In 2008, the RIAA and the MPAA started negotiating with Internet service providers to create a system that would warn consumers who use file-sharing services to download copyrighted material that their behavior is illegal, or at least against their service agreements. If the deal is completed, it would not call for enforcement as strict as the Digital Economy Act does in the U.K., according to several executives familiar with the progress of the negotiations in early 2011: Internet access could not be limited before the sixth notice, users could ask for an independent review, and penalties would probably involve a cut in speed rather than outright disconnection.

In summer 2008, Andrew Cuomo, then New York State attorney general, pressured Verizon, Sprint, and Time Warner Cable to block access to message boards and Web sites they hosted that contained child pornography. Universal Music executives subsequently contacted Cuomo to point out that similar material was also being traded on the file-sharing service LimeWire. So Cuomo put some pressure on Internet service providers to start negotiating with labels on a way to limit file-sharing, both of illegal pornography and of copyrighted works. The MPAA and the National Cable & Telecommunications Association joined the talks, which seemed so promising that at the end of 2008 the RIAA announced it would abandon its suits against individual infringers, which had run their course anyway.

As of early 2011, no agreement had been announced. Even if the deal never happens, however, the relationship between media companies and Internet service providers has fundamentally changed. For a decade and a half, they had found themselves on opposite sides of an issue: the same piracy that hurt labels and studios made broadband Internet access more valuable to consumers. But now that most consumers already have broadband, Internet service providers want to control costs by limiting the activities of the small number of downloaders who account for a disproportionate share of data traffic.[34] And the service providers and media companies have common foes in Google and other technology companies that champion net neutrality. Although the government has not been involved in these negotiations, the White House is said to approve, at least to some degree. "It's the beginning of a shift to responsible companies acting responsibly," says one executive involved.

Not everyone wants that. On a fundamental level, some online activists and the companies that fund them are so attached to the idea of a perfectly open Internet that they won't accept any action that protects the rights of creators. Remember that the Electronic Frontier Foundation was co-founded by John Perry Barlow, who told the governments of the world, "You have no sovereignty where we gather."[35] In May 2010, the organization made the very reasonable suggestion that creators need to stop suing individual copyright infringers.[36] Then, a few months later, it objected to COICA on the grounds that it constituted censorship.

So what, exactly, *should* creators do to enforce their rights? And if the answer is nothing, how can any kind of legitimate market develop online? It would be both ironic and tragic if the United States finally developed an information economy only to find that information isn't actually worth anything.

The future isn't what it used to be.

Back in 1993, when Bruce Lehman began to think about crafting a copyright policy for the online world, almost everyone predicted the information superhighway would be a huge boon to the culture business. Good jobs would be created by new opportunities to sell music, movies, and other forms of entertainment still being developed. Independent artists would be able to sell their work without studios or labels. Media would improve in quality, as well as quantity.

The Internet has brought forth many wonders, from the silly to the sublime to the skateboarding bulldog on YouTube (which is both). Newspapers no longer have a monopoly on serious journalism, and their mistakes are promptly challenged. Anyone can create culture instead of simply consuming it. It's never been easier to distribute creative work. At the same time, it's never been harder to get paid for it.

The Internet has been an impressive engine of economic growth. But a great deal of that growth has gone to a small number of technology companies. They depend on informative journalism to make their search engines useful, and they depend on compelling music and movies to make digital players worth owning. But the companies that fund those cultural products have never been in worse shape. They're cutting jobs, and with them the ability to create and market new work. Those search engines and players won't be nearly as valuable without them.

The current situation is slowly robbing the Internet of its potential. Rather than encourage innovation and excellence, it rewards cost cutting and crowdsourcing. The effects can be underwhelming. In his book *You Are Not a Gadget: A Manifesto*, the computer scientist Jaron Lanier points out that two of the most widely acclaimed results of the remarkable technological advances of the Internet are *Wikipedia* and Linux, a free encyclopedia and a new version of the Unix operating system.

We can do better.

No one believes that piracy could be stopped by a law like COICA or an agreement between media companies and Internet service providers. And even stopping it completely wouldn't solve all of the culture businesses' problems. But regulations like these, whether private or public, would allow a working market to emerge. Creators would sell, consumers would buy, and both would benefit. Music and movie companies will probably never enjoy the kinds of profit margins they did in the 1990s, but they could return to stability by persuading creators that they still have value in a world of digital distribution. Artists would have the option of working with big companies or making their own way in an online economy that allowed them to do business, not just take donations.

In a functioning market, online media would get better, not just cheaper. And this, in turn, would fuel the growth of more technology companies. This wouldn't break the Internet; it would help it live up to its potential.

ACKNOWLEDGMENTS

As I point out elsewhere, the enthusiasm over digital technology has made it fashionable to suggest that authors can write books on their own, in their spare time. Maybe so. But I wouldn't have been able to write this one without the support of a publisher and agent, and it would have been very different without the editing and extra reporting that vastly improved the manuscript.

My agent, David Kuhn, believed in this idea when it was just notes on a napkin at City Bakery, and it would have stayed there were it not for his enthusiasm and dedication. I was fortunate that this book went to Doubleday, where senior editor Kris Puopolo believed in it from the beginning and never lost faith during a hectic home stretch. Doubleday editor in chief Bill Thomas also saw this project's potential, and assistant editor Stephanie Bowen helped make sure it stayed in one piece.

Several friends and colleagues provided perspective along the way. Michael Hogan provided an invaluable sounding board. Melissa Maerz, Marty Beiser, and John Raeside helped me separate signal from noise and streamline prose. At various points, I also benefitted from the suggestions of Vanessa Grigoriadis, Greg Lindsay, Ethan Brown, Gabe Kahn, and, especially, Ann Donahue.

Kara Cutruzzula provided invaluable research, a sharp eye, and a sympathetic ear. Jennifer Netherby and Adam Auriemma came in at the end to help out with extra reporting and fact-checking that let me meet my deadline – or at least come closer to it than I otherwise might have. All three are talented journalists in their own right. The legal eagle-eyed

Terry Hart, who runs a smart blog about copyright at www.copyhype. com, read the manuscript to look for mistakes and helped me understand some thorny issues. Tim Caspar Boehm, Julian Sancton, Scott Sayare, and Helienne Lindvall helped with foreign reporting, and Kaitlin Paulson reported on an event I couldn't cover.

I spoke to more than a hundred sources for this book, and it would be difficult to thank them all. But a few went beyond the call of duty to help out: Cary Sherman, Michael Fricklas, Rick Cotton, Ellen Seidler, Daniel Raimer, Fred von Lohman, Michael Nash, Danny Goldberg, Mitch Singer, Mark Teitell, Friz Attaway, Paul Aiken, Andrew Bridges, and Marybeth Peters. David Bakula at Nielsen SoundScan helped out with valuable statistics, and Jane Ginsburg at Columbia Law School provided a nuanced perspective on issues that are usually reduced to talking points. Andy Kim, a great friend, was kind enough to help me unravel the complexities of the modern movie business.

I started exploring many of the ideas in this book in stories for other publications. I learned much of what I know about business reporting from Bruce Headlam at *The New York Times*, who has a better sense for what makes a story than anyone I know. Evelyn McDonnell gave me the space and the freedom to explore some of these ideas at Moli.com. And I learned a great deal about the music business from my colleagues at *Billboard*, especially Bill Werde, Lou Hau, Cortney Harding, Chris Walsh, David Prince, and Ben Sheffner.

Over the course of my career, I've been lucky enough to learn a lot from some talented editors and writers, including Michael Caruso, Michael Hainey, Mark Kemp, Larry Carlat, Alan Light, Caroline Miller, Jason Fine, and Charles Mann. Longer ago than I'd like to admit, Abe Peck taught me everything I know about magazines, and much else besides. Anthony DeCurtis has always been a great mentor and a good friend.

As I worked on this book, I got a place to stay in Los Angeles from Allan Levine and Kathleen McQuade and encouragement from Tricia Romano, Duff McDonald, Laura Levine, and Jordan Frank. As always, Sia Michel was a valuable source of support and advice. And Joe Spiegel helped me move, hung out when I was sick, and generally kept me from going nuts.

My parents raised me with a love for learning and a respect for books (and my dad found copy errors that everyone else missed). Nina Ida Levine, who arrived as I was writing, provided the most adorable distractions ever, and I'm grateful for every single one of them. Most of all, Kerstin convinced me I could do this, put up with me while I did, and continues to inspire me.

NOTES

A NOTE ON SOURCES

In the course of writing *Free Ride*, I conducted more than a hundred interviews, examined scores of legal and financial documents, and read most of the books that have been written about the online media business and copyright law. The book also draws from the decade and a half I've spent reporting on how the Internet changed the music business, as well as living through the way it is redefining journalism.

I conducted all the interviews between November 2009 and January 2011. Most sources spoke on the record. Due to language barriers, I hired researchers to help with a few interviews, and I note when that was the case; they also helped translate articles and documents.

The financial impact of online piracy is notoriously difficult to measure, and the exaggerations of most Hollywood-funded studies have become a running joke. (It's worth pointing out, however, that studies funded or conducted by opponents of copyright are no less ridiculous.) So I relied only on studies that seemed sound, and I explain my thinking in the notes below. (For example, I refer to an Envisional study funded by NBC Universal because it's based on underlying data provided by technology companies.) Although it's hard to quantify piracy exactly, its effects are easy to see.

INTRODUCTION
THE ONLINE FREE-FOR-ALL

1. Rachel Layne, "GE Exiting NBC Universal Brings Immelt Cash, Scrutiny," Bloomberg News Service, December 3, 2009.

2. Bill Carter, "Fox Erodes NBC's Hold on Young Viewership," *New York Times*, March 3, 2003.

3. General Electric did not break out financial figures for NBC Universal, but the *Times* got the number from a source familiar with its financial results. Tim Arango, "NBC's Slide to Troubled Punch Line," *New York Times*, January 16, 2010.

4. Under the terms of the proposed deal, Comcast would pay $6.5 billion in cash and merge $7.25 billion in cable assets with NBC Universal to create a new entity; it would own 51 percent and have the option to buy out GE's stake in eight years.

5. Sharon Waxman, "Comcast: It's a Brave New World, and Cable Runs It," TheWrap.com, December 3, 2009.

6. John Biggs, "A Video Clip Goes Viral, and a TV Network Wants to Control It," *New York Times*, February 20, 2006.

7. "Top 10 Most Pirated TV Shows on BitTorrent," *TorrentFreak* (blog), May 5, 2009.

8. Brooks Barnes and Michael Cieply, "In Hollywood, Grappling with Studios' Lost Clout," *New York Times*, January 18, 2010.

9. Stephen Morris and Anne-Sylvaine Chassany, "Hands Interested in EMI for Less Than Citigroup Seeks at Auction," *Bloomberg Businessweek*, February 10, 2011.

10. Said by the *Washington Post*'s executive editor, Marcus Brauchli. Howard Kurtz, "Washington Post Shutters Last U.S. Bureaus," *Washington Post*, November 24, 2009.

11. According to Forrester Research, total revenue from recording sales and licensing declined from $14.6 billion in 1999 to $6.3 billion in 2009.

12. *State of the News Media 2010* (Pew Research Center Publications, March 15, 2010).

13. From an Electronic Frontier Foundation white paper by Fred von Lohmann, *A Better Way Forward: Voluntary Collective Licensing of Music File Sharing* (April 2008).

14. According to data from IHS Screen Digest, an independent analyst firm that covers the media business.

15. *Technical Report: An Estimate of Infringing Use of the Internet* (Cambridge, U.K.: Envisional, January 2011).

16. *New Media, Old Media: How Blogs and Social Media Agendas Relate and Differ from Traditional Press* (Pew Research Center Publications, May 23, 2010).

17. Ed Felten, "Census of Files Available via BitTorrent," *Freedom to Tinker* (blog), January 29, 2010.

18. Richard MacManus, "Top 10 YouTube Videos of All Time," Readwriteweb. com, December 7, 2010. The list includes two by Eminem and one each by Justin Bieber, Lady Gaga, Shakira, Pitbull, and Miley Cyrus. (Cyrus has a recording contract with Disney, which is not technically one of the four major labels, but I counted it as one for this purpose.) Another two involve cute babies.

19. As of February 1, 2011, Apple's market cap was $317.9 billion, Microsoft's $239.5 billion, and Google's $151.8 billion.

20. From Steve Jobs's Stanford University Commencement address, June 12, 2005.

21. Edwin McDowell, "Publishing: The Computer Software Race Is On," *New York Times*, April 22, 1983.

22. Anderson, *Free*, p. 173.

23. Auletta, *Googled*, p. 125.

24. One definition: "A person or organization who benefits from a public good but neither provides it nor contributes to the cost of collective provision." John Black, Nigar Hashimzade, and Gareth Myles, *Oxford Dictionary of Economics*, 3rd ed. (New York: Oxford University Press, 2009).

25. Anthony DeRosa, "The Death of Platforms," *Soup* Tumblr, January 17, 2011.

26. This is discussed in chapter 3.

27. Stephen E. Siwek, *Copyright Industries in the U.S. Economy: The 2003–2007 Report* (prepared for the International Intellectual Property Alliance, June 2009).

28. Estimated by the media business analyst Rick Edmonds; see Olga Kharif, "The Online Experiments That Could Help Newspapers," *Bloomberg Businessweek*, March 8, 2009.

CHAPTER ONE: HOW CONGRESS CREATED
YOUTUBE—AND MEDIA'S BIG PROBLEM

1. "Musical Myopia, Digital Dystopia: New Media and Copyright Reform," hosted by McGill University's Centre for Intellectual Property Policy and the Schulich School of Music, March 23, 2007. Quotations taken from conference video.

2. Title I of the Digital Millennium Copyright Act, the WIPO Copyright and Performances and Phonograms Treaties Implementation Act, makes it illegal to "circumvent a technological measure that effectively controls access to a work" or "manufacture, import, offer to the public, provide, or otherwise traffic in" something primarily designed or promoted for that purpose. The law also includes exceptions, as well as a rule-making process under which more can be created.

3. Title II of the Digital Millennium Copyright Act, the Online Copyright Infringement Liability Limitation Act, outlines a Transitory Network Communications Safe Harbor, a System Caching Safe Harbor, and an Information Location Tools Safe Harbor. The most relevant part of the law has been section 512(c), which offers a Safe Harbor Provision for Online Storage as long as the service provider does not receive "a financial benefit directly attributable to the infringing activity," have "actual knowledge" of infringing activity or knowledge of "facts or circumstances from which infringing activity is apparent"—a so-called red flag. The law also includes several other provisions that have not been as important.

4. "In many respects, he plays that role in a de facto way," Secretary of Commerce Ron Brown said, as quoted in Teresa Riordan, "Even in a 'Big Tent,' Little Insults, Little Compromises," *New York Times*, May 29, 1994.

5. Under the Copyright Act of 1790, U.S. copyright lasted for fourteen years, with a second fourteen-year term available to those who registered for it. The Copyright Act of 1976 extended the term to the life of the author, plus fifty years, or seventy-five years for works owned by corporations, such as films. The Copyright Term Extension Act of 1998 extended that term even further—and set off an anti-copyright backlash that continues today.

6. Technically, in this example, copyright is a monopoly granted to Bruce Springsteen, who has chosen to enter into a contract with Columbia. But the ability of artists to grant and license their copyrights makes it practical for companies to invest in them.

7. *Sony Corp. of America v. Universal City Studios Inc.*, 464 U.S. 417 (1984).

8. *Home Recording of Copyrighted Works: Hearings Before the Subcommittee on Courts, Civil Liberties, and the Administration of Justice of the House Judiciary Committee*, 97th Cong., 2nd sess. (April 12, 1982) (Jack Valenti testimony).

9. These are the basic principles of a very complicated legal doctrine. Although fair use is codified in the Copyright Act of 1976, it depends mostly on judicial precedent.

10. *Nimmer on Copyright* was written by Melville Nimmer and is periodically updated by David. Although lawyers see these issues differently, David Nimmer is one of the country's foremost authorities on copyright law.

11. *Universal City Studios Inc. v. Eric Corley*, 273 F.3d 429 (2d Cir. 2001).

12. The Defense Advanced Research Projects Agency (DARPA) played a key role in the development of the Advanced Research Projects Agency Network (ARPANET), an early network that became a precursor to the Internet. It also funded most of the research behind the TCP/IP protocol at the heart of the Internet. And

from 1986 to 1995, the National Science Foundation ran an Internet "backbone" that handled massive amounts of traffic between large networks.

13. The 1998 Internet Tax Freedom Act, which has been extended until 2014.

14. *XPLORA1: Peter Gabriel's Secret World*, developed by Real World Studios and published by MacPlay. At the time, this was a *big deal*.

15. The use of the past tense is deliberate, since this could change. In October 2009, Senator Patrick Leahy introduced the Performance Rights Act, which would require traditional radio stations to pay the owners of recordings and the artists who perform on them.

16. *Religious Technology Center v. Netcom On-Line Communication Services, Inc.*, 907 F. Supp. 1361 (N.D. Cal. 1995).

17. *Fonovisa Inc. v. Cherry Auction Inc.* , 76 F.3d 259 (9th Cir. 1996). In this case, the court held a flea market liable for the actions of vendors selling pirated copies of albums on the Latin music label Fonovisa.

18. Pamela Samuelson, "The Copyright Grab," *Wired*, January 1996.

19. Barlow wrote songs with Dead guitarist Bob Weir, including "Cassidy," "Hell in a Bucket," and "Feel Like a Stranger." He didn't perform with the band.

20. John Perry Barlow, "A Declaration of the Independence of Cyberspace" (February 8, 1996). Barlow has the same Quirky Approach to Capitalization as the Founding Fathers.

21. *Harper & Row Publishers Inc. et al. v. Nation Enterprises et al*, 471 U.S. 539 (1985).

22. On July 17, 1997, Howard Coble (R-N.C.) introduced bill H.R. 2180 to limit secondary liability; on July 29, 1997, he also introduced H.R. 2281 to implement the WIPO Copyright Treaty. On July 31, 1997, Senator Hatch introduced S. 1121 to implement the WIPO Copyright Treaty. On September 3, 1997, Senator John Ashcroft (R-Mo.) introduced S. 1146 to limit secondary liability.

23. *Hearing of the Courts and Intellectual Property Subcommittee of the House Judiciary Committee*, 105th Cong., 1st. sess. (September 16, 1997).

24. This became H.R. 2281, the Digital Millennium Copyright Act.

25. This became S. 2037, the Digital Millennium Copyright Act.

26. The DeCSS code was released online by Jon Lech Johansen, who became known as DVD Jon. He wrote it with several online collaborators who preferred to remain anonymous.

27. Tim Wu, "Does YouTube Really Have Legal Problems?" *Slate*, October 26, 2006.

28. Kevin Delaney, "YouTube Magic: Now You See It, Now You Don't," *Wall Street Journal*, August 8, 2007.

29. Viacom's Statement of Undisputed Facts in Support of its Motion for Partial Summary Judgment, *Viacom Intl. Inc., et al v. YouTube Inc. et al*, No 07-CV-02103, items 57, 104 (S.D.N.Y. filed March 18, 2010).

30. Officially, it's the Directive 2001/29/EC of the European Parliament and of the Council of 22 May 2001.

CHAPTER TWO: FACING THE MUSIC:
HOW THE INTERNET DEVASTATED THE MUSIC BUSINESS

1. Goodman, *Fortune's Fool*, pp. 132, 133.

2. According to a study released on May 15, 2000, by the now-defunct research company Webnoize, 73 percent of U.S. college students surveyed reported using Napster at least once a month.

3. Goodman, *Fortune's Fool*, p. 131.

4. Ibid., p. 132.

5. According to Forrester Research.

6. *A&M Records Inc. et al. v. Napster Inc.* , 114 F. Supp. 2d 896 (N.D. Cal. 2000).

7. Menn, *All the Rave*, p. 100. The document in question, written in October 1999, came out in litigation, during the discovery process.

8. Complaint, *A&M Records v. Napster.*

9. "Napster quietly paid Chuck D $100,000 and made the most of his endorsement, offering $5,000 for the best pro-Napster lyric written to accompany 'donated' music by Public Enemy." Menn, *All the Rave*, p. 136.

10. The bill was the Intellectual Property and Communications Omnibus Reform Act of 1999, enacted on November 29, 1999.

11. Bill Holland, "New Work-for-Hire Law to Be Examined: The Arguments from Both Sides," *Billboard*, May 20, 2000.

12. The 1976 Copyright Act gives authors and some heirs the right to "terminate" their grant of copyright to a company after a certain amount of time by filing a notice to that effect. The length of time varies according to when a work was created, but works registered after 1978 can revert to authors after thirty-five years. This could create major problems for record labels, especially since sales of older albums have become more important in recent years.

13. Bill Holland, "Work for Hire Bill Repealed," *Billboard*, October 28, 2000. Technically, the entire bill wasn't repealed, but "sound recordings" were removed from the list of works for hire by the Work Made for Hire and Copyright Corrections Act of 2000.

14. Bill Holland, "Work-for-Hire Talks Stalled," *Billboard*, August 5, 2000.

15. From a speech Bronfman made at a RealNetworks conference, on May 26, 2000, in San Jose, California.

16. *Music on the Internet: Is There an Upside to Downloading?: Hearing Before the Senate Judiciary Committee*, 106th Cong., 2nd sess. (July 11, 2000).

17. Order, *A&M Records v. Napster.*

18. Knopper, *Appetite for Self-Destruction*, p. 142. Disclosure: Knopper is a friend.

19. To get this admittedly inexact estimate, I divided the total number of iTunes accounts activated worldwide by the number of iTunes songs sold. Some people may have more than one account, while some accounts may be used by more than one person.

20. Levy, "Download," in *Perfect Thing*.

21. Levy, *Perfect Thing*, p. 143.

22. Shawn Tully, "Big Man Against Big Music," *Fortune*, August 14, 2000.

23. Several other RIAA employees of the time confirmed that these threats were legitimate enough to take seriously.

24. Statistical analysis done by Field Research Corporation, *A&M Records v. Napster* (9th Cir. 2001).

25. Menn, *All the Rave*, p. 232.

26. Order, *A&M Records v. Napster* (9th Cir. 2001).

27. Expert Report of Professor Lawrence Lessig, *A&M Records v. Napster* (N.D. Cal. 2000).

28. John Perry Barlow, "The Next Economy of Ideas," *Wired*, October 2000. Barlow has a habit of name-dropping Hezbollah in discussions of opposition to copyright. Reasonably enough, many anti-copyright activists find this unfair to their views.

29. Menn, *All the Rave*, p. 236.

30. Barlow, "Next Economy of Ideas."

31. Litman, *Digital Copyright*, p. 169.

32. Although the statistic of forty million is often repeated, estimates vary. The National Motorists Association, which lobbies for looser speeding laws, estimates that between twenty-five million and fifty million tickets for moving violations are issued in the United States each year. AOL's Autoblog has reported that thirty-four million tickets are issued each year.

33. It also sent the matter back to the district court to craft an injunction that required copyright holders to identify specific works for Napster to filter.

34. Menn, *All the Rave*, pp. 291–96.

35. *Leiber v. Bertelsmann AG*, No. C 04-1671 MHP (S.D.N.Y. filed Feb. 19, 2003).

36. Simon Thiel, "Bertelsmann Posts First-Half Loss on Napster Charges," Bloomberg, September 4, 2007. The settlements are private, but Bertelsmann's finance chief, Thomas Rabe, said that they would probably cost the company €393 million (about $550 million).

37. For business reasons, the manager declined to identify the band.

38. Glenn Peoples, "The Long Tale?" *Billboard*, November 14, 2009. Disclosure: I assigned and helped edit this article, which showed that the so-called long tail applies to sales of albums, but not individual tracks.

39. Kevin Kelly, *The Technium* (blog), March 4, 2008.

40. "He certainly fronted them some regular living expense money in that critical year of 1966, when they were first getting established. He's been occasionally described as their 'patron.'" Author interview with Blair Jackson, author of *Garcia: An American Life* (New York: Viking, 1999). Stanley, a talented audio engineer, also designed the band's sound systems, and the album *History of the Grateful Dead, Vol. 1 (Bear's Choice)* was titled after his nickname, Bear.

41. "There were a few busts of T-shirt sellers in the parking lots outside shows, some cease-and-desist orders to some of the larger T-shirt makers (especially ones who made what were clearly mass-manufactured shirts that violated copyrights)." Jackson, interview with author. T-shirts could involve copyrights, trademarks, or both.

42. According to Nielsen SoundScan.

43. Antony Bruno, "The Soulja Boy Conundrum: What Is the Value of a Million-Plus Twitter Following?" Billboard.biz, December 17, 2010.

44. In 2007, "Crank That (Soulja Boy)" spent seven weeks at No. 1 on the *Billboard* Hot 100, which tracks sales and airplay. In 2010, the first single from Soulja Boy's third album only reached No. 34 on the same chart.

45. Three of the most popular file-sharing services of the time—Grokster, Kazaa, and Morpheus—all used the FastTrack protocol, which designated some users as "supernodes." This provided both the technological advantages of centralization and the legal advantages of decentralization.

46. Grokster operated under its own name, Kazaa was owned by Sharman Networks, and Morpheus was owned by the company MusicCity, which became StreamCast Networks. I'm using the names of the services in the interest of simplicity.

47. Michael Eisner testimony before the Senate Committee on Commerce, Science, and Transportation, February 28, 2002.

48. "Is it the responsibility of the world at large to protect an industry whose business model is facing a strategic challenge?" Intel's chairman, Andy Grove, asked in a *New York Times* interview following Eisner's testimony. "Or is it up to the entertainment industry to adapt to a new technical reality and a new set of consumers who want to take advantage of it?" Amy Harmon, "Piracy or Innovation? It's Hollywood vs. High Tech," *New York Times*, March 14, 2002.

49. Speech given at the Optical Storage Symposium in San Francisco, September 17, 2002.

50. According to StopBadware.org.

51. On August 11, 2003, it sent a Digital Millennium Copyright Act takedown notice to that effect to Google, which can be seen on chillingeffects.org.

52. Todd Woody, "The Race to Kill Kazaa," *Wired*, February 2003. Disclosure: I had a role in assigning this story when I worked at *Wired*, but I didn't edit it.

53. Writ of certiorari from the Supreme Court to the Ninth Circuit.

54. In 2001, Felten said he was threatened with an RIAA lawsuit for planning to present his research on breaking a copy-protection system; the RIAA denied this.

55. *Metro-Goldwin-Mayer Studios, Inc., et al v. Grokster, Ltd., et al*, 259 F. Supp. 2d 1029 (C.D. Cal. 2003).

56. *MGM Studios v. Grokster*, 380 F. 3d 1154 (9th Cir. 2004). Specifically, the Ninth Circuit Court of Appeals upheld the decision on secondary liability and remanded the case to the lower court to resolve the remaining issues.

57. The RIAA targeted individuals for violating the copyright holder's exclusive right to distribution. In many cases, it added an allegation of violating the exclusive right of reproduction—that is, downloading.

58. U.S. Copyright Act, 17 U.S.C. §504(c)(2).

59. The RIAA sued Sarah Ward, sixty-six, in 2003 and the late Gertrude Walton in 2005. The RIAA had been identifying unauthorized distributors of major-label music by their IP addresses, then asking Internet service providers to match them with a name and address. The organization then sent a letter asking that person to contact the RIAA and—if it seemed he or she wasn't responsible—dropped the case. If the person didn't contact the RIAA, it would move ahead with a case.

60. *Virgin Records America v. Jammie Thomas*, No. 06-CV-1497 (D. Minn. trial began October 2, 2007). The case became *Capitol Records v. Jammie Thomas* after Virgin Records merged into Capitol in 2007.

61. Thomas was accused of uploading more than seventeen hundred songs, but, as in most cases, labels only sued over certain tracks.

62. The RIAA does not comment on the specifics of its legal strategy. But it was almost certainly less interested in collecting money than in avoiding a precedent that went against it.

63. "NPD Digital Music Study" (2006–2009). In 2006 through 2008, this was only

a decrease in the percentage of Internet users. In 2009, the number of individuals using file-sharing services declined as well.

64. Stan Liebowitz, "Policing Pirates in the Networked Age" (Cato Institute's Policy Analysis No. 438, May 15, 2002).

65. Damien Cave, "File Sharing: Innocent Until Proven Guilty," *Salon*, June 13, 2002.

66. Robert Wilonsky, "Do the Math," *Dallas Observer*, August 8, 2002.

67. Lawrence Lessig, "End the War on Sharing," *Financial Times*, June 19, 2002.

68. Damien Cave, "File Sharing: Guilty as Charged?" *Salon*, August 23, 2002.

69. In the early 1980s, when he was teaching at the University of Western Ontario, Liebowitz conducted studies for the Canadian government that showed photocopying didn't hurt publishers and that cable retransmission of network television wasn't bad for broadcasters.

70. www.utdallas.edu/~liebowit.

71. Felix Oberholzer-Gee and Koleman Strumpf, "The Effect of File-Sharing on Record Sales: An Empirical Analysis" (March 2004).

72. Stan Liebowitz, "How Reliable Is the Oberholzer-Gee and Strumpf Paper on File-Sharing?" (September 2007). Available online but not yet officially published.

73. Birgitte Andersen and Marion Frenz, "The Impact of Music Downloads and P2P File-Sharing on the Purchase of Music: A Study for Industry Canada" (Study for Industry Canada, May 2007).

74. David Blackburn, "Online Piracy & Recorded Music Sales," Harvard University working paper (2004); Norbert Michel, "The Impact of Digital File-Sharing on the Music Business: An Empirical Analysis," *Topics in Economic Analysis & Policy*, vol. 6, issue 1 (2006); Martin Peitz and Patrick Waelbroeck, "The Effect of Internet Piracy on Music Sales: Cross-Section Evidence," *Review of Economic Research on Copyright Issues*, vol. 1, issue 2 (2004); Rafael Rob and Joel Waldfogel, "Piracy on the High C's: Music Downloading, Sales Displacement, and Social Welfare in a Sample of College Students," *Journal of Law and Economics*, vol. 49, issue 1 (April 2006); Alejandro Zentner, "Measuring the Effect of Music Downloads on Music Purchases," *Journal of Law and Economics*, vol. 49, issue 1 (April 2006).

75. According to Nielsen SoundScan. "Catalog albums" are releases—not material—that are more than eighteen months old and don't meet any other definition of a current title. For example, *Thriller* qualifies as a catalog album, but a new collection of Michael Jackson material would not. Catalog sales declined more than overall sales in 2010, but that was because the Beatles reissues and the

death of Michael Jackson made 2009 an exceptionally successful year for older releases.

76. According to October 2010 data from the Nielsen Company; the European average is 23 percent.

77. *Recording Industry in Numbers 2010* (IFPI, 2010).

78. William Hochberg, "Land of the Rising Disc," *Wired*, July 2011. There are also other reasons why CDs sell well in Japan, including a vital rental market.

79. Felix Oberholzer-Gee and Koleman Strumpf, "File-Sharing and Copyright" (paper presented at Vienna Music Business Research Days, June 9 and 10, 2010).

80. According to the U.S. Bureau of Labor Statistics, based on quarterly census of employment and wages for musical groups and artists, NAICS code 71113.

81. According to Nielsen SoundScan.

82. According to the NPD Group, 19 percent of music by track is acquired from legal download sites, while 23 percent is from file-sharing services. This doesn't count online streaming.

83. Exact estimates of Apple's share of the personal computer market in 2001 vary from 2.5 percent (Gartner Dataquest) to 4.5 percent (IDC). I used the 3 percent figure in the interest of simplicity.

84. Bronfman spoke at the Goldman Sachs Communacopia investor conference in New York on September 22, 2005. He was responding to a comment by Steve Jobs that music executives were "greedy."

85. Antony Bruno and Glenn Peoples, "The Price You Pay," *Billboard*, June 27, 2009. The article analyzes Nielsen SoundScan data. Disclosure: I edited this story when I was at *Billboard*.

86. Bob Pegoraro, "Beatles Finally Allowing Digital Downloads on Apple's iTunes," *Washington Post*, November 16, 2010.

87. According to Nielsen SoundScan.

88. According to data provided by BigChampagne, downloads increased slightly for a few days, decreased slightly for a few days, and then climbed significantly for two weeks.

89. According to sales data from Nielsen SoundScan, No. 4 was Kid Rock's *Rock n Roll Jesus*, and No. 5 was AC/DC's *Black Ice*. This actually understates the success of *Rock n Roll Jesus*, which came out in October 2007.

90. According to Nielsen SoundScan.

91. According to the media measurement company BigChampagne.

92. Andrew Orlowski, "Apple, Tesco 'Most to Blame' for Music Biz Crisis," *The Register*, October 19, 2007. Based on a Capgemini study.

93. Anita Elberse, "Bye Bye Bundles: The Unbundling of Music in Digital Channels," *Journal of Marketing* vol. 74, issue 3 (May 2010). The study ran from January 2005 to April 2007.

94. According to the RIAA, $14.6 billion of music was shipped in 1999.

95. *MGM Studios v. Grokster*, 545 U.S. 913 (2005).

96. Ibid.

97. Fred von Lohmann, *"What Peer-to-Peer Developers Need to Know About Copyright Law* (Electronic Frontier Foundation, January 2006).

98. "Supreme Court Ruling Will Chill Technology Innovation" (Electronic Frontier Foundation press release, June 27, 2005).

99. Michael Arrington, "This Is Quite Possibly the Spotify Cap Table," *TechCrunch*, August 7, 2009.

CHAPTER THREE: GEEKS BEARING GIFTS:
GOOGLE'S WAR ON COPYRIGHT

1. Complaint, *Viacom v. YouTube*, No. 07-CV-2103 (S.D.N.Y. filed March 13, 2007).

2. *Viacom v. YouTube*, 718 F. Supp. 2d 514 (S.D.N.Y. 2010).

3. *Viacom v. YouTube*, No. 10-3270 (2d. Cir. filed August 11, 2010).

4. Lawrence Lessig, "Make Way for Copyright Chaos," *New York Times*, March 18, 2007.

5. "Google Inc. Pledges $2M to Stanford Law School Center for Internet and Society" (Stanford Law School press release, November 29, 2006).

6. Bobbie Johnson, "Search Giant Sets Aside $200M for YouTube Court Cases," *Guardian*, November 15, 2006.

7. "Google Inc. Pledges $2M to Stanford Law School Center for Internet and Society," Stanford University press release.

8. "To avoid any conflict of interest, CIS avoids litigation if it involves Google." From "About the Stanford Center for Internet and Society," Stanford Center for Internet and Society Web site.

9. In 2009, Google had about $11 billion in U.S. revenue, according to the company's financial statements; the entire recorded music business made $6.5 billion.

10. "We wage war against our children and our children will become the enemy." Lessig, *Remix*, p. 293.

11. *Eric Eldred, et al v. Janet Reno, Attorney General*, 74 F. Supp. 2d 1 (D.D.C. 1999); *Eldred v. Reno*, 239 F. 2d 372 (D.C. Cir. 2001).

12. David Streitfeld, "The Cultural Anarchist vs. the Hollywood Police State," *Los Angeles Times*, September 22, 2002.

13. *Eldred v. Ashcroft*, 537 U.S. 186 (2003).The case changed its name because John Ashcroft replaced Janet Reno as United States attorney general.

14. Vishesh Kumar and Christopher Rhoads, "Google Wants Its Own Fast Track on the Web," *Wall Street Journal*, December 15, 2008.

15. Lawrence Lessig, "Required Reading: News," *Lessig.org* (blog), December 12, 2008.

16. Jia Lynn Yang and Nina Easton, "Obama & Google (a Love Story)," *Fortune*, October 26, 2009.

17. Stephanie Clifford, "For Inauguration, Google Plans a Party to Cross Party Lines," *New York Times*, January 11, 2009.

18. Tony Romm, "White House Official Reprimanded for Consulting with Google Colleagues," Thehill.com, May 17, 2010.

19. Full quotation: "PS we've tee'd it up for the OIC [Open Internet Coalition] gang, so some of those folks will have your back." Davidson to McLaughlin, e-mail, November 23, 2009.

20. "Google CEO Named Chairman of Washington Think Tank," *Chronicle of Philanthropy*, February 7, 2008.

21. "Can You Hear Me Now? Why Your Cell Phone Is So Terrible: A Future Tense Event from Slate Magazine and the New America Foundation" (New America Foundation office, April 2, 2010).

22. According to the Public Knowledge Web site.

23. "Public Knowledge Proposes New Copyright Reform Act" (Public Knowledge press release, February 15, 2010).

24. "Digital Freedom Campaign Launched" (Consumer Electronics Association press release, October 30, 2006).

25. *Sony BMG Music Entertainment et al. v. Joel Tenenbaum*, No. 07-CV-11446 (D. Mass. filed August 7, 2007).

26. Full quotation: "Law in the court of public opinion is what shapes law in the courts and in the real world. This could be 'Civil Action II.' " John Schwartz, "Tilting at Internet Barrier, a Stalwart Is Upended," *New York Times*, August 10, 2009. Nesson was a lawyer in the case that became the subject for the movie *A Civil Action*.

27. "A Sensible Compromise," *Harvard Crimson*, December 13, 2010.

28. Hyde, *Common as Air,* p. 5.

29. Stephen Manes, "The Trouble with Larry," Forbes.com, March 29, 2004.

30. Jane Ginsburg, " 'Une Chose Publique?' The Author's Domain and the Public Domain in Early British, French, and U.S. Copyright Law," *Cambridge Law Journal*, vol. 645, issue 3, pp. 636–70, November 2006.

31. Guiguo Wang, *Business Law of China* (Hong Kong: Butterworths Asia, 1993), p. 462.

32. Ray Corrigan, "Colmcille and the Battle of the Book: Technology, Law, and Access to Knowledge in 6th Century Ireland" (paper presented at GikII 2 workshop on the intersections between law, technology, and popular culture at University College London, September 19, 2007).

33. Ibid. It says something about our conflicted attitudes toward intellectual property that Finnian and Colmcille were both canonized—the latter became Saint Columba.

34. "Simon Marion's Plea on Privileges" (1586), Primary Sources on Copyright, www.copyrighthistory.org.

35. *Harper & Row v. Nation Enterprises.*

36. Stephen Manes, "The Trouble with Larry." Forbes.com, 29 March 2004.

37. *Steamboat Willie* is often described as a parody of *Steamboat Bill Jr.* , but it's hard to see what they have in common.

38. Disney bought the rights for *101 Dalmatians* from Dodie Smith, the rights for *Lady and the Tramp* from Ward Greene, and the rights for *Dumbo* from Helen Aberson. The rights for *Bambi* came from MGM, which had acquired them from the book's author. The family of Joel Chandler Harris sold Disney the rights for *Song of the South.* And Disney bought the rights to *Peter Pan* from Great Ormond Street Hospital, where the author J. M. Barrie had donated them.

39. Jacob Grimm died in 1863, his brother four years before that. Under today's copyright term, which lasts seventy years past the life of the author, their work would have entered the public domain in 1933. Disney's *Snow White and the Seven Dwarfs* came out in 1937. I am *not* defending the current term of copyright, which I think is too long—just showing how Lessig's logic doesn't hold up under scrutiny.

40. "The opposite of a free culture is a 'permission culture'—a culture in which creators get to create only with the permission of the powerful, or of creators from the past." Lessig, *Free Culture*, p. 6.

41. *Campbell, aka Skyywalker, et al v. Acuff-Rose Music Inc. ,* 510 U.S. 569 (1994). Justice David Souter appended to his opinion the lyrics to 2 Live Crew's "Pretty Woman," which pretty much set a precedent for *awesome.*

42. *Don Henley et al. v. Charles S. Devore et al,* 733 F. Supp. 2d 1144 (C.D. Cal.

2010). Under U.S. copyright law, a song's writer—or, in this case, writers—have the right to synchronize it with video, or license these "sync" rights. And the courts have delineated a difference between parody and satire. The first, which is almost always fair use, involves using part of a work to comment on the work itself; the second, which has less protection, involves using part of a work to comment on something else.

43. Henley answered questions via e-mail. He knows more about copyright law than many major-label executives and brought up Lessig's ideas unprompted.

44. *David Byrne et al. v. Charlie Crist et al*, No. 8:10-CV-1187 (M.D. Fla. filed May 24, 2010).

45. David Byrne, "Yours Truly vs. the Governor of Florida," David Byrne's blog, May 25, 2010.

46. Terry Hart, "Creative vs. Consumptive Infringement," Copyhype.com, September 22, 2010. Disclosure: I hired Hart, a law school graduate who did not yet have a job, to read this book for legal mistakes. I used his description because it's one of the clearest I've read.

47. Sousa used this phrase as the title of a 1906 article he wrote for *Appleton's Magazine*.

48. Sousa testified in front of Congress in June 1906 about the issues Congress addressed in the Copyright Act of 1909.

49. Patrick Warfield, "John Philip Sousa and 'The Menace of Mechanical Music,'" *Journal of the Society for American Music*, vol. 13, issue 4, October 2009.

50. Ibid.

51. Patrick Warfield (Sousa scholar and music professor at the University of Maryland), interview with author.

52. "Nonetheless, newspapers and magazines repudiated his assault on the phonograph. It was bound to improve public taste in the long run." Neil Harris, John Philip Sousa, and the Culture of Reassurance, Performing Arts Encyclopedia (online), Library of Congress.

53. Viacom's Statement of Undisputed Facts, *Viacom v. YouTube*, items 57, 104. Chen said in an e-mail that "i know that if we remove all that content. we go from 100,000 views a day down to about 20,000 views or maybe even lower." Dutton said in an instant message that "the truth of the matter is, probably 75-80% of our views come from copyrighted material" [both *sic*].

54. Ibid., item 145.

55. Class Plaintiffs Statement of Uncontroversial Material Facts in Support of Their Motion for Partial Summary Judgment, *Football Assn. Premier League Ltd. et al. v. YouTube Inc. et al*, No 07-CV-2103 (S.D.N.Y. filed March 18, 2010).

56. Viacom's Statement of Undisputed Facts, *Viacom v. YouTube.*

57. YouTube's Counterstatement to Viacom's Statement of Undisputed Facts, *Viacom v. YouTube.*

58. Viacom's Statement of Undisputed Facts, *Viacom v. YouTube.*, items 148, 149.

59. Ibid., items 161, 162.

60. *Viacom v. YouTube*, Hohengarten exhibits 312, 314, and 315.

61. Ibid., Hohengarten exhibit 315.

62. Ibid., Schapiro exhibit 173.

63. Hurley said YouTube "had agreed to use [filtering technology] to identify and possibly remove copyrighted material from Warner Music, and it would discuss a similar arrangement with Viacom as part of a broader deal." Geraldine Fabrikant and Saul Hansell, "Viacom Tells YouTube: Hands Off," *New York Times*, February 3, 2007.

64. YouTube's Memorandum of Law in Support of Defendant's Motion for Summary Judgment, *Viacom v. YouTube.*

65. *Viacom v. YouTube*, Schapiro exhibits 49, 51, and 53.

66. *Robert Tur v. YouTube Inc.* , CV-06-04436 (C.D. Cal. filed July 14, 2006).

67. Although the case is often referred to as a class-action lawsuit, as of early 2011 it was not yet certified as one.

68. Complaint, *Premier League v. YouTube.*

69. *Viacom v. YouTube*, 718 F. Supp. 2d 514 (S.D.N.Y. 2010).

70. Matthew Karnitschnig and Julia Angwin, "Media Firms Say Google Benefited from Film Piracy," *Wall Street Journal*, February 12, 2007. The depositions themselves are under seal.

71. Legally, this is unexplored terrain. The Digital Millennium Copyright Act doesn't cover ad networks, and some of the sites in question aren't in the United States.

72. Ellen Seidler, "Google-Go-Round, Profits from Pirates" (blog).

73. *Warner Bros. Entertainment Inc. et al v. Triton Media, LLC*, No. CV-10-6318 (C.D. Cal. filed August 24, 2010).

74. Ito responded to questions via e-mail.

75. Joi Ito, Hal Abelson, and Laurie Racine are on the boards of both Creative Commons and Public Knowledge. Creative Commons also has close ties with both Stanford and the Berkman Center at Harvard; of the group's board members, Glenn Otis Brown, now at YouTube, went to Harvard Law School and taught a class with Lessig at Stanford; Eric Saltzman is the Berkman Center's former execu-

tive director; and Molly Shaffer Van Houweling has been a fellow at both Stanford Law School and the Berkman Center.

76. Josh Quittner, "The Flickr Founders," *Time*, April 30, 2006.

77. Oliver Lindberg, " 'Business Will Overcome Its Opposition to Creative Commons or Perish,' " TechRadar.com, July 25, 2010.

78. "How Copyright Threatens Democracy: A Conversation with Cory Doctorow" (New America Foundation office, June 28, 2010). I hired a local reporter to take notes on this event and checked Losey's and Doctorow's quotations against a video of the speech.

79. Ibid.

80. Tim Wu, "YouTube as Video Store," *Slate*, January 29, 2010. Wu, "The Apple Two," *Slate*, April 6, 2010.

81. Wu responded to questions via e-mail.

82. Patry, *Moral Panics and the Copyright Wars*, p. 15.

83. Ibid., p. 17. I took the sales numbers from Take-Two Interactive's 2010 second quarter results. If Patry's mistake sounds reasonable, think for a moment about that number: *ninety-five million.* There aren't even that many video game consoles that can *play Grand Theft Auto IV.*

84. U.S. Government Accountability Office, *Intellectual Property Observations on Efforts to Quantify the Economic Effects of Counterfeit and Pirated Goods* (GAO-10-423, Report to Congressional Committees, April 12, 2010).

CHAPTER FOUR: THE SIREN SONG OF "FREE":
WHY NEWSPAPERS STRUGGLED ONLINE

1. From the annual Hugh Cudlipp Lecture by Alan Rusbridger, January 26, 2010.

2. Ibid.

3. This anecdote appeared in the *Media Diary* blog of the *Australian* on November 13, 2010, and was confirmed by Rusbridger's assistant, who said the technical staff had accidentally unplugged his laptop.

4. Stephen Brook, "Current Losses Unsustainable, GNM Managing Director Warns Staff," *Guardian*, September 15, 2009.

5. Tim Luckhurst, "Is the Guardian Beating Its Head Against a Paywall?" *Independent*, March 27, 2010.

6. According to the Newspaper Association of America.

7. *New Media, Old Media: How Blogs and Social Media Agendas Relate and Differ from Traditional Press* (Pew Research Center Publications, May 23, 2010).

8. According to the Newspaper Association of America.

9. According to the American Society of News Editors.

10. According to the blog *Paper Cuts*, which tracks the decline of the newspaper business.

11. "How Newsrooms Are Coping with Cutbacks" (Pew Research Center's Project for Excellence in Journalism, May 11, 2010).

12. These are reliable estimates, based on interviews with executives and analysts, but the price of newspaper advertising varies by city, circulation, size, section, and other factors.

13. With a nod to the work of Ryan Chittum, who figured out such numbers for a previous year in the *Columbia Journalism Review*, I calculated this by dividing Newspaper Association of America data on advertising revenue by the number of readers for each medium.

14. Mercedes Bunz, "Huffington Post and Politico Set to Make 2009 Profit," *Digital Content* (blog), *Guardian*, January 4, 2010.

15. According to the Interactive Advertising Bureau.

16. *The Media Show*, BBC Radio 4, May 18, 2010.

17. Brian Morrissey, "News Corp.'s James Murdoch Bets on Paid Model," *Adweek*, November 12, 2010.

18. According to News Corporation.

19. "Times and Sunday Times Readership Falls After Paywall," BBC News, November 2, 2010.

20. "We have talked to News Corp and other companies for months on these sorts of things." Maija Palmer, "Google Looks to Make Peace with Murdoch," *Financial Times*, May 18, 2010.

21. Arif Durrani, "Why News Corp. Really Pulled the Plug on Project Alesia," BrandRepublic.com, October 21, 2010.

22. According to the Audit Bureau of Circulations.

23. According to the Newspaper Association of America.

24. In March 2010, the annual report of the Pew Research Center's Project for Excellence in Journalism found that 19 percent of loyal news consumers would pay for online content. An October 2009 Boston Consulting Group survey put that number at 48 percent.

25. "After Three Months, Only 35 Subscriptions for *Newsday's Web Site*," *New York Observer*, January 26, 2010.

26. According to comScore.

27. Maureen Orth, "Arianna's Virtual Candidate," *Vanity Fair*, November 1994.

28. Rahuk K. Parikh, "The Huffington Post Is Crazy About Your Health," *Salon*, July 30, 2009.

29. Ken Doctor, *News Users 2009* (Outsell, December 10, 2009).

30. Arnon Mishkin, "The Fallacy of the Link Economy," PaidContent.org, August 13, 2009.

31. Jake Dobkin, "How the New York Times Lost an Entire Generation of Readers," BusinessInsider.com, February 2, 2010.

32. *International News Service v. Associated Press*, 248 U.S. 215 (1918).

33. *National Basketball Association v. Motorola Inc.*, 105 F.3d 841 (2d Cir. 1997).

34. *The Associated Press v. All Headline News Corp. et al*, No. 08 Civ. 323 (S.D.N.Y. filed January 14, 2008).

35. *Barclays Capital Inc. et al v. TheFlyOnTheWall.com*, 700 F. Supp. 2d 310 (S.D.N.Y. March 18, 2010).

36. Consent Judgment and Permanent Injunction, *Dow Jones & Co. Inc. v. Briefing.com Inc.*, No. 10 Civ. 3321 (S.D.N.Y. filed November 15, 2010).

37. In 1999, a cinema chain's case against Moviefone was dismissed on the grounds that Moviefone's use of its information did not reduce its incentive to publish its film schedule. In 2009, a court dismissed a case in which the *Scranton Times-Tribune* sued a rival for rewriting its obituaries.

38. *The Future of Journalism: Hearing Before the Communications, Technology, and the Internet Subcommittee of the Senate Commerce, Science, and Transportation Committee*, 111th Cong., 1st sess. (May 6, 2009) (Arianna Huffington testimony).

39. Knight Commission on the Information Needs of Communities in a Democracy, *Informing Communities: Sustaining Democracy in the Digital Age* (Washington, D.C.: Aspen Institute, October 2, 2009).

40. At a 2009 Senate Commerce Committee hearing on the future of journalism, Alberto Ibargüen testified that "nothing Congress can do is as important as providing universal, affordable digital access and adoption." At a December 2009 Federal Trade Commission (FTC) workshop on the same topic, Eric Newton testified that "consumers must have universal broadband access"—an issue that isn't under the FTC's purview.

41. "Public Knows Basic Facts About Politics, Economics, but Struggles with Specifics" (Pew Research Center for the People & the Press, November 18, 2010).

42. Alan Mutter, "Non-profits Can't Possibly Save the News," *Reflections of a Newsosaur* (blog), March 30, 2010.

43. "How News Happens: A Study of the News Ecosystem of One American City" (Pew Research Center's Project for Excellence in Journalism, January 11, 2010).

44. Ibid.

45. Such joint operating agreements, which held newspapers exempt from parts of antitrust law, were set up to allow multiple papers to survive in some U.S. cities.

46. Number of unique visitors in January 2011, according to comScore.

47. Number of unique visitors in January 2011, according to comScore.

CHAPTER FIVE: THE REVOLUTION MAY NOT BE TELEVISED: HOW THE INTERNET COULD KILL *MAD MEN*

1. Estimates vary, but $32 billion was the figure used in Ronald Grover, Tom Lowry, and Cliff Edwards, "Revenge of the Cable Guys," *Bloomberg Businessweek*, March 11, 2010.

2. *An Examination of the Proposed Combination of Comcast and NBC Universal: Hearing Before the Subcommittee on Communications, Technology, and the Internet of the House Energy and Commerce Committee*, 111th Cong., 2nd sess. (February 4, 2010) (Jeff Zucker testimony).

3. Avner Ronen, "Boxee Responds to NBC's Jeff Zucker," *Boxee* (blog), February 4, 2010.

4. Derek Baine (analyst, SNL Kagan), interview with author.

5. Exact estimates vary but SNL Kagan's Baine says 54 percent.

6. *Consumers Consider Axing the Coax* (Yankee Group, April 27, 2010).

7. SNL Kagan reports, August 23 and November 17, 2010.

8. Sallie Hofmeister, "News Corp. Ups Ante in the All-News Game," *Los Angeles Times*, May 7, 1996.

9. Research note, Pali Research, January 4, 2010.

10. Andrew Wallenstein, "Peter Chernin to Old Media: Be Afraid. Be Very Afraid," PaidContent.org, November 17, 2010.

11. Alex Witchel, "'Mad Men' Has Its Moment," *New York Times Magazine*, June 22, 2008.

12. According to Nielsen Media Research. The number of viewers for a first broadcast undercounts the popularity of *Mad Men*, which reached an average of 3.3 million viewers within the week each episode aired. But subsequent viewers on digital video recorders are worth less because many of them skip commercials.

13. Derek Baine (analyst, SNL Kagan), interview with author.

14. Brian Steinberg, "Why 'Mad Men' Has So Little to Do with Advertising," *Advertising Age*, August 2, 2010.

15. "Monthly Household Spending on Communications Services" (Centris research note, October 29, 2010).

16. Alex Ben Block, "Why NBC's Jay Leno Plan Makes Sense," *Hollywood Reporter*, May 29, 2009.

17. Andrew Wallenstein, "Which TV Channels Can't Cord-Cutters Live Without?," PaidContent.org, December 6, 2010.

18. Hulu has said it made $263 million in revenue in 2010.

19. This is a rough estimate, since network advertising costs vary widely—by show, time of day, demographic of audience, and method of consumption (live, on demand, digital video recorder, and so on). At the risk of oversimplifying, let's assume that network ads sell for a CPM of $30, compared with a Hulu CPM of $40. Let's also assume that Hulu runs twelve thirty-second ads an hour, half of what a network would. (Networks run sixteen minutes of advertising an hour, but some of that consists of promotions for other shows.) That means a network show would bring in $720 per thousand viewers, while Hulu would bring in two-thirds of that. This calculation doesn't count carriage fees.

20. *Nielsen Q2 2010 State of the Media Report* (Nielsen Media Research, November 2010).

21. Diane Bartz, "U.S. Senator Asks NBC About Olympic Site Pay-TV Link," Reuters, February 26, 2010.

22. Richard Greenfield, "Dear Media Executives: Do Not Destroy Your Future, Think Long-Term; Read Comments from BTIG Survey" (research note, October 4, 2010).

23. Brian Stelter, "ESPN Study Shows Little Effort to Cut Cable," *New York Times*, December 5, 2010.

24. *Piracy of Live Sports Broadcasting over the Internet: Hearing Before the House Judiciary Committee.* 111th Cong., 1st sess. (December 16, 2009) (Ed Durso testimony).

25. Matt Burns, "9 Great Gifts for the Media Pirate in Your Life," *TechCrunch*, November 22, 2010.

26. David Goldman, "Internet TV Sales Up—but No One Uses It," CNNMoney.com, January 4, 2011.

27. According to the research company iSuppli.

28. "Changing Models: A Global Perspective on Paying for Content Online" (Nielsen Company, February 2010).

29. An article in the *Wall Street Journal* also said Disney asked Google to do this. See Sam Schechner and Amir Efrati, "Networks Block Web Programs from Being Viewed on Google TV," *Wall Street Journal*, October 22, 2010.

30. Les Moonves, "The Networks Strike Back: How Old Media Has Adapted to the New World" (speech, University of Texas, October 4, 2010).

31. Alexia Tsotsis, "ABC, CBS, and NBC Shut Out Google TV: Fox and MTV Still Available," *TechCrunch*, October 21, 2010.

32. Diane Brady, with Sarah Rabil, "Jeff Bewkes and the Apple Trap," *Bloomberg Businessweek*, January 30, 2011.

33. Ibid.

34. "Public Knowledge Criticizes 'TV Everywhere' " (Public Knowledge press release, June 24, 2009).

35. Comments of Public Knowledge & New America Foundation in the Matter of Video Device Competition, Before the Federal Communications Commission, filed July 13, 2010.

36. Comments of Google Inc. in the Matter of Video Device Competition, Before the Federal Communications Commission, filed July 13, 2010.

CHAPTER SIX: BOOKS OR KINDLE-ING?
HOW TECHNOLOGY COULD TURN THE PAGE ON PUBLISHING

1. Rory Maher, "Here's Why Amazon Will Win the eBook War," BusinessInsider.com, January 13, 2010. Amazon's share of the e-book market has fallen since then.

2. In addition to interviews, I got details of the Seattle meeting from Ken Auletta, "Publish or Perish," *New Yorker*, April 26, 2010.

3. Jay Yarow, "9 Charts That Show Why Amazon Investors Have Nothing to Worry About," BusinessInsider.com, February 17, 2010. This article quoted a Credit Suisse report that said Amazon had 22 percent of the overall book market and 19 percent of the print book market in 2009.

4. "Announcement: Macmillan E-books," Amazon.com Kindle Community, from the Amazon Kindle team. Amazon's announcement dripped condescension toward publishers, saying, "Customers will at that point decide for themselves whether they believe it's reasonable to pay $14.99 for a bestselling e-book."

5. Auletta, "Publish or Perish."

6. No one at Random House asked for any special consideration as I wrote this book. I interviewed Richard Sarnoff, since he was a key figure in negotiating the Google Books settlement, but I arranged the interview through the Random House publicity department, just as any other journalist would.

7. Eric Engelman, "Amazon Stops Selling Some Penguin, Hachette E-books," *TechFlash,* April 1, 2010.

8. Henry Blodget, "Hey, John Sargent, CEO of Macmillan Books, Screw You!" BusinessInsider.com, January 31, 2010. Yes, that's really the title of the article.

9. John Mutter, "A Standing O for Macmillan," *Shelf Awareness* (blog), February 4, 2010.

10. Sergey Brin, "A Library to Last Forever," *New York Times*, October 8, 2009.

11. Roy MacLeod, *The Library of Alexandria: Centre of Learning in the Ancient World* (New York: I. B. Tauris, 2000), p. 5. According to MacLeod, customs officials confiscated texts from passing ships, as well as visitors. They took originals for the library and returned copies to the owners.

12. There are two common views of whether Google's book-scanning project qualifies as fair use. One, held by copyright reform activists, is that scanning books in order to create an index is no different from a card catalog, so it obviously falls under fair use. The other is that such a big project by a private company couldn't possibly qualify. A court would probably find the issue less obvious than either side makes it out to be. On the one hand, Google's use would further the aim of copyright law, and it could raise the value of the books in question by making them easier to find. On the other, Google is scanning entire books, and the project is commercial, not educational, in nature.

13. *Authors Guild Inc. et al, Assn. of American Publishers v. Google Inc.*, No. 05-CV-8136 (S.D.N.Y. filed October 19, 2005).

14. Settlement Agreement, *Authors Guild, Assn. of American Publishers v. Google*, No. 05-CV-8136 (S.D.N.Y. filed October 28, 2008). Amended Settlement Agreement, *Authors Guild, Assn. of American Publishers v. Google*, No. 05-CV-8136 (S.D.N.Y. filed November 13, 2009).

15. The Book Rights Registry would have been run by a board made up of authors and publisher representatives from the United States, the U.K., Canada, and Australia.

16. Jeffrey Toobin, "Google's Moon Shot," *New Yorker*, February 5, 2007.

17. Competition and Commerce in Digital Books: The Proposed Google Book Settlement Hearing Before the House Judiciary Committee, 111th Cong., 1st sess. (September 10, 2009) (Marybeth Peters testimony.)

18. *Authors Guild, Assn. of American Publishers v. Google*, No. 05-CV-8136 (S.D.N.Y. filed March 22, 2011).

19. Ibid.

20. Auletta, "Publish or Perish."

21. The practice of selling less expensive paperbacks after a title had been sold in hardcover dates from 1935, when the London-based Penguin Books acquired rights to reprint ten books from their original publishers. Pocket Books brought Penguin's

model to the United States in 1939. John Feather, *A History of British Publishing* (London: Routledge, 1988), p. 177.

22. Arik Hesseldahl, "The True Cost of Amazon's New Kindle," *Bloomberg Businessweek*, April 22, 2009.

23. Brad Stone and Motoko Rich, "Stephen R. Covey Grants E-book Rights to Amazon," *New York Times*, December 15, 2009.

24. Auletta, "Publish or Perish."

25. "Amazon to Launch 'Kindle Singles'—Compelling Ideas Expressed at Their Natural Length" (Amazon.com press release, October 12, 2010).

26. Ibid.

CHAPTER SEVEN: MOVING PICTURES:
CAN HOLLYWOOD CONQUER THE CLOUD?

1. According to Hollywood.com.

2. According to Hollywood.com, 2010 box office revenue for the United States and Canada was $10.55 billion, although attendance was down more than 5 percent.

3. Alex Ben Block, "ShoWest 2010," *Hollywood Reporter*, March 16, 2010. In the early 1980s, about 30 percent of theatrical revenue came from foreign countries; in 2008, those markets accounted for 65 percent.

4. According to data from IHS Screen Digest, revenue from U.S. DVD and Blu-ray sales and rentals was $21.9 billion in 2004 but fell to $16.3 billion in 2010. As recently as 2008, it was $19.3 billion.

5. Dawn C. Chmielewski, "Disney Chief Executive Bob Iger Outlines Role of Modern Studio Chief," *Company Town* (blog), *Los Angeles Times*, October 17, 2009.

6. Brooks Barnes and Michael Cieply, "In Hollywood, Grappling with Studios' Lost Clout," *New York Times*, January 18, 2010.

7. I didn't go to Cham; the description of the RapidShare office is from Dirk Von Gehlen, "RapidShare—der unbekannte Web-Star," *Süddeutsche Zeitvung*, June 16, 2008.

8. *2009 Global Broadband Phenomena* (Sandvine, October 20, 2010).

9. According to comScore. RapidShare does not disclose details about its number of users.

10. Hollywood's estimate of RapidShare's earnings comes from a presentation that looked at RapidShare's traffic, estimated how much of that traffic consisted of RapidPro customers, and deducted costs for storage and bandwidth. It concluded that the company had an annual profit of between $45 million and $340 million.

The numbers and assumptions look realistic—and the lifestyles of some other people in the online locker service business make it clear how lucrative it can be—but I used the low end of the range to attempt to correct for the bias of the source.

11. *ATLAS Internet Observatory* (Arbor Networks, 2009).

12. "Technical Report: An Estimate of Infringing Use of the Internet," Envisional Ltd. research report, January 2011. This study was funded by NBC Universal, but the estimate of online traffic was derived from other companies' information, and the 90 percent figure seems realistic given the use of file-sharing services.

13. *Fall 2010 Internet Phenomena* (Sandvine, October 20, 2010).

14. *Disney Enterprises, Inc., et al v. Hotfile Corp., Anton Titov, and DOES 1-10*, No. 11-CV-20427-UU (S.D. Fla. Filed February 8, 2011).

15. Rebecca Lewis, "Multi-millionaire Hacker Buys Chrisco Mansion," *New Zealand Herald*, February 14, 2010.

16. Based on data provided by BigChampagne.

17. According to BoxOfficeMojo.com.

18. Ibid.

19. Ben Fritz, "'X-Men Origins: Wolverine' Kicks Off High-Stakes Summer Movie Season," *Los Angeles Times*, May 1, 2009.

20. A 2005 MPAA-funded LEK study, "The Cost of Movie Piracy," showed that studios lost $6.1 billion to piracy, but the MPAA has retracted the parts of that study related to illegal downloading among college students.

21. This ratio was used in the March 2010 Terra Consultants study "Building a Digital Economy: The Importance of Saving Jobs in the EU's Creative Industries."

22. According to Nash Information Services.

23. According to BigChampagne.

24. This ratio was also used in the Terra Consultants study.

25. Robert Booth, "WikiLeaks Cable: Jihad? Sorry, I Don't Want to Miss Desperate Housewives," *Guardian*, December 7, 2010.

26. Ricardo H. Cavazos Cepeda, Douglas C. Lippoldt, and Jonathan Senft, "Policy Complements to the Strengthening of IPRs in Developing Countries" (OECD Trade Policy Working Paper No. 104, Organization for Economic Cooperation and Development, September 14, 2010).

27. David Lieberman, "Disney Chief Offers a Ray of Encouragement to UltraViolet Movie Coalition," *USA Today*, November 11, 2010.

28. ComScore stopped tracking RapidShare, making exact comparisons difficult. But all reliable statistics on Internet traffic say that RapidShare is extremely popular and that it got less so over the course of 2010.

29. *Perfect 10 Inc. v. Rapidshare AG et al,* No. 09-CV-2596 H (S.D. Cal. Filed November 18, 2009).

30. Ibid., notice of settlement.

31. Jon Lech Johansen, better known as DVD Jon, broke the code with two collaborators who have never been identified.

CHAPTER EIGHT: DISQUIET ON THE EUROPEAN FRONT: WHY FRANCE FAVORS ART OVER THE INTERNET

1. The law is formally known as *Loi favorisant la diffusion et la protection de la création sur Internet,* or "Law promoting the distribution and protection of creative works on the Internet." It's managed by the Haute Autorité pour la Diffusion des Oeuvres et la Protection des Droits sur Internet, or the High Authority for the Distribution of Artworks and the Protection of (Copy)Rights on the Internet.

2. *Report from the Commission to the European Parliament, the Council, the European Economic and Social Committee, and the Committee of the Regions, Application of Directive 2004/48/EC of the European Parliament and the Council of 29 April 2004 on the Enforcement of Intellectual Property Rights* (European Commission, December 22, 2010). The report reviewed the effectiveness of the 2004 Directive on Intellectual Property Rights.

3. *La loi des 13–19 janvier 1791,* or the Law of 13–19 January 1791.

4. As of February 2011, Amazon did not sell the Kindle or its e-books from Amazon.de; searches for "Kindle" on that site linked to Amazon.com, from which Germans can order the device.

5. Thomas Crampton, "France Weighs Forcing iPods to Play Other Than iTunes," *New York Times*, March 17, 2006.

6. Elisabeth Niggemann, Jacques de Decker, and Maurice Lévy, *The Net Renaissance: Report of the "Comité des Sages" Reflection Group on Bringing Europe's Cultural Heritage Online* (European Commission, January 2011).

7. Ibid., p. 3.

8. Ibid.

9. David Hearst, "Yahoo! Faces French Fines for Nazi Auctions," *Guardian*, July 24, 2000.

10. Ibid., p. 7.

11. Lisa Guernsey, "Welcome to the Web. Passport, Please?" *New York Times*, March 15, 2001.

12. This idea was introduced during the 1993 negotiations for the General Agreement on Tariffs and Trade and allows France to protect its movie business with quotas.

13. French law prohibits the release of a film on DVD within the first four months of its theatrical release, unless the studio gets an official exemption.

14. *Le développement et la protection des oeuvres culturelles sur les nouveaux réseaux* (Department of Culture and Communication, November 2007).

15. *Digital Britain Report* (U.K. Department for Culture, Media, and Sport, June 16, 2009). It was based on a 2007 report by the Work Foundation, a private company.

16. Charles Arthur, "Controversial Digital Economy Bill Amendment Follows Lobbyists' Draft," *Guardian*, March 11, 2010.

17. "The Rise and Rise of Digital Music" (Ipsos MediaCT, June 2010).

18. "2010 Digital Entertainment Survey" (Wiggin LLP and Entertainment Media Research, May 2010).

19. "Quand vous redeviendrez de gauche, vous saurez où nous trouver," *Le Monde*, May 5, 2009.

20. French National Assembly hearing, July 23, 2009.

21. In 2006, the Spanish attorney general issued a circular that advised courts to treat the use of file-sharing services as "private copying," much like taping a friend's CD. While this is not binding, few courts have found otherwise.

22. *IFPI Digital Music Report 2011* (IFPI, January 2011).

23. Ben Fritz, "In Spain, Internet Piracy Is Part of the Culture," *Los Angeles Times*, March 30, 2010.

24. In Sweden, as in some other European countries, for-profit copyright infringement is often prosecuted as a criminal case. The Pirate Bay founders faced a criminal case with civil damages.

25. Dan Simmons, "The Views from the Pirate Bay," *Click*, BBC, November 30, 2007.

26. Anders Rydell and Sam Sundberg, *Piraterna* (Stockholm: Ordfront, 2009).

27. Daniel Roth, "The Pirates Can't Be Stopped," *Condé Nast Portfolio*, January 14, 2008. Disclosure: I contributed a few short pieces to *Portfolio* but had nothing to do with this one.

28. Paul Douglas, "15 Memorable Quotes from the Pirate Bay's Peter Sunde," TechRadar.com, March 14, 2010.

29. For translation of Swedish e-mails and reporting about the legal aspects of the Pirate Bay case, I hired Helienne Lindvall, a Swedish journalist who writes a column for the *Guardian*. Disclosure: Lindvall is also a professional songwriter.

30. Emanuel Sidea, "Högerextremist sponsrar filpirater," *Veckans Affärer*, April 23, 2007.

31. Lundström to John Goldie, e-mail, March 10, 2005; translated from Swedish.

32. Lundström to Sergei Kuznetsov, e-mail, March 15, 2005; translated from Swedish.

33. Oded to Lundström and Gottfrid, e-mail, May 26, 2006.

34. Staffan Olsson, "Pirate Bay drar in miljonbelopp," *Svenska Dagbladet*, July 8, 2006.

35. Ibid.

36. Neij to Gottfrid, e-mail, February 7, 2006; translated from Swedish.

37. Neij to Gottfrid, another e-mail, February 7, 2006; translated from Swedish.

38. Sofia Benholm, "Det kommer bli väldigt skårt att röra The Pirate Bay nu," SVT. se, May 18, 2010.

39. Peter Sunde criminal case, Court of Appeals for Skåne and Blekinge, verdict, February 10, 2009.

40. There are exceptions: books can be discounted after a year, as can damaged volumes.

41. Exact comparisons are difficult, but in 2008, Germany had 3,800 bookstores and 94,000 new books published, according to the Börsenverein. In 2010 the United States had 10,600 bookstores and, in 2009, 275,000 books published, according to the Association of American Publishers.

42. According to the Börsenverein and Amazon.com, respectively.

43. Frank Patalong, "E-Books und Buchpreisbindung: Schuss in den eigenen Fuß," *Spiegel Online*, February 1, 2010.

44. Memorandum of Law in Opposition to the Settlement Proposal on Behalf of the Federal Republic of Germany, *The Authors Guild, Assn of American Publishers v Google Inc*, No 05-CV-8136 (S.D.N.Y. filed August 31, 2009).

45. Sylvain Dejean, Thierry Pénard, and Raphaël Suire, "Une première évaluation des effets de la loi HADOPI sur les pratiques des Internautes français" [A first evaluation of the effects of the HADOPI law on the practices of French Internet users] (Marsouin, March 2010).

46. "Statement on OFCOM Draft Code on Implementing Digital Economy Act" (TalkTalk press release, May 28, 2010).

47. George Osborne and Eric Schmidt, "Innovation Is the Secret of Economic Success," *Telegraph*, November 3, 2010.

48. David Cameron, "East End Tech City Speech," November 4, 2010.

49. Andrew Orlowski, "Theft Scribe Picked for Intellectual Property Review," *Register*, December 7, 2010.

CHAPTER NINE: BLANKET PROTECTION:
TURNING COPYRIGHT INTO COPY*RISK*

1. *Music on the Internet: Is There an Upside to Downloading? Hearing Before the Senate Judiciary Committee*, 106th Cong., 2nd sess. (July 11, 2000) (Jim Griffin testimony).

2. Peter L. Bernstein, *Against the Gods: The Remarkable Story of Risk* (New York: John Wiley & Sons, 1996). Starting in 1696, the coffeehouse owner Edward Lloyd tracked information about the shipping business and provided a place to buy and sell insurance for it. Those who wanted to accept risk would write their names under a particular ship, which is where we get the term "underwriter"; the famous British insurance company took its name from the coffeehouse itself.

3. In 1941, when ASCAP was sued on antitrust grounds by the Department of Justice, the case was settled with a consent decree; BMI signed a similar decree the same year. Both have been modified since.

4. Philippe Crocq, "The SDRM Story," *Billboard*, May 22, 1993.

5. *Herbert v. Shanley Co.*, 242 U.S. 591 (1917).

6. Bennett Lincoff, "Everyone Covered by Blanket Licenses," *Billboard*, December 16, 1995.

7. *Hearing of the Courts and Intellectual Property Subcommittee of the House Judiciary Committee*, 105th Cong., 1st sess. (September 16, 1997) (John Bettis testimony).

8. The tribunal is a special court that has legal authority to set license rates when companies cannot come to terms. Its closest U.S. equivalent would be a rate court. As of early 2011, it had not yet ruled.

9. Although the labels favor TDC, the Danish tribunal has declined their request to intervene in court.

10. Sam Gustin, "Fee for All," Portfolio.com, March 27, 2008. Many journalists who covered Griffin's plan believed the phrase "compulsory license" meant consumers would be required to pay, whether or not they listened to music online. But it would be compulsory for *copyright holders*, not consumers.

11. This was confirmed by the general counsel at Warner Music Group, who handled the matter.

12. The Higher Education Opportunity Act makes certain federal financial aid for students conditional on informing students of penalties for online copyright infringement, creating a plan to reduce infringement, and offering legal alternatives, to the extent that it's possible.

13. Michael Arrington, "The Music Industry's New Extortion Scheme," *TechCrunch*, March 27, 2008. Arrington quoted Akamai's David Barrett, even though, as a trained lawyer, he ought to know better. If collecting money for services rendered qualifies as extortion, every bill collector in the United States is guilty.

14. If a garage band wants to cover "Born to Run," it doesn't have to get permission from the song's writer, Bruce Springsteen—it just has to pay a "mechanical royalty." But it would have to get permission if it wanted to use his recording of the song or change it enough that its version would be considered a derivative work.

15. In 1995, Congress passed the Digital Performance Right in Sound Recordings Act, which allows labels and performers to collect money when their works are streamed, although traditional radio has only paid songwriters. It only covers "online radio"; services that let consumers pick exactly what they want to hear must negotiate directly with labels.

16. OECD Broadband Portal, Organization for Economic Cooperation and Development.

17. As of 2008, there were 116,783 households in the United States, according to the Census Bureau.

18. These estimates are based on the current price of subscriptions, a rough idea of how many U.S. residents buy music, and what such a service might cost to run.

19. The companies are Amazon, Apple, Nokia, EMI Music Publishing, Universal Music Publishing, SACEM, the English collecting society PRS for Music, and the Swedish collecting society STIM.

20. Volker Grassmuck, "The World Is Going Flat(-Rate)," Intellectual Property Watch Web site, May 11, 2009.

21. Eircom sells individual downloads, as well as two package deals: €5.99 for fifteen downloads a month, and €12.99 for forty downloads a month.

22. *Between EMI Records et al and UPC Communications Ireland Limited*, the High Court (of Ireland).

CHAPTER TEN: THE FUTURE OF THE FUTURE:
CHOOSING COMMERCE OR CHAOS?

1. Chris Anderson, "The Web Is Dead. Long Live the Internet," *Wired*, September 2010.

2. *Wired* used estimates from Cisco. Data traffic on the Web is still growing, but it's losing ground to other platforms on a relative basis, as a percentage of overall online traffic.

3. Josh Bernoff and Shar VanBoskirk, *The Splinternet: Preparing for an Internet Fragmented by Devices and Passwords* (Forrester Research, January 26, 2010).

4. "Comments of Google," filed to the Federal Communications Commission, July 13, 2010.

5. Most notably, Google campaigned to get its Google Voice app in Apple's App Store. But it has expressed its desire for open mobile networks in a variety of other ways as well.

6. John Koblin, "Condé Nast Banks on Scott Dadich," *Women's Wear Daily*, October 15, 2010.

7. Most net neutrality regulations that have been proposed apply only to "legitimate content." But they would give Internet service providers an incentive not to block sites filled with pirated movies, lest they accidentally make inaccessible a few Creative Commons videos.

8. Ryan Kim, "FCC Hears Net Neutrality Arguments at Stanford," *San Francisco Chronicle*, April 18, 2008.

9. One of the most impressive examples was how the *Daily Kos* had readers look through Justice Department documents. "Crowdsourcing the Torture Memos," *Daily Kos*, April 16, 2009. In the U.K., the *Guardian* used a similar strategy to sift through 458,832 pages of documents about politicians' expenses. "Investigate Your MP's Expenses," *Guardian*, June 2009.

10. Gartner estimates that nine out of ten apps sold in 2010 were for Apple. *Forecast: Mobile Application Stores, Worldwide, 2008–2014* (Gartner, January 26, 2011).

11. Tim Berners-Lee, "Long Live the Web: A Call for Continued Open Standards and Neutrality," *Scientific American*, December 2010.

12. David Goldman, "Android and Qualcomm Are the New Wintel," CNNMoney.com, November 12, 2010. The article references a study by the consultancy PRTM—which coined the term "Quadroid"—that says three-quarters of new Android phones use Qualcomm chips. And it predicts this uniformity will put pressure on device makers' profit margins, just as it did for PC makers.

13. Michael Wolff, "Who's to Blame: Them?" *Wired*, September 2010.

14. Tim Wu, "The Apple Two," *Slate*, April 6, 2010.

15. "Can You Hear Me Now? Why Your Cell Phone Is So Terrible: A Future Tense Event from Slate Magazine and the New America Foundation" (New America Foundation office, April 2, 2010).

16. As of February 1, 2011, Apple was worth $317.9 billion, Microsoft $239.5 billion, and Google $151.8 billion.

17. Cory Doctorow, "Why I Won't Buy an iPad (and Think You Shouldn't, Either)," *Boing Boing* (blog), April 2, 2010.

18. David Goldman, "Final Nail in Coffin for Net Neutrality?" CNNMoney.com, November 2, 2010.

19. *In the Matter of Preserving the Open Internet Broadband Industry Practices* (Federal Communications Commission report and order, December 23, 2010).

20. The Internet Freedom, Broadband Promotion, and Consumer Protection Act of 2011, introduced by Cantwell and Senator Al Franken (D-Minn.).

21. Ashby Jones, "Verizon Files Early Challenge to Latest 'Net Neutrality' Rules," *Law Blog, Wall Street Journal,* January 21, 2011.

22. Sarah McBride and Ethan Smith, "Music Industry to Abandon Mass Suits," *Wall Street Journal,* December 19, 2008.

23. "100,000 P2P Users Sued in US Mass Lawsuits," *TorrentFreak* (blog), January 30, 2011.

24. Greg Sandoval, "Biden to File Sharers: 'Piracy Is Theft,' " CNet.com, June 22, 2010.

25. Although Obama appointed Espinel, he didn't create the position. That came from the 2008 PRO-IP Act—formally known as the Prioritizing Resources and Organization for Intellectual Property Act.

26. Victoria Espinel, "2010 Joint Strategic Plan on Intellectual Property Enforcement" (Executive Office of the President of the United States, June 2010).

27. Ibid.

28. Michael Arrington, "Here's How the Government Can Fix Silicon Valley: Leave It Alone," *TechCrunch,* June 7, 2010.

29. Quick civics refresher: Espinel, who works for the White House, doesn't have the power to change laws; Congress does that. Arrington, who's a lawyer, should know this.

30. The seized domains were TVshack.net, Movies-Links.TV, FilesPump.com, Now-Movies.com, PlanetMoviez.com, ThePirateCity.org, ZML.com, Ninja-Video, and NinjaThis.net.

31. "Censorship of the Internet Takes Center Stage in 'Online Infringement' Bill," Electronic Frontier Foundation blog, September 21, 2010.

32. Several consumer review sites, including trustpilot.com and sitejabber.com, contain stories of unexpected charges to credit cards.

33. *Harper & Row v. Nation Enterprises.*

34. According to Cisco, the busiest 1 percent of broadband connections account for more than 20 percent of all online traffic, and the busiest 10 percent for more than 60 percent of all traffic.

35. Barlow, "A Declaration of the Independence of Cyberspace."

36. "Creators Must Move Beyond Suing the Audience," Electronic Frontier Foundation Deeplinks blog, May 28, 2010.

BIBLIOGRAPHY

BOOKS

Alderman, John. *Sonic Boom: Napster, MP3, and the New Pioneers of Music.* Cambridge, Mass.: Perseus, 2001.

Anderson, Chris. *Free: The Future of a Radical Price.* New York: Hyperion, 2009.

———. *The Long Tail: Why the Future of Business Is Selling Less of More.* New York: Hyperion, 2006.

Auletta, Ken. *Googled: The End of the World as We Know It.* New York: Penguin, 2009.

Battelle, John. *The Search: How Google and Its Rivals Rewrote the Rules of Business and Transformed Our Culture.* New York: Portfolio, 2005.

Coburn, Pip. *The Change Function: Why Some Technologies Take Off and Others Crash and Burn.* New York: Portfolio, 2006.

Coleman, Mark. *Playback: From the Victrola to MP3, 100 Years of Music, Machines, and Money.* New York: Da Capo, 2003.

Darnton, Robert. *The Case for Books: Past, Present, and Future.* New York: PublicAffairs, 2009.

Epstein, Edward Jay. *The Big Picture: The New Logic of Money and Power in Hollywood.* New York: Random House, 2005. Essential reading for anyone who wants to understand how Hollywood works.

———. *The Hollywood Economist: The Hidden Financial Reality Behind the Movies.* Brooklyn: Melville House, 2010.

Epstein, Jason. *Book Business: Publishing Past, Present, and Future.* New York: W. W. Norton, 2001.

Fisher, William W., III. *Promises to Keep: Technology, Law, and the Future of Entertainment.* Stanford, Calif.: Stanford Law and Politics, 2004.

Goldsmith, Jack, and Tim Wu. *Who Controls the Internet? Illusions of a Borderless World.* New York: Oxford University Press, 2006. A prescient look at the future of law online and a thoroughly researched rejoinder to anyone who thinks it won't have one.

Goldstein, Paul. *Copyright's Highway: From Gutenberg to the Celestial Jukebox.* Stanford, Calif.: Stanford Law and Politics, 2003. An excellent introduction to copyright—thorough enough for almost anyone, but accessible enough for beginners.

Gomez, Jeff. *Print Is Dead: Books in Our Digital Age.* Basingstoke, U.K.: Palgrave Macmillan, 2008.

Goodman, Fred. *Fortune's Fool: Edgar Bronfman Jr., Warner Music, and an Industry in Crisis.* New York: Simon & Schuster, 2010.

Gorman, Robert A., and Jane C. Ginsberg. *Copyright: Cases and Materials.* 7th ed. New York: Foundation Press, 2006.

Hafner, Katie, and Matthew Lyon. *Where Wizards Stay Up Late: The Origins of the Internet.* New York: Touchstone, 1996.

Helprin, Mark. *Digital Barbarism: A Writer's Manifesto.* New York: Harper, 2009.

Henry, Neil. *American Carnival: Journalism Under Siege in an Age of New Media.* Berkeley: University of California Press, 2007.

Hyde, Lewis. *Common as Air: Revolution, Art, and Ownership.* New York: Farrar, Straus and Giroux, 2010.

Johns, Adrian. *Piracy: The Intellectual Property Wars from Gutenberg to Gates.* Chicago: University of Chicago Press, 2009.

Jones, Alex. *Losing the News: The Future of the News That Feeds Democracy.* New York: Oxford University Press, 2009.

Keen, Andrew. *The Cult of the Amateur: How Blogs, MySpace, YouTube, and the Rest of Today's User-Generated Media Are Destroying Our Economy, Our Culture, and Our Values.* New York: Doubleday, 2007.

Knee, Jonathan A., Bruce C. Greenwald, and Ana Seave. *The Curse of the Mogul: What's Wrong with the World's Leading Media Companies.* New York: Portfolio, 2009.

Knopper, Steve. *Appetite for Self-Destruction: The Spectacular Crash of the Record Industry in the Digital Age.* New York: Free Press, 2009.

Lanier, Jaron. *You Are Not a Gadget: A Manifesto.* New York: Alfred A. Knopf, 2010.

Lardner, James. *Fast Forward: Hollywood, the Japanese, and the VCR Wars.* New York: W. W. Norton, 1987. A genuinely thrilling account of Sony's introduction of the VCR and the legal case that followed.

Lessig, Lawrence. *Code and Other Laws of Cyberspace.* New York: Basic Books, 1999.

————. *Code: Version 2.0.* New York: Basic Books, 2006. Although I find Lessig's arguments on copyright unconvincing, this defined the debate over online regulation in ways that still echo today.

————. *Free Culture: The Nature and Future of Creativity.* New York: Penguin Books, 2005.

————. *The Future of Ideas: The Fate of the Commons in a Connected World.* New York: Vintage Books, 2001.

————. *Remix: Making Art and Commerce Thrive in the Hybrid Economy.* New York: Penguin Press, 2008.

Levy, Steven. *The Perfect Thing: How the iPod Shuffles Commerce, Culture, and Coolness.* New York: Simon & Schuster, 2006.

Liebowitz, Stan. *Re-thinking the Network Economy: The True Forces That Drive the Digital Marketplace.* New York: AMACOM, 2002.

Litman, Jessica. *Digital Copyright.* Amherst, N.Y.: Prometheus Books, 2001.

Menn, Joseph. *All the Rave: The Rise and Fall of Shawn Fanning's Napster.* New York: Crown Business, 2003. The definitive take on one of the most interesting business stories of the decade.

Merriden, Trevor. *Irresistible Forces: The Business Legacy of Napster and the Growth of the Underground Internet.* Oxford: Capstone, 2001.

Meza, Philip E. *Coming Attractions? Hollywood, High Tech, and the Future of Entertainment.* Stanford, Calif.: Stanford Business Books, 2007.

Palmer, Shelly. *Television Disrupted: The Transition from Network to Networked TV.* 2nd ed. White Plains, N.Y.: York House Press, 2008.

Passman, Donald S. *All You Need to Know About the Music Business.* 7th ed. New York: Free Press, 2009. The ultimate reference book by one of today's smartest music lawyers.

Patry, William. *Moral Panics and the Copyright Wars.* New York: Oxford University Press, 2009.

Poundstone, William. *Priceless: The Myth of Fair Value (and How to Take Advantage of It).* New York: Hill and Wang, 2010. A fascinating look at why things *really* cost what they do.

Reback, Gary L. *Free the Market! Why Only Government Can Keep the Marketplace Competitive.* New York: Portfolio, 2009.

Shapiro, Carl, and Hal R. Varian. *Information Rules: A Strategic Guide to the Network Economy.* Boston: Harvard Business School Press, 1999.

Ulin, Jeffrey C. *The Business of Media Distribution: Monetizing Film, TV, and Video Content in an Online World.* Amsterdam: Focal Press, 2010.

Wu, Tim. *The Master Switch: The Rise and Fall of Information Empires.* New York: Alfred A. Knopf, 2010.

Zittrain, Jonathan. *The Future of the Internet and How to Stop It.* New Haven, Conn.: Yale University Press, 2008.

WEB SITES

Ars Technica, arstechnica.com. Some of the smartest reporting on these issues available online.

Billboard.biz, www.billboard.biz.

CNET News Media, news.cnet.com. Especially Greg Sandoval's Media Maverick column at news.cnet.com/media-maverick.

Content Bridges, www.contentbridges.com.

Copyhype, www.copyhype.com. (Terry Hart, who writes this blog, helped check my legal reporting and became a friend.) A historical analysis of copyright issues, full of references to case law.

Copyrights & Campaigns, copyrightsandcampaigns.blogspot.com.

Edward Jay Epstein's Web Log, edjayepstein.blogspot.com.

Media Decoder (blog), *New York Times*, mediadecoder.blogs.nytimes.com.

Music Technology Policy, musictechpolicy.wordpress.com.

Public Knowledge *Policy Blog*, www.publicknowledge.org/blog.

Reflections of a Newsosaur, newsosaur.blogspot.com.

The Register, www.theregister.co.uk.

TorrentFreak, torrentfreak.com.

Wired.com, www.wired.com. Especially Eliot Van Buskirk's music business coverage at www.wired.com/epicenter.

INDEX